D1570142

The Constitution of Empire

GARY LAWSON
AND GUY SEIDMAN

The Constitution
of Empire

TERRITORIAL EXPANSION AND
AMERICAN LEGAL HISTORY

Yale University Press
New Haven &
London

Copyright © 2004 by Yale University. All rights reserved. This book may not be reproduced, in whole or in part, including illustrations, in any form (beyond that copying permitted by Sections 107 and 108 of the U.S. Copyright Law and except by reviewers for the public press), without written permission from the publishers.

Printed in the United States of America by Sheridan Books, Ann Arbor, Michigan.

Library of Congress Cataloging-in-Publication Data
Lawson, Gary, 1958–
The constitution of empire : territorial expansion and American legal history /
Gary Lawson and Guy Seidman.
     p.   cm.
Includes bibliographical references and index.
ISBN 0-300-10231-3 (cloth : alk. paper)
1. United States — Territorial expansion. 2. United States — Politics and
government — Philosophy. 3. United States — Territories and possessions —
Politics and government. 4. Imperialism — History. 5. Constitutional history —
United States. 6. Constitutional law — United States. I. Seidman, Guy. II. Title.
E179.5.L36 2004
342.73′0413 — dc22
2003016909

A catalogue record for this book is available from the British Library.

The paper in this book meets the guidelines for permanence and durability of the Committee on Production Guidelines for Book Longevity of the Council on Library Resources.

10 9 8 7 6 5 4 3 2 1

To Patty, Nathaniel, and Noah Lawson

To Ady and in loving memory of Lea Seidman

Contents

Acknowledgments

Portions of this book appeared previously in Gary Lawson and Guy Seidman, *The First "Establishment" Clause: Article VII and the Post-Constitutional Confederation*, 78 Notre Dame L Rev 83 (2002); Gary Lawson and Guy Seidman, *The Hobbesian Constitution: Governing without Authority*, 95 Nw UL Rev 581 (2001); and Gary Lawson, *Territorial Governments and the Limits of Formalism*, 78 Cal L Rev 853 (1988). We are grateful to the *Notre Dame Law Review*, the *Northwestern Law Review*, and the *California Law Review* for permission to reproduce those materials.

We are indebted to Boston University School of Law and the Interdisciplinary Center, Herzliya, for their support during the production of this book. We would also like to thank Northwestern University School of Law for introducing us to each other and for supporting us during the formative stages of the book's development.

We received helpful comments on portions of this manuscript from David Golove, Vasan Kesavan, and the participants at a workshop at Boston University School of Law. We are especially grateful to Professor Golove, who took considerable time and effort to provide us with comments despite regarding much of our project as misconceived. Akhil Reed Amar and Sanford Levinson provided much-needed encouragement at various stages.

We are grateful for the editorial assistance and support that we have received through Yale University Press, especially from Marie Blanchard, Keith Condon, Dan Heaton, and Lara Heimert. We thank Kathy Ellis and Barbara Granger for helping make available the time to write this book. Most of all, we thank Patricia B. G. Lawson for just about everything.

The Constitution of Empire

Introduction:
From Sea to Shining Sea . . . and Beyond

In 1809, Thomas Jefferson wrote to James Madison that "no constitution was ever before so well calculated as ours for extensive empire."[1] Our goal is to evaluate Jefferson's statement by undertaking a constitutional and historical survey of American territorial acquisition and governance. History has largely validated Jefferson's imperial enthusiasm. It is less clear that the Constitution does so.

Gorham's Ghost

When the last of the original colonies ratified the Constitution in 1790, the United States consisted of thirteen geographically contiguous states clustered on or near the Atlantic Ocean plus a large federal territory, destined for statehood, which extended westward to the Mississippi River. Six years before citizen Jefferson penned his 1809 letter to Madison, President Jefferson—notwithstanding some now-famous constitutional doubts about the country's capacity to acquire new territory—had doubled the original land mass of the United States through the Louisiana Purchase, which extended American borders west to the Rocky Mountains and south to the Gulf of Mexico. In his 1809 letter, Jefferson expressed no doubts about the constitutionality of territorial expansion. He told Madison that he expected America eventually to acquire East and West Florida, Cuba, and Canada, which would show the world "such an empire for liberty as she has never surveyed since the creation."[2]

Jefferson was wrong (thus far) about the ultimate destiny of Cuba and Canada, which ended up as independent rather than American states, but by the end of the nineteenth century, American sovereignty extended across the North American continent, into the Caribbean, and as far across the Pacific Ocean as the Philippines. Today, America includes the noncontiguous states of Alaska and Hawaii and island possessions in both the Pacific and Atlantic Oceans.

The founding generation was intensely interested in the geographical extent of the American polity. Madison's famous defense of the extended republic in *The Federalist*[3] was a response to the widespread belief that the United States of the late eighteenth century was already larger than republican institutions could sustain. Madison encountered some of those concerns at the Constitutional Convention. On August 8, 1787, Madison objected to a proposal that there be one representative in the House of Representatives for every forty thousand people, on the ground that "[t]he future increase of population if the Union shd. be permanent, will render the number of Representatives excessive." Nathaniel Gorham, who served at the Convention as chairman of the Committee of the Whole and sat on the Committee of Detail, replied: "It is not to be supposed that the Gov't will last so long as to produce this effect. Can it be supposed that this vast Country including the Western territory will 150 years hence remain one nation?"[4]

At one level, of course, Madison was right: the nation endures. But at another level, the ghost of Gorham can still raise a challenge. The nation has endured, but has it endured as the same nation that Madison and Gorham helped construct? There are dimensions to that question that partake of political science, sociology, history, philosophy, and many other disciplines, but we concentrate in this book solely on the dimension of constitutional meaning. Has American expansion taken place pursuant to or outside the bounds of the United States Constitution that Madison and Gorham were drafting in the summer of 1787? Was Jefferson's effervescent (at least in 1809) attitude toward the Constitution's ability to accommodate empire justified?

Imperial Constitution or Constitutional Imperialism?

It is hard to form a strong conviction of any sort about the Constitution's suitability as an instrument for empire from a casual inspection of the text. The Constitution is noticeably terse when it comes to territorial acquisition and governance. There is no express clause concerning the acquisition of territory. The Admissions Clause in Article IV provides that "[n]ew States may be admitted by the Congress into this Union," but there is no clear declaration that new states can come from foreign territory acquired after the Constitution was ratified rather than from the original Northwest Territory or cessions from the original states. Indeed, the rest of the Admissions Clause speaks only of territory that is already part of existing states.[5] There are two clauses that obviously concern governance of federal territory: one grants to Congress power "[t]o exercise exclusive Legislation in all Cases whatsoever" over the nation's capital and federal enclaves located within the boundaries of states, and another gives Congress power "to dispose of and make all needful Rules and Regulations respecting the Territory or other Property belonging to the United States."[6] Many other clauses, of course, can plausibly be construed to affect territorial matters in some fashion, but the list of provisions directly addressed to problems of territorial acquisition and governance is very short.

These sparse texts leave open a great many questions. Does the Constitution in fact permit or accommodate territorial expansion? If so, in what forms? To what extent? With what conditions or limitations? Through which institutional mechanisms? Are the provisions for territorial governance subject to the same kinds of constitutional restrictions as other federal powers? To what extent do structural principles, such as the separation of powers or federalism, control the forms of acquisition and governance? Do inhabitants of federal territories have the same rights as inhabitants of the states? Does the President have inherent power to govern territory? Can Congress grant him[7] that power? Does it matter whether the nation is at war or peace? These are all very basic questions about American constitutional government, and none of them is answered by express texts in the Constitution. Accordingly, the search for answers requires a careful examination of constitutional text, structure, and principles. As with so many problems encountered when expounding the Constitution, the problems of territorial acquisition and governance require a serious exercise in interpretation.

We perform that interpretative exercise by uncovering the Constitution's original meaning—which, as we shall soon explain, is not necessarily the same operation that often takes place, or is often thought to take place, under the label of "originalism." Applying that conception of constitutional meaning, our conclusion is that Jefferson was partly right and partly wrong, a conclusion that reflects a basic ambiguity about the meaning of an American "empire."

One could mean by that term an expansive polity of affiliated, self-governing states, which was clearly Jefferson's conception. Alternatively, one could mean something along the lines of European empires, in which the mother country rules over subservient colonies — an arrangement with which the founding generation had some familiarity (and generally little sympathy). Jefferson was largely, though not entirely, right about the Constitution's suitability for empire if he simply meant that the Constitution accommodates the addition of new states. Notwithstanding President Jefferson's 1803 qualms about territorial acquisition, the Constitution provides ample authorization for the acquisition of new territory for the purpose of creating new states, and the Admissions Clause permits the admission of new states from territory acquired after ratification of the Constitution. The Constitution is thus well suited to the addition of new states to the union.

The one possible complication concerns governance of territory following its acquisition and prior to its admission as a state. The Territories Clause expressly gives Congress broad power to govern federal territory, but that power is not unlimited. We maintain that the power to govern federal territory is subject to check by some, though not all, of the same structural and prohibitory limitations that apply to federal power in other contexts. Most significantly, those limitations place obstacles in the path of institutions of self-governance during the territorial phase. As we will explain, however, those obstacles can be overcome with a small amount of creativity. On the whole, Jefferson was basically right about an empire of affiliated states: the Constitution is not perfectly designed for such expansion, but it does the job adequately.

It is far less clear whether the Constitution is well suited to "empire" on a colonial model. Whereas there is no constitutional problem with the acquisition of territory that is intended as a future state, there are serious questions about the ability of the United States to add territories that are not slated for statehood. Historically, this calls into question a number of nineteenth-century acquisitions, most notably the acquisition of the Philippine Islands in 1899. Furthermore, just as territorial governance in preparation for eventual statehood may call for institutions of self-government, territorial governance for colonial purposes may call for the opposite. Many staples of the American constitutional order, such as jury trials, may be poorly suited to the long-term occupation of territories that have experienced legal traditions that do not employ the full range of Anglo-American institutions. If the Constitution always requires such institutions to be implemented in federal territory — and, contrary to modern law, we think that it does — that could effectively prevent many kinds of acquisitions by making it difficult or impossible to govern the territory once it is acquired.

Parts I and II of this book explore these issues of territorial acquisition and governance in some depth. Part I concerns the constitutional rules and mechanisms for the acquisition of new territory. Chapter 1 uses the Louisiana Purchase as a vehicle for discussing the most obvious method of adding territory to the United States: acquisition from a foreign sovereign by treaty, either by purchase or, as happened at the end of the Mexican-American War and the Spanish-American War, as part of a peace settlement. In trying to understand the Constitution's Treaty Clause, which starkly states that the President "shall have Power . . . to make Treaties, provided two thirds of the Senators present concur,"[8] we are drawn once again to Thomas Jefferson. Jefferson propounded a theory of the treaty power that was quite different from the consensus of his time, radically different from the consensus of the past two hundred years, and ultimately correct.

The conventional wisdom (and that is not a term of derision — conventional wisdom is often conventional precisely because it is wisdom) holds that the federal treaty power is, in the representative words of Gerald Neuman, "an independent grant of power to the federal government to enter into treaties that enact rules that Congress might not otherwise have been able to enact."[9] This view has prevailed as a matter of constitutional law at least since 1920, when the Supreme Court held in *Missouri v Holland*[10] that the President and Senate could regulate by treaty matters that Congress could not constitutionally regulate by statute. Jefferson, by contrast, viewed the treaty power as an *implementational* power that permits the President and Senate to carry into effect national powers in the international arena but does not give the national government jurisdiction beyond its other enumerated powers. On this understanding, the Treaty Clause in Article II, section 2 is analogous to the Sweeping Clause of Article I, section 8: both are capable, but *only* capable, of executing other national powers. We defend that position at great length, albeit ultimately on the less-than-satisfying ground that its many serious problems are less grave than the problems faced by every other possible understanding of the federal treaty power.

In the context of territorial acquisition, federal treaty makers are capable of adding territory to the United States, but only as a means of carrying into effect other national powers, such as the power to admit new states or to provide and maintain a navy. Thus every acquisition by treaty must implement an enumerated power, which casts serious doubt on acquisitions of territory that go beyond military needs and do not contemplate future statehood for the acquired territory. The Louisiana Purchase, in which all of the acquired territory was clearly destined for, and eventually achieved, statehood, easily satisfies that standard. Subsequent acquisitions are not always such easy cases.

In Chapters 2 and 3, we apply our theory of the treaty power to the American acquisitions of territory after 1803, and in particular to the acquisitions of noncontiguous territory, such as Alaska and the Philippines, for which there was contemporary doubt about the prospects for statehood. We also explore the other two mechanisms for permanently adding territory to the United States: discovery, which formed the basis for the American claim to Oregon, and statutory annexation, which was employed to add Texas and Hawaii to the nation. The latter method proves to be easily constitutional. The former is more problematic, especially if the executive is left to its own devices and is not acting as a direct agent of Congress.

In the end, the only acquisition that we are prepared to say was unconstitutional was the acquisition of the Philippines. That problem was "cured" in a fashion when the Philippines received independence in 1948, but the half century of American governance of the Philippines still requires constitutional justification. Some other acquisitions, furthermore, are close calls and raise issues that are serious enough and interesting enough, from the standpoint of both history and constitutional meaning, to warrant careful examination.

Part II addresses problems of territorial governance. Chapter 4 introduces the sparse constitutional provisions that authorize territorial governance and begins discussion of the permissible governmental structures that may be established in the territories. It demonstrates that some familiar institutions of territorial self-government, such as elected territorial legislatures and governors, are unconstitutional, although the Constitution permits the construction of "shadow" institutions of self-government that can achieve many of the same goals as the forbidden mechanisms. Chapter 5 demonstrates that federal judges in the territories, as is true of federal judges anywhere else in the country, must conform to the requirements of Article III. Most territorial judges dismally fail this test. In both Chapters 4 and 5, we sketch the history by which the legal system has validated such constitutionally forbidden institutions as elective territorial officials and non–Article III courts to show that Congress and the courts have never answered the serious constitutional arguments against these institutions.

Chapter 6 explores some problems that arise when Congress fails to exercise its constitutional power to govern territory and the executive department tries to fill the void. We study in detail the events in California during the "interregnum" of 1848–50, during which California was governed by federal military officials without statutory authorization. The Supreme Court approved that peculiar form of governance in 1854. We do not. More to the point, neither does the Constitution.

Chapter 7 deals with the application of provisions such as the Bill of Rights to territorial citizens. As does virtually everyone else who has considered the issue, we disagree with the current doctrine that permits Congress to deprive at least some territorial inhabitants of at least some of these constitutional protections. Territorial inhabitants obviously do not stand in precisely the same relation to Congress as do state inhabitants, but neither do they stand in precisely the same relation to Congress as do staplers, paper clips, and the other "Property belonging to the United States" mentioned in the Territories Clause.

The substantial historical component of Part II illustrates how far the actual operations of territorial governance have strayed from the Constitution's original meaning over the course of two hundred years. Gorham's ghost may thus have triumphed in the end: the nation, with territories in tow, has endured beyond Gorham's expectations, but the Constitution that he helped draft got left behind in the wake.

Whose Meaning?

Because this work is primarily an exercise in constitutional interpretation, methodology is critical. Clearly, it would require a separate book even to introduce the myriad problems of constitutional interpretation, and that is not our project here. But the reader does need, or at least deserve, to know what we mean when we make assertions about constitutional meaning.

We approach the task of constitutional interpretation from a perspective that is best labeled "originalist." But our use of the label *originalist* is somewhat nonstandard, though it is far from idiosyncratic.[11] Rather than argue over labels, we simply describe our interpretative approach and let the reader determine what to make of it.

In the context of constitutional interpretation, originalism is a theory about the point in time at which the meaning of the federal Constitution is fixed — namely, a particular point in the document's history somewhere near the origin. As such, originalism is *not* a theory of interpretation. It cannot be a theory of interpretation, because an interpretative theory must, at a minimum, specify *what counts* toward establishing meaning and not simply *the point in time* at which the values of the relevant interpretative variables are fixed.[12] Is meaning determined by the semantic meaning of the document's text at the critical moment in time? The concrete expectations held by a certain group of historical persons at the critical moment in time? The evolving standards of morality held by a certain group of historical persons at the critical moment in time? Any of these theories, and countless others, would represent a species of originalism.

Most self-described constitutional originalists, however, combine their temporal leanings with rules of interpretative relevance that give primacy to some set of historically concrete mental states. The great divide in modern times within originalist circles has concerned *whose* historically concrete mental states determine original meaning: some privileged group of drafters, some privileged group of ratifiers, or a somewhat more amorphous group of actors who one might call, for lack of a better phrase, the educated affected public. On any such understanding, original meaning is a historical fact. It may be a difficult historical fact to ascertain given the problems of (1) determining whether the relevant mental states represent linguistic understandings, expectations of consequences, and/or resolutions of specific paradigm cases, (2) identifying and aggregating the relevant mental states (in the face of the evidentiary problems caused by temporal distance), and (3) establishing the proper social and historical context in which the mental states must be understood — but it is a historical fact nonetheless.

We share many important premises with this conception of originalism. We agree that the meaning of a document such as the Constitution must be determined by reference to the public audience to which the document is most plausibly addressed. The Constitution is not a diary or a poem. It is a set of directives that gives every indication of being addressed to a relatively wide audience. Those directives are sets of words with referents — things and relations in the world which the words signify — and the trick is to figure out what things and relations a public audience at a particular point in time would have attached to these words in the context in which they appear.

We will not defend this aspect of our approach at length. Nor is a lengthy defense really necessary, because this approach, at least in its broad outlines, follows from the nature of the Constitution as a public communicative instrument containing directives. The Constitution addresses itself to a general audience, and indeed to an audience that stretches quite far in time and space, not to a small secret society. The best understanding of "the meaning" of that document accordingly must focus on the public audience to which the document presents itself. Moreover, the nature of the document points toward the *original* meaning of the document in the event that there is ever a divergence between the original and current public meanings of the document. This is in keeping with standard conventions concerning human communication. The use of original meaning is, as Sai Prakash has termed it, a "'Default Rule'"[13] that need not be expressly specified in the communicative instrument. If an instruction manual written in 1789 said, "Keep a screwdriver handy during assembly," whether the term *screwdriver* refers to a tool or an alcoholic beverage is determined by public understandings of 1789 rather than of 2003.[14]

Indeed, this mode of discerning constitutional meaning is at all controversial only because many people import normative force to that meaning and accordingly contaminate the interpretative inquiry with concerns about real-world decision-making. No one, we trust, would ever think of interpreting the Confederate Constitution or the original corporate charter for Rhode Island according to contemporary public meanings, evolving social values, or any interpretative method other than some variant of original public meaning. But letting normative concerns drive interpretation conflates the question what the Constitution means with the very different question whether the Constitution, given its meaning, is a sound basis for decision-making.[15] We view the interpretation of the Constitution as an enterprise conceptually separate from an assessment of its normative force and accordingly take the interpretative methodology of original public meaning, in the broad sense sketched above, as self-evident.

We part company from much of contemporary originalism, however, in this critical respect: we do not believe that original meaning necessarily represents historically real mental states. There is ultimately no way to divorce meaning from mental states — that would truly be an absurd attempt to formulate "law without mind"[16] — but the critical question is which mental states are constitutive of meaning. The mental states in which we ground meaning are not historical but rather are *hypothetical* and *counterfactual*: What would a fully informed public audience at the relevant point in time, in possession of all relevant information about the Constitution and the world around it, have understood the Constitution to mean?

This approach best captures the real nature of argumentation concerning documentary meaning. Documents that address themselves to the public have objective meanings that are capable of being grasped or missed by their authors, their readers, or even both. Otherwise, it would not be possible (as ordinary people, uncorrupted by advanced degrees, know that it is possible) to "misinterpret" a document or statement or to be told, quite reasonably, that even if one intended or read X, the words used really meant Y. This familiar attitude toward documents only makes sense on the assumption that the proper object of inquiry is a *hypothetical* mental state, not an actual mental state. Indeed, the attempts by many modern originalists to ground meaning in historical mental states probably has much less to do with reflection on the nature of interpretation than with concerns about the normative status of the Constitution. The mental states held by a concrete group of framers or ratifiers is a more plausible-sounding (even if not actually more plausible) basis for the binding quality of a document than is a set of hypothetical mental states that may never have existed. But that is no reason to fudge the process of interpretation.

Of course, one should not overstate the difference between actual and hypothetical understandings; they merge whenever a particular understanding was so widely held by an actual historical audience that any reasonable interpreter in that audience would necessarily have held it. But there are some contexts in which actual and hypothetical understandings do not merge. Suppose that a large number of actual readers interprets a text to mean one thing, a smaller but non-zero number of actual readers interprets the same text to mean something different, and the contending parties engage in a dialogue concerning the document's true meaning. If meaning is truly a function of measuring (through whatever weighting formula is appropriate) actual mental states, then that dialogue cannot possibly consist of anything other than: "There are more/better interpreters on my side than on your side"; "yes, you win/no, you lose." There would literally be nothing to the concept of meaning beyond nose counts. That may be the view favored by some philosophers, but it is not the way in which such dialogues about documentary meaning are conducted, were conducted in the late eighteenth century, or ever will be conducted by ordinary people. Then and now, people give *reasons* for their views of meaning, and those reasons do not inevitably reduce to some method for adding actual mental states. Those reasons can involve pointing out some feature of the document that one's opponents have not yet seen, or have undervalued, or have refused to acknowledge for political or other reasons. In other words, they refer to mental states that *would* or *might* exist under counterfactual circumstances. Those reasons can also, of course, include reference to actual mental states; one can certainly invoke the numbers, the eminence, or both of the proponents of a particular viewpoint. But those actual mental states are *evidence* of meaning; they are not *constitutive* of meaning. That is how dissenting voices on meaning can maintain, without absurdity, that they are right and the majority is wrong. And majorities typically do not consider it a full and complete response to any arguments about meaning to point out that the dissenting voices are not as loud as the majority's.

The meaning of a document such as the Constitution is a hypothetical construct that represents the hypothetical conclusion of a hypothetical dialogue in which all of the factors that bear on meaning are given their due weight. If a fully informed observer of this hypothetical dialogue, after considering all of the relevant arguments and after applying the appropriate interpretative baselines, would have concluded that a dissenting voice on the meaning of a document had the better of the argument, that dissenting voice would reflect the document's objective public meaning. Furthermore, the hypothetical mental states that constitute a document's meaning are not (necessarily) the mental states that would have been held by fully informed authors or ratifiers of the document. The set of people whose hypothetical mental states count depends on the kind of document at issue. The Constitution purports to establish binding directives for the governance of a social order. (Whether those directives are in fact binding is entirely beside the point here; we are trying to discern the Constitution's *meaning*, not its *authority*, and for that purpose its pretensions are more important than its reality.) As a brute social fact, such a document will not succeed in its mission if it is accepted only by its authors or a small set of ratifiers. It will only succeed if a sufficiently large percentage of the people with muskets choose not to shoot them in a particular direction. The addressees of the Constitution are the general public (or at least the armed general public). The Constitution's meaning is therefore the meaning that would have prevailed in a broad public dialogue if all relevant arguments and information had been presented.

An understanding (even if not an acceptance) of this approach is critical to an understanding of the arguments that we construct in this book. Under an approach such as ours that privileges an objective, hypothetical meaning, statements by concrete historical persons about their understandings of the Constitution, or actions by those persons that can be taken to represent such statements, are potentially interesting and potentially probative, but they are hardly the primary tools of interpretation. Assuming that the mental states are known,[17] those mental states are only good evidence of meaning if they were formed by someone (1) who considered all of the relevant arguments, (2) was capable of synthesizing all of the relevant arguments, and (3) was unlikely to be unduly influenced by various biases that would interfere with sound processing of the evidence. As one of us has written elsewhere, "one must always be prepared to ask whether an expressed understanding would have been different if the utterer had known or thought about X, Y, and Z."[18] Of course, expressed mental states help establish the linguistic plausibility of an interpretation and are therefore relevant, but the search for meaning does not consist of counting noses on expressive faces. A view that received only minimal expression during the founding era could nonetheless represent the meaning of the Constitution *if* one concludes that a fully informed audience, after considering all of the relevant arguments, including arguments that may not have occurred to anyone at the time, would have accepted that view as correct.

For the same reasons, views reflected in legal practices — whether legislative, executive, or judicial — are also potentially interesting and probative but not decisive. Accordingly, we use historical episodes and decided cases to illustrate problems and questions, especially in Part II, but we do not consider those sources to be strong evidence of constitutional meaning.

So how does one construct a hypothetical dialogue at a point more than two hundred years in the past? How does one evaluate the hypothetical strength of arguments that were never actually presented or considered (or were presented to and considered by only a small percentage of the relevant public audience)? This problem is easy to overstate. People frequently argue about, and have always argued about, meaning in the fashion that we describe. The actual mechanics of our originalism are not dramatically different from the mechanics of more familiar interpretative approaches: we look at the semantic meaning of the text, the instrument in which the specific text is embedded, general linguistic usages and patterns, historical contexts, and background understandings. The difference between our approach and others concerns the *weight* of various items of evidence more than it does the *admissibility* of such evidence.

Put as simply as possible, our approach downplays, though it does not eliminate, the relevance of actual expressions of mental states and emphasizes the relevance of arguments from textual structure and documentary character. By "textual structure" we mean the text, organization, and context of the document considered as a whole. One never interprets a specific clause of the Constitution. One always interprets the Constitution, with special attention to the role and meaning of a specific clause. As Professor Laurence Tribe has elegantly put it: "Read in isolation, most of the Constitution's provisions make only a highly limited kind of sense. Only as an interconnected whole do these provisions meaningfully constitute a frame of government for a nation of states."[19] By "documentary character" we mean attention to the kind of document that is being interpreted—in this case an externally addressed set of directives for social governance—and the general interpretative principles that accompany that kind of document. In our approach, arguments from structure and "first principles" can easily outweigh even very impressive evidence about concrete historical understandings. Original *understandings* were not necessarily original *meanings*.

History and the Constitution

Our inquiry in this book is, of course, academic in the purest sense of the term. American expansion is a historical fact, and it is far too late, as a matter of real-world politics, to retrace the road now. We did not write this book in order to influence the course of world events. Our goals, instead, are twofold. First, we think it is useful to tell the story of American expansion from the perspective of constitutional lawyers. We are not historians. We have no new insights to offer on Napoleon's motives in selling Louisiana, the significance of Spain's steadily declining influence from the eighteenth century onward, or the social forces that drove American expansion through the nineteenth century.

Many of the narratives in this book, especially in Part I, are based on secondary rather than primary sources. Nonetheless, we have found it valuable to examine the saga of American expansion through the lens of constitutional meaning, and we hope that others find it of similar value. Second, we think it is important, even if only for purposes of intellectual clarity, to understand the Constitution's original scheme of territorial acquisition and governance.

There are two major sets of questions pertaining to territorial affairs that we put aside — for lack of space, not for lack of interest. First, all of the expansion in the continental United States, including the original European expansion that generated the colonies, has involved the displacement (to use a much-too-polite euphemism) of the native inhabitants. Those inhabitants have a unique legal status that is expressly recognized by the Constitution, which grants Congress power separately to regulate commerce "with foreign Nations, and among the several States, and with the Indian Tribes."[20] That status, and its implications for territorial acquisition and governance, is outside the scope of our survey. Second, there might have been a major federal acquisition, or reacquisition, of territory following the Civil War, depending upon whether one regards the Southern secession as legally effective. And once the Southern states were acquired/occupied/restored, serious and unique questions arose about the scope and form of, and authorization for, federal governance of that region. Those questions are also beyond our project.[21] We are concerned only with the initial acquisition of territory that was not previously part of the United States and with the governance of that territory's non-Indian population. Those concerns present problems enough for one book.

PART I

Acquiring Territory

I

Fundamentals: Lessons from Louisiana

The story of the Louisiana Purchase has been often told.[1] In large measure, it is a story of simple expansionism: "because it's there" is a tempting (even if ultimately inadequate) explanation for most any American territorial acquisition. In the case of the Louisiana Purchase, however, the key plot elements were trade and navigation.

The eastern portion of the United States in the late eighteenth century had ready access to the Atlantic Ocean. The territory west of the Allegheny Mountains did not. As late as 1817, a trip from Cincinnati to New York took at least fifty days, while a trip from Liverpool to New York took only forty. Overland transportation costs were correspondingly, and often prohibitively, high.[2] For the region west of the Alleghenies, river transport was essential to economic development. And for anything other than local traffic, the heart of the transportation system was the Mississippi River.

Under the 1783 Treaty of Peace with Great Britain, the Mississippi River marked the western boundary of the United States. From its source in Minnesota, the Mississippi River runs south along the present-day states of Minnesota, Wisconsin, Iowa, Illinois, Missouri, Kentucky, Tennessee, Arkansas, Mississippi, and Louisiana. Along the way, it intersects a host of other important midwestern and mideastern rivers, most notably the Ohio River, which runs from eastern Pennsylvania along the Ohio/West Virginia, Ohio/

Kentucky, and Indiana/Kentucky borders. When one adds to the mix the tributaries that feed these rivers, it is no wonder that James Madison described the Mississippi River as in the eyes of westerners "the Hudson, the Delaware, the Potomac, and all the navigable rivers of the Atlantic states, formed into one stream."[3]

The Mississippi River empties into the Gulf of Mexico in southern Louisiana. In the late eighteenth century, Louisiana belonged to Spain, as did most of the present-day United States west of the Mississippi River.[4] Americans, as the owners of a good portion of the east bank of the Mississippi River, had joint navigation rights with Spain over much of the river's length. But "on its last two hundred miles or so, Spain controlled both banks. . . . No one, therefore, could navigate the lower Mississippi any more than one could travel by land across Spanish territory, without permission from Spain."[5] In addition, Spain owned East and West Florida, which encompassed the present state of Florida plus a strip extending from the Florida Panhandle through present-day Alabama and Mississippi all the way to the Mississippi River.[6] This meant that literally all of the land, and therefore all of the river mouths, on the Gulf of Mexico was in Spanish territory. Spain thus controlled ocean access for virtually all of the rivers in the American West and Southeast: the Pearl and Pascagoula Rivers in present-day Mississippi, the Tombigbee River in Mississippi and Alabama, the Alabama River in Alabama, the Apalachicola River system, which includes the Chatahoochee, that runs along the Georgia/Alabama border, and the Flint, which flows through Georgia. As Henry Adams described the situation: "From the mouth of the St. Mary's, southward and westward, the shores of Florida, Louisiana, Texas, and Mexico were Spanish; Pensacola, Mobile, and New Orleans closed all the rivers by which the United States could reach the gulf. The valley of the Ohio itself, as far as Pittsburgh, was at the mercy of the King of Spain; the flour and tobacco that floated down the Mississippi, or any of the rivers that fell into the Gulf, passed under the Spanish flag, and could reach a market only by permission of Don Carlos IV."[7]

During this time, the United States, as an upstream owner of the rivers, had a plausible argument at international law that it had navigational rights extending to the sea; the Spanish governor of West Florida even seemed to accept this argument in 1808. In any event, the right to navigation on the Mississippi River was resolved by agreement between Spain and the United States after 1788 and then finalized in the Treaty of San Lorenzo, which was signed on October 27, 1795, and ratified on April 25, 1796. The Treaty of San Lorenzo, in addition to guaranteeing American navigational rights on the Mississippi River in Article IV, declared in Article XXII that Spain "will permit the citizens of the United States for the space of three years from this time to deposit their merchandizes and effects in the port of New Orleans, and to export them from thence without paying any other duty than a fair price for the hire of the stores, and his Majesty promises either to continue this permission if he finds during that time that it is not prejudicial to the interests of Spain, or if he should not agree to continue it there, he will assign to them, on another part of the banks of the Mississippi, an equivalent establishment."[8] This right to store goods on land duty-free pending their shipment was known as the "right of deposit." The right of deposit obviated the need to load goods sent down the Mississippi immediately onto shipping vessels or to store them on riverboats until they could find transportation.

On October 18, 1802, acting on secret orders from the Spanish court that were unknown even to the governor of Louisiana, the Spanish intendant of Louisiana — a colonial fiscal officer whose primary responsibilities involved customs matters — terminated the right of deposit at New Orleans. Spain did not, under the terms of Article XXII of the Treaty of San Lorenzo, "assign . . . , on another part of the banks of the Mississippi, an equivalent establishment" of a right of deposit, and the closure thus appeared to be palpably unlawful. Although the Mississippi River remained open to Americans, and the closure of the deposit probably had few actual effects on traffic, the closure created such a stir that it seriously threatened war between the United States and Spain. After vigorous American protests, the Spanish officials, many of whom were as surprised by the action as were the Americans, relented and restored the right of deposit in New Orleans on May 17, 1802.

At least some founding-era Americans had had their eyes on the territory to the south and west of their borders for quite some time, but these events on the Mississippi River intensified the pressure to acquire the port of New Orleans and/or other access to the Gulf of Mexico. One option, which had plenty of adherents in the early 1800s, was a straightforward war of acquisition. A less dramatic, and perhaps cheaper, option was to attempt to purchase New Orleans and the Floridas from Spain. New Orleans, however, had already found a new owner.

Spain had originally acquired the Louisiana Territory from France in 1762. French negotiators had actively sought to reacquire it at least since 1795, and on October 1, 1800, in the Treaty of San Ildefonso, Spain agreed to give it back in exchange for Napoleon's setting up the king of Spain's son-in-law as king of Tuscany. This was not necessarily a bad deal for Spain: the costs of maintaining Louisiana as a colony exceeded any plausible financial benefits; the king of Spain thought that he had "traded the 'vast wilderness of the Mississippi and of the Missouri' for Tuscany, the flower of Italy, 'the beautiful and learned home of Galileo, of Dante, or Petrarch'";[9] and Spain was, in any event, in no condition to stand up to Napoleon. The French, however, did not actually carry through their part of the bargain,[10] and the king of Spain did not formally order the transfer of Louisiana to France until October 15, 1802. Even then, Spain conditioned the transfer on a promise from France not to alienate Louisiana after taking dominion, a condition to which Napoleon agreed.

Because the Treaty of San Ildefonso was kept secret, and because French possession of Louisiana was delayed by bickering over performance and by a slave revolt in Santo Domingo (now Haiti) that drained off many French troops, no one in America could be certain until 1802 that a transfer had taken place. But France's ambitions on the North American continent were not a secret, and rumors of a transfer of Louisiana to France circulated even before the Treaty of San Ildefonso was signed. By March 1802, copies of the treaty were published in American newspapers. Although France did not then occupy Louisiana, and indeed officially continued to deny that it owned Louisiana at all for a considerable time after the treaty was signed, the United States began inquiring about a possible purchase of New Orleans (and the Floridas as well, if France had acquired them). After several months of maneuvering,[11] France offered and the United States negotiators accepted the sale of the territory that France had acquired in the Treaty of San Ildefonso,[12] which the latter treaty defined as "Louisiana with the Same extent that is now in the hands of Spain, & that it had when France possessed it; and Such as it Should be after the Treaties subsequently entered into between Spain and other States."[13]

This territory included at least enough land to double the area of the United States. It unambiguously encompassed all or major parts of the present states of Louisiana, Arkansas, Missouri, Iowa, Minnesota, North Dakota, South Dakota, Nebraska, Kansas, Oklahoma, Colorado, Wyoming, and Montana; and it was argued at various times — with, as we shall see, varying degrees of plausibility — to include Texas (along with parts of Oklahoma, New Mexico, and Colorado), pieces of Mississippi, Alabama, and Florida, and even the Pacific Northwest. The treaty was actually signed in early May 1803, but the signatures were backdated to April 30, 1803. Ratifications were exchanged on October 20, 1803.

Apart from the rather vague specification of the boundaries of the acquired territory, to which we will later attend, there were two potential problems with this purchase: it was unclear whether France had the power to sell Louisiana and it was unclear whether the United States had the power to buy it. As for the former problem, France had not actually fulfilled the conditions set forth in the Treaty of San Ildefonso, and it had explicitly promised Spain not to alienate Louisiana, either of which would call into question France's title to the territory. President Jefferson, however, regarded these as problems for France and Spain to work out, and Spain dropped its objections. Had Spain not relented, it is unclear why that would not have been America's problem as well; if Spain still owned Louisiana, France had nothing to sell. The more pertinent problem from our standpoint, however, concerns the power of the United States to acquire Louisiana. That problem raises profound questions of American constitutional law, to which we will now turn.

The Constitution and Acquisitions

There were moments when President Jefferson doubted the ability of the United States to acquire Louisiana. The Constitution does not contain an express "Territorial Acquisition Clause." This fact did not escape Jefferson's notice. In an 1803 letter to John Dickinson, Jefferson stated that "[t]he general government has no powers but such as the constitution has given it; and it has not given it a power of holding foreign territory, and still less of incorporating it into the Union. An amendment of the Constitution seems necessary for this."[14] Jefferson expressed this view repeatedly during the summer of 1803 and even floated for discussion a number of proposed constitutional amendments to authorize the acquisition, although at other points he seemed to assume that the Constitution permitted territorial acquisitions.[15] In the end, of course, Jefferson and others who had doubts about the nation's constitutional power to acquire Louisiana either swallowed those doubts or had them buried at the bottom of the Gulf of Mexico.

In 1828, a quarter-century after the Louisiana Purchase became a fact of national life, Chief Justice John Marshall declared for a unanimous Supreme Court that "[t]he Constitution confers absolutely on the government of the Union, the powers of making war, and of making treaties; consequently, that government possesses the power of acquiring territory, either by conquest or treaty."[16] But a search for constitutional meaning cannot take even late-eighteenth-century or early-nineteenth-century understandings as givens. It is worth asking, if only as a historical matter, whether and in what fashion the Constitution permits the United States to expand its territory.

Chief Justice Marshall located the source of his assumed power of acquisition in the war powers ("by conquest") and the treaty power ("or treaty"). Because the Jefferson Administration engineered the Louisiana Purchase and not the Louisiana Conquest, the events of 1803 do not implicate the constitutional propriety of conquest as a mode of territorial acquisition. Subsequent nineteenth-century events, of course, raise that issue with a vengeance, and we will in due time address the extent to which the Constitution permits the conquest of territory. Similarly, we will later address the extent to which the United States can constitutionally acquire territory through discovery. But as far as the Louisiana Purchase is concerned, the proper focus of attention would seem to be the treaty power.

That assumption proves to be correct, at least in part: the treaty power was an essential tool in the acquisition of Louisiana. A number of participants in the debates concerning the Louisiana Purchase in 1803, however, sought to ground the acquisition in other sources of constitutional power. It is worthwhile to consider those sources as well, if only to clear the air for a detailed examination of the federal treaty power.

Acquisitions and Enumerations

Several members of Congress, in discussing ratification and implementation of the treaty for the acquisition of Louisiana, maintained that acquisition of territory is a necessary incident of sovereignty and therefore requires no specific constitutional authorization. For instance, Representative Samuel Latham Mitchill argued that a power of territorial expansion is "inherent in independent nations." Representative Thomas Sandford similarly argued that because the Constitution does not affirmatively exclude a power to acquire property, such a power "must be considered as possessed by Government." Representative John Smilie considered "a right of annexing territory incidental to all Governments," and the power was accordingly "vested in some department of Government in the United States." A similar argument was advanced by Senator John Taylor, who suggested that "[n]either the means nor the right of acquiring territory are forbidden to the United States."[17]

Presented this baldly, the argument fundamentally misunderstands the Constitution and the very concept of a limited government. The distinctive genius of the American Constitution is the idea, clearly codified in the Tenth Amendment,[18] that every exercise of national power must be traceable to an explicit or implicit grant of power in the document. On this understanding, it is entirely possible for all other governments in the world to possess certain powers and prerogatives that are not possessed by the United States. As Representative Samuel Thatcher correctly said in response to Mr. Sandford, "the only sound doctrine is, not that which has been stated by the gentleman from Kentucky (Mr. SANFORD,) that whatever power is not prohibited by the Constitution is agreeable to it, but that such powers as are not given are still held by the States or the people. No arguments have been addressed to prove that the Constitution delegates such a power."[19]

Similar considerations undermine the slightly subtler arguments put forward by other members of Congress that used the presumed prerogatives of sovereignty as an interpretive tool. Representative Joseph Nicholson, for instance, grounded the power to acquire territory in the Constitution's treaty and war-making powers — as did Chief Justice Marshall twenty-five years later. But Representative Nicholson concluded that these enumerated constitutional powers must include a power of territorial acquisition because "[t]he right must exist somewhere. It is essential to independent sovereignty."[20] Representative Randolph similarly argued that the national government must have constitutional power to acquire territory because the Confederation government clearly had such power and because there is no express or inferred limitation on acquisition in the Constitution. "If the old Confederation — a mere government of States — a loosely connected league . . . could rightfully acquire territory in their allied capacity, much more is the existing Government competent to make such an acquisition."[21]

These are not valid arguments in the context of the federal Constitution. The limited government of the United States might well lack certain powers possessed by unlimited governments. It is even conceivable that there could be governmental powers possessed neither by the states nor by the United States if the Constitution denies those powers to the states and fails to grant them to the federal government. That is precisely the point driven home by the Tenth Amendment's declaration that "[t]he powers not delegated to the United States by the Constitution, nor prohibited by it to the States, are reserved to the States respectively, *or to the people.*" This does not mean that Representatives Nicholson and Randolph were necessarily incorrect about the scope of federal power, but it does mean that one cannot reason to that conclusion from abstract premises about governmental power severed from the concrete scheme of power embodied in the Constitution.

Representative Caesar Rodney, like most participants in the debate over Louisiana, read the treaty power to include a power of territorial acquisition,[22] but he advanced as well a number of alternative grounds for the legality of the Louisiana Purchase. The first clause of Article I, section 8, the section that enumerates most of the powers of Congress, states that Congress has power to "lay and collect Taxes, Duties, Imposts and Excises, to pay the Debts and provide for the common Defence and general Welfare of the United States; but all Duties, Imposts and Excises shall be uniform throughout the United States."[23] Representative Rodney seized on the phrase "provide for the common Defence and general Welfare," maintaining that "[t]he import of these terms is very comprehensive indeed. . . . I cannot perceive why, within the fair meaning of this general provision is not included the power of increasing our territory."[24]

Representative Rodney's comments raise the ancient and long-lived debate concerning whether the so-called General Welfare Clause (and the accompanying language "to pay the Debts and provide for the common Defence") is a distinct grant of power to the national government. Jeffrey Renz has aptly identified three versions of the power claimed by Representative Rodney: the "strong Hamiltonian" interpretation, which states that "the General Welfare Clause granted Congress power to enact all laws that it deems for the general welfare"; the more moderate interpretation advanced by Joseph Story, and at times by Hamilton, that "would grant Congress the power to spend for any purpose that it deems in furtherance of the general welfare"; and the Madisonian view, which treats the clause as a grant of power "to spend and to enact laws pursuant to the powers enumerated in Section 8 [of Article I]."[25] The modern Supreme Court has effectively adopted the second, "soft" Hamiltonian position.[26]

The intramural debate among Hamilton, Madison, Story, and others is fascinating,[27] but any position that treats the phrase "to pay the Debts and provide for the common Defence and general Welfare of the United States" as a grant of power in any form is fundamentally wrong. The language "to pay the Debts and provide for the Common Defence and general Welfare of the United States" sets forth a limitation on and clarification of the previously granted power to tax; it does not authorize the expenditure of tax revenues for the stated purposes. It would take an article to establish this point, but, fortunately, the article has already been written: Professor Renz has exhaustively demonstrated that none of the variations that treat the General Welfare Clause as a power grant mesh with the Constitution's text, structure, or history. Textually, the General Welfare Clause reads as a limitation on the power to tax rather than as a grant of power: taxes and duties may be levied only to pay the debts and provide for the common defense and general welfare, and they must be uniform throughout the United States. Structurally, reading the clause as a grant of power largely unravels the entire scheme of enumerated power that is so carefully laid out elsewhere in the Constitution. If one takes the strong Hamiltonian view, the unraveling is obviously total; Congress would effectively become a legislature of general jurisdiction. If one takes the moderate Hamiltonian view, as has the modern Supreme Court, the unraveling is more subtle (because spending authority and regulatory authority are not the same thing), but it would be at least a bit odd to have a government limited in every way except its authority to spend. The Madisonian view that ties spending to enumerated powers turns out, as we shall see shortly, to be an essentially correct account of federal spending authority, but that spending authority stems from a source other than the General Welfare Clause. Historically, treating the General Welfare Clause as a limitation on and clarification of the taxing power elegantly meshes with founding-era understandings about the nature and dangers of taxation; by making clear that "duties" may be levied for the "general Welfare," the clause affirms the congressional power to use excises and duties for regulatory as well as revenue-raising purposes.[28] All things considered, there is little to be said for any reading of the General Welfare Clause other than the one that rather plainly emerges from the text: Congress may levy taxes only for certain enumerated purposes.

Representative Rodney invoked yet another clause in support of a power of territorial acquisition. The District Clause gives Congress power "To exercise exclusive Legislation in all Cases whatsoever, over such District (not exceeding ten Miles square) as may, *by Cession of particular States, and the Acceptance of Congress*, become the Seat of the Government of the United States, and to exercise like Authority over *all Places purchased by the Consent of the Legislature of the State in which the Same shall be*, for the Erection of Forts, Magazines, Arsenals, dock-Yards, and other needful Buildings."[29] This clause, argued Representative Rodney, "is predicated on the right to purchase territory . . . and only limits that purchase by the consent of the States. If Congress have the right of purchasing territory from a State, how can gentlemen contend that they have not the right of purchasing territory elsewhere . . . ?"[30]

The argument does indeed support a power of territorial acquisition, but not necessarily the power that Representative Rodney sought to establish. The District Clause *presupposes* that the United States can acquire territory from states either by cession or purchase. The clause grants the power to govern such territory, but it assumes rather than grants the logically prior power of acquisition, which must therefore stem from some other constitutional source. That source, of course, cannot be the treaty power. The United States cannot make treaties with its own states. Treaties, by their nature, are compacts among sovereign nations, not agreements among units within a political community. Accordingly, whatever power justifies the acquisition of territory by the federal government within the domain of the United States does not necessarily justify acquisition of territory from foreign sovereigns. It might in fact do so, but one can only discover the answer by identifying the precise source of power to acquire domestic territory and examining whether that power extends to transactions such as the Louisiana Purchase.

So where in the Constitution does the federal government get the power to receive or buy land from a state? Consider a far more basic question: where does the federal government get the power to buy any kind of property, such as paper clips from a private contractor? The question is not as trivial as it may seem. Not only does the Constitution fail to contain an express "Territorial Acquisition Clause," it fails (apart from the various taxing and borrowing authorizations, which permit the "acquisition" of money) to contain an express "Acquisition Clause" for any kind of property. If one takes the principle of enumerated powers seriously, as one should, one needs to find something in the Constitution that can authorize property acquisitions. And because constitutional clauses that grant power often do so only in a limited form and fashion, power-granting clauses are often primary sources of constitutional limitations; the character of the grant often defines the scope and limits of the power. The search for a proper source of the power to acquire property cannot be taken lightly.

The modern answer to this problem is quite straightforward: the Constitution's Spending Clause authorizes the federal government to spend funds to acquire property. What could possibly be simpler? But although the Spending Clause is well enough known today to be the subject of Supreme Court opinions and academic symposia,[31] there is one small problem with using the Spending Clause as a source of power to acquire property: there is no Spending Clause in the federal Constitution. The text most often identified as a "Spending Clause" is in fact a taxing clause: the provision, invoked by Representative Rodney, which authorizes Congress to levy uniform taxes to pay the debts and provide for the common defense and general welfare. The only power granted by this clause is the power to lay and collect taxes; everything else in the clause limits, qualifies, and justifies this basic grant. Of course, there is no reason to bring in tax revenues unless one is going to spend them, but that does not mean that the taxing and spending powers must come from the same source. Indeed, one might well expect the contrary if one thinks that there are likely to be different internal limitations on taxing and spending authority; there is no reason, for instance, to suppose that the Constitution would impose a geographical uniformity requirement on spending in the same manner that it imposes a uniformity requirement on taxation. Nor are taxes the only source of funds for the national government. As Professor David Engdahl has noted, "[f]or generations, public debts were paid and a large part of the federal budget was supported by proceeds from the sale of public domain lands; but nothing in the Taxing Clause even implicitly contemplates spending such funds."[32] In modern times, of course, a major source of federal revenue has been the Borrowing Clause, which authorizes Congress "[t]o borrow Money on the credit of the United States."[33] This clause "makes no reference to spending at all, and the spending allusion in the Taxing Clause does not even colorably reach borrowed sums."[34] It is clear textually, structurally, and historically that the Taxing Clause is not an authorization to spend. As an eighteenth-century

Freudian might have observed: Sometimes a power to lay and collect taxes really is just a power to lay and collect taxes.

Nor does the Constitution's Appropriations Clause authorize the spending of funds. The Appropriations Clause states: "No money shall be drawn from the Treasury, but in Consequence of Appropriations made by Law; and a regular Statement and Account of the Receipts and Expenditures of all public Money shall be published from time to time."[35] This clause is a limitation on executive or judicial action rather than a grant of any power — which is why it appears in Article I, section 9, the portion of the original Constitution that is devoted to direct limitations on various federal actors. It makes appropriations statutes a precondition to any federal spending, so that presidents and judges cannot spend on their own authority, but it does not itself authorize such statutes.

Of course, the Constitution somewhere contains the power to spend money. It matters a great deal, however, from where that power comes, as the textual source of the power defines the scope and limits of the grant. So where in the Constitution can one find the undoubted power to enact spending statutes to acquire property or for any other purpose? There are two possible sources: one is limited but certain, the other is broader but more problematic.

The broadest potential source of spending power would be the Property Clause of Article IV, which states that "Congress shall have Power to dispose of and make all needful Rules and Regulations respecting the Territory or other Property belonging to the United States."[36] If this clause authorizes spending statutes, then there is no direct textual limitation on the purposes for which money can be spent; the clause is simply a bare authorization to Congress to "dispose of . . . Property belonging to the United States." Disposal of money in return for paper clips, tanks, or Louisiana would be permissible.

Professor David Engdahl has mounted a spirited argument that this clause indeed authorizes spending statutes,[37] and his position has much to commend it. Textually, money that reaches the United States Treasury, whether from taxes, proceeds from sales, or borrowing, seems clearly to be "[p]roperty belonging to the United States." Money is clearly "property" for purposes of the Fifth Amendment's Due Process and Takings Clauses, and one normally presumes that words in the Constitution (even words separated by two years' time, as is true of the Property Clause and the Fifth Amendment) are used consistently. The Property Clause unambiguously authorizes Congress to "dispose of" property, and what could more clearly constitute a disposition of money than an appropriations statute? Indeed, founding-era sources contain a number of explicit references to "disposal" of money, such as tax revenues,[38] so there is nothing linguistically peculiar about a clause that would authorize

Congress to "dispose of" money. Structurally, the generalized spending power that would come from the Property Clause fits well with the language of the Taxing Clause, which permits taxation "to pay the Debts and provide for the common Defence and general Welfare of the United States." And historically, Professor Engdahl labors hard to link the Property Clause to earlier-proposed provisions that even more clearly would have authorized spending without internal textual limitation.

Nonetheless, we do not think that the Property Clause can bear this much weight. The basic problem is the clause's location in the Constitution. Article I contains the vast majority of congressional powers, including specific powers over fiscal affairs. The taxing clauses are all in Article I, along with all of the clauses expressly dealing with appropriations or other financial matters.[39] It would be nothing short of bizarre if the Constitution located its central authority to spend in the bowels of Article IV. An ordinary reader in 1788 would expect to find federal spending authority somewhere in Article I, along with the taxing, appropriations, and fiscal management provisions, instead of in the grab bag of miscellaneous provisions that constitute Article IV.

The move from property disposal to spending is even less plausible when one considers the rest of the Property Clause. The clause authorizes both disposal of property and the enactment of "all needful Rules and Regulations respecting the Territory or other Property belonging to the United States; and nothing in this Constitution shall be so construed as to Prejudice any Claims of the United States, or of any particular State." The phrase "all needful Rules and Regulations" clearly authorizes Congress to govern land held by the United States. It also clearly authorizes Congress to regulate the use of personal property held by the United States. It is much harder to see how the clause relates to money held in the treasury.

Most fundamentally, the primary object of the Property Clause is clearly "Territory belonging to the United States." The clause provides authorization for governance of the Northwest Territory and any other territory ceded to the United States, authorization for disposal (sale) of such territory, and a stipulation that land claims by states will be unaffected by the clause or anything else in the Constitution. If one judges words by the company that they keep, the inclusion in this clause of the phrase "or other Property" would most naturally be taken as a reference to "other Property similar in character to the Territory belonging to the United States that is the primary subject of this clause." Tangible items, such as land or paper clips, are sensible subjects for a clause that deals with authority to "dispose of" and to make "Rules and Regulations respecting" such property, while money is a much poorer fit. Notwithstanding the presumption in favor of construing words in the Constitution consistently, there is a strong contextual case for treating the word "Property" in the Property Clause differently from the same word as it appears in the Fifth and Fourteenth Amendments.[40] Stated more precisely, the phrase "Territory or other Property belonging to the United States" is not coextensive with "property" or "private property" held by individuals.

The improbability of a reasonable, fully informed founding-era public observer's understanding the Property Clause as a general authorization for appropriations can be illuminated by comparing the clause with the proposal that Professor Engdahl regards as its ancestor. On August 22, 1787, the Committee of Detail proposed a clause granting the Congress power "to provide, as may become necessary, from time to time, for the well managing and securing the common property and general interests and welfare of the United States in such manner as shall not interfere with the Governments of individual States in matters which respect only their internal Police, or for which their individual authorities may be competent."[41] Had this provision been ratified, it would have been easily understood as a general authorization of the national government to take measures, whether through appropriations or regulations, to promote the "general . . . welfare" of the nation. Such authority would have extended only to matters that were deemed to be beyond the competence of the state governments, but subject to that qualification, it would have provided broad authority outside of the specific enumerations of power found elsewhere in the Constitution. Indeed, those specific enumerations would either have been mere illustrations of the all-encompassing general welfare principle or perhaps exceptions to the "beyond state competence" qualification (allowing, for instance, Congress to enact copyright legislation without first demonstrating that the subject was beyond the competence of the states). Such a "well managing clause" would have vastly altered the character of the national government from one of limited and enumerated legislative powers to one of general powers, of appropriation or otherwise, in all matters beyond state competence. Its import would not have escaped public notice.

Contrast the likely informed public understanding of this "well managing clause" with the likely informed public understanding of the Property Clause, which as we noted appears in Article IV rather than in Article I, in which the vast bulk of enumerated legislative powers are found: "The Congress shall have Power to dispose of and make all needful Rules and Regulations respecting the Territory or other Property belonging to the United States." Even if some of the participants in the Constitutional Convention believed (as Professor Engdahl argues) that the Property Clause incorporated the "well managing clause's" general appropriations authorization, though not its general regulatory authorization,[42] is it plausible to think that an informed general public would so read this provision in Article IV? If one is looking for authorization for appropriations, the Property Clause does not present itself as a likely candidate.

Of course, if that clause was the only possible source of authorization for federal spending, a fully informed audience would probably take the leap. It is more likely that the Constitution contains an ill-suited, inconspicuous appropriations authorization than none at all. But the Constitution contains another provision that unquestionably authorizes appropriations statutes. The certain source of appropriations authority is the clause at the end of Article I, section 8 that grants to Congress ancillary powers to effectuate the national government's other granted powers: "The Congress shall have Power . . . To make all Laws which shall be necessary and proper for carrying into Execution the foregoing Powers, and all other Powers vested by this Constitution in the Government of the United States, or in any Department or Officer thereof."[43] This "Sweeping Clause," as the founding generation called it,[44] unquestionably includes the power to enact spending laws that are "necessary and proper" for effectuating federal powers. And the Sweeping Clause, of course, appears in Article I, along with the rest of the Constitution's financial provisions, which is exactly where one would expect to find the federal government's spending authority.

The critical difference between the Sweeping Clause and the Property Clause as sources of spending authority concerns the internal textual limitations on the granted authority. The Property Clause, if it functioned as a grant of spending authority, would impose no limits on the purposes for which Congress could spend. There would be no question, for example, that the clause provided sufficient authorization for the purchase of land from private parties, states, or foreign sovereigns. The Sweeping Clause, by contrast, only authorizes laws, including spending laws, that are "necessary and proper for carrying into Execution" other enumerated federal powers. Congress can therefore spend only if the appropriation is tied to the execution of one of the federal government's granted powers. The Sweeping Clause does not provide a stand-alone grant of spending authority, and certainly not an authority to spend for a nonspecific "general welfare of the United States." In this respect, the federal spending power that emerges from the Sweeping Clause closely approximates the federal spending power that James Madison believed came from his construction of the General Welfare Clause. Madison, recall, believed that the General Welfare Clause authorized federal spending, but only pursuant to Congress's Article I, section 8 powers. He was right that Congress can spend money only to carry into execution other granted powers, but he was wrong about the source and scope of that power. The source of that power is the Sweeping Clause, not the General Welfare Clause. And the power extends to implementing any powers granted to any federal institution, not merely the powers of Congress enumerated in Article I, section 8.

If the Sweeping Clause authorizes the purchase of land, that purchase must be pursuant to some enumerated power of some federal institution. In the context of the Louisiana Purchase, the Sweeping Clause would authorize the federal government to spend money for the acquisition of Louisiana *if but only if* that spending was "necessary and proper" for carrying into execution an independent power of acquisition. The Sweeping Clause helps to *effectuate* any power of acquisition contained in the Constitution, but it does not itself provide a power of acquisition.

Admittedly, there are problems with viewing the Sweeping Clause as the sole source of federal spending authority. It is entirely possible that some participants in the drafting and ratification of the Constitution expected the federal government to be able to spend for certain purposes beyond the enumerated powers of Congress.[45] Such expectations, however, do not rise to the level of constitutional meaning unless they conform to the understandings of the Constitution's words and structure that would have been held by an informed general public after consideration of all relevant arguments.[46]

A more troubling interpretative problem is the provision in the Taxing Clause stating that taxes are authorized "to pay the Debts and provide for the common Defence and general Welfare of the United States." It is, to say the least, odd to authorize the raising of revenue for the general welfare if there is no corresponding power to spend for the general welfare, and the Sweeping Clause generates no such power. The reference in the Taxing Clause to the general welfare supports the idea that a power to spend for the general welfare exists somewhere in the Constitution.

There are, however, two understandings of the general welfare phrase in the Taxing Clause that harmonize with our reading of the rest of the constitutional structure. First, and most straightforwardly, one could simply take it at face value as a limitation on the power to tax. The Taxing Clause requires all excises to be "uniform throughout the United States," but that does not prevent all possible uses of the taxing power as a tool of sectional rivalry. Suppose, for instance, that a majority in Congress imposes a "uniform" excise tax on goods that are produced only in one disfavored region or state. Such taxes survive scrutiny under the uniformity provision of the Taxing Clause, but if the obvious purpose of the taxes is to punish the disfavored region or state, one could argue that they were not imposed in order "to pay the Debts and provide for the common Defence and general Welfare of the United States." The general welfare language thus serves as an additional check on the use of the taxing power as a weapon of political combat.

Additionally, as Professor Renz has eloquently argued, one could view the general welfare phrase in the Taxing Clause as a guarantee of Congress's power to use duties and excises as a regulatory tool, which was a practice familiar to and approved by the founding generation. Without the "general welfare" language, duties and excises could be used only to raise revenues, not to regulate or promote commerce. On this understanding, the General Welfare Clause does not grant power, but it confirms and clarifies the nature of the power to levy duties and excises.

The Sweeping Clause is the natural home for the Constitution's undoubted spending authority. It is a more natural home than any of the alternative sources, including the alternative that would attribute to an informed general public an understanding that the unpromising language of the Property Clause authorizes spending measures without limit.

If spending authority is limited by the terms of the Sweeping Clause, one is left to find a power of territorial acquisition that the Sweeping Clause can help carry into execution; the Sweeping Clause itself cannot be the source of such power. The most obvious candidate for such a power is the Treaty Clause, which is where this discussion began and to where it will now return.

Enumerations and Treaties

The Treaty Clause of the Constitution states that the President "shall have Power, by and with the Advice and Consent of the Senate, to make Treaties, provided two thirds of the Senators present concur."[47] Louisiana was acquired from France by a treaty executed by the President and confirmed by two-thirds of the Senate. There is nothing in the text of the Treaty Clause that suggests that treaties of acquisition, which certainly were among the kinds of treaties that were most familiar to the founding generation, are not within its compass. Indeed, there is nothing in the text of the Treaty Clause that indicates *any* limitation on the kinds of treaties that can be executed. Accordingly, there would seem to be no question that the United States could properly acquire the Louisiana Territory by means of a treaty. The consideration for the acquisition, of course, had to be appropriated by Congress, but the President plus two-thirds of the Senate would seem to be constitutionally competent to enter into the deal.

In the case of the Louisiana Purchase, matters do turn out to be as simple as they seem. Indeed, if the Louisiana Purchase were the only acquisition of territory in American history, one could dispose of the constitutional problem of territorial acquisition in very short order. A wide range of understandings of the treaty power would all lead to the conclusion that the purchase was constitutional; it is actually quite difficult to imagine a remotely plausible understanding of the treaty power under which the Louisiana Purchase would not be constitutional.

Nonetheless, we undertake in this chapter an extensive analysis of the scope and limits of the federal treaty power. We have our reasons. The Louisiana Purchase was an easy case, but it was easy because of considerations that often escape notice. The Louisiana Purchase was not easily constitutional simply because one can wave the Treaty Clause at it. It was easily constitutional because a number of constitutional provisions and principles worked in conjunction with the Treaty Clause to make it easy. And once one gets beyond 1803, into the second half of the nineteenth century, matters become considerably more complex. We cannot long escape the problem of accurately defining the federal treaty power, so we might as well face it up front.

TAKING THOMAS JEFFERSON SERIOUSLY

The scope of the treaty power has been the subject of substantial debate from the nation's earliest days to the present. The framing generation worried about such questions as whether the President and a two-thirds majority of the Senate can cede some or all of a state's territory to a foreign power.[48] Early-twentieth-century thinkers, echoing previous debates, wondered whether the treaty power could be used to create regulatory laws that are beyond the enumerated legislative powers of Congress.[49] Modern scholars debate whether treaties can override otherwise applicable constitutional limitations, such as the prohibition on federal commandeering of state governmental processes.[50] Overlying these debates is the perennial question whether and when treaties are self-executing — that is, take effect as domestic law without legislative implementation.[51] And the prevalence of executive agreements, with or without congressional approval, raises the additional question whether the treaty power is the exclusive mechanism by which the United States can make binding international commitments.[52]

It is unclear under modern law what, if anything, limits the scope of the treaty power. The Supreme Court has never invalidated a treaty provision as unconstitutional, but it has suggested that treaties cannot bind the United States to violate certain rights guaranteed by the Bill of Rights.[53] Scholars have suggested limitations ranging from restraints on the kinds of negotiations that treaties can embody to restraints grounded in federalism and/or separation of powers.[54] Most of these claimed restraints are contested, either as too limiting, not limited enough, or both. Debates about the treaty power are plentiful, lively, and vibrant.

One key question that need not concern us here is whether treaties can extend only to a limited range of subjects that are properly a matter for international agreement. The answer turns on the eighteenth-century meaning of the word *treaty*. Does that term, in its constitutional context, mean any agreement between sovereign nations on any subject, or does it refer only to a subset of agreements dealing with such matters as war, peace, trade, and comity? It is possible that the word *treaty* was generally understood in 1788 to refer only to a certain class of international agreements.[55] Mercifully, we need not address this potentially vexing question here, because treaties of acquisition are clearly within the compass of the treaty power on any plausible understanding of its scope. One can argue about whether so-called human rights treaties that concern only the treating nations' regulation of their own citizens fall within the constitutional meaning of the term *treaty*,[56] but acquisitions of territory, whether as part of a peace settlement or otherwise, are paradigmatic examples of treaties.

Historically, the most important question concerning the treaty power has concerned whether the treaty power extends to matters beyond the legislative competence of Congress. This question whether there is a precise congruence between the scope of the treaty power and the scope of Congress's legislative power was the basis for founding-era objections to treaty provisions dealing with such matters as alien ownership of real property.[57] It was central to the Southern antebellum critique of the federal treaty power and particularly of the force of federal treaties that interfered with Southern regulation of slavery.[58] It was the precise issue decided by the Supreme Court in its landmark 1920 decision in *Missouri v Holland*, which held that Congress could implement treaties creating international commitments regarding migratory birds even though Congress and the President could not (under then-existing understandings) constitutionally regulate that subject under any of the enumerated Article I legislative powers.[59] In the wake of *Holland*, the relation between the treaty power and Congress's legislative powers was the subject of the attempt led by Senator John Bricker half a century ago to amend the Constitution, most dramatically by a provision that would have stipulated (either as clarification or alteration of the Treaty Clause) that "[a] treaty shall become effective as internal law in the United States only through legislation which would be valid in the absence of treaty."[60] This question has been the subject of extensive legal commentary for a century. And it misconceives the real constitutional issue concerning the treaty power.

There is no reason to suppose that the treaty power can extend only to subjects within Congress's enumerated powers. Vasan Kesavan has endeavored to demonstrate that at least one accepted function of treaties — the cession of territory to another country, generally as part of a treaty of peace — is beyond the enumerated powers of Congress.[61] A much simpler example, however, is readily available: Congress does not have the power to end a war, but the President and the Senate can formalize the end of a war by treaty. Congress, of course, can *effectively* end a war by refusing to fund the war effort, but it has no formal power, either internationally or domestically, to terminate a war.[62] A treaty power that does not include the power to enter into peace treaties would be like an executive power that does not include the power to execute the laws; it would require overwhelming evidence (which does not exist) to attribute this understanding to a fully informed eighteenth-century audience. Thus, if the debate really focuses on whether the Constitution's presidential/senatorial treaty-making power is precisely coextensive with the congressional/presidential lawmaking power, it is much ado about nothing.

We submit that this focus on whether the treaty power and the legislative power are congruent reflects a fundamental misconception about the Treaty Clause that has been with us for a long time. The Treaty Clause has almost universally been understood as a grant of governmental power that stands independently of the other enumerated national powers. As Gerald Neuman elegantly describes the prevailing view, "[t]he treaty power was designed as an independent grant of power to the federal government to enter into treaties that enact rules that Congress might not otherwise have been able to enact."[63] We think that the Treaty Clause has a much different, and more limited, role in the constitutional structure. The treaty power, as Thomas Jefferson suggested more than two hundred years ago, is a vehicle for implementing otherwise-granted national powers in the international arena. It may be used to carry into effect national powers found in the Constitution, but it cannot function as a free-standing power, divorced from connection to the exercise of some other enumerated power. In this respect, the Treaty Clause is analogous to the Sweeping Clause of Article I: the Sweeping Clause permits Congress to implement otherwise-granted national powers domestically, while the treaty power permits the President and Senate to implement otherwise-granted national powers — and by "national powers" we mean *any* granted federal powers, not just the legislative powers of Congress--internationally by entering into agreements with foreign sovereigns. The treaty power, in other words, is *implementational* rather than *jurisdiction extending*.

In order to understand this "Jeffersonian" position, a good place to start is with the distinctive nature of the treaty power. What can one do through treaties that cannot be done by some other legal act? The answer is that domestic legislation cannot legally bind either foreign sovereigns or future American governmental actors. Congress can, within its constitutional authority, bind citizens, states, and the national government. It can even create legal rights in foreign governments and give those governments enforcement power in American courts. But Congress cannot extend its legislative influence to foreign sovereigns or prevent itself or future Congresses from altering statutory rights granted to foreign governments. For that, the nation needs treaties: legally binding consensual arrangements between or among sovereigns.

Suppose that the United States and France want to enter into an agreement providing for reciprocal duty-free entry of perfumes. Congress can pass a law exempting French perfumes from all American duties. But if Congress later changes that law, the French government would have no legal recourse. The French government could change its own domestic law, make diplomatic hay, begin a trade war, or even begin a shooting war, but the American action would not violate any legal norm. If, however, the arrangement is embodied in a treaty, then subsequent legislation contrary to the terms of the treaty would violate international law. Congress could still pass legislation in violation of the treaty that would be fully effective as a matter of domestic law. Such legislation would not be "unconstitutional." But a treaty that "locks in" the agreement raises the cost of such legislation by whatever amount a violation of international law is considered or expected to entail. Similarly, a treaty, and only a treaty, can secure an internationally binding agreement from a foreign sovereign.

Treaties are thus an essential means for implementing national powers in the international arena. The Sweeping Clause permits Congress to execute national powers domestically (provided that such executory laws are "necessary and proper"). The Treaty Clause similarly permits the United States, through the President and the Senate, to implement national powers internationally by locking in intergovernmental agreements.

At least, that is the most *minimal* function of the Treaty Clause. It is another matter altogether to say that it is the *maximal* or *only* function. Thomas Jefferson took that next step. Jefferson was, at least much of the time, deeply suspicious of the federal treaty power, in terms of both its constitutional scope and the wisdom of its frequent exercise. Although some scholars allege that at least some aspects of his views on the treaty power reflected a dominant consensus, others powerfully (and persuasively) disagree.[64] For our purposes, it does not matter which view of Jefferson and his contemporaries is correct. Our goal is to determine whether Jefferson's view is, all things considered, the best reading of the Treaty Clause, not whether it commanded a clear majority of his contemporaries.

Jefferson succinctly expressed his constitutional view of treaties in a manual on parliamentary practice that he wrote for the Senate while he was Vice President:

> By the Constitution of the United States, this department of legislation is confined to two branches only, of the ordinary Legislature; the President originating, and Senate having a negative. To what subject this power extends, has not been defined in detail by the Constitution; nor are we entirely agreed among ourselves. 1. It is admitted that it must Concern the foreign nation, party to the contract, or it would be a mere nullity res inter alias acta. 2. By the general power to make treaties, the Constitution must have intended to comprehend only those objects which are usually regulated by treaty, and cannot be otherwise regulated. 3. It must have meant to except out of these the rights reserved to the States; for surely the President and Senate cannot do by treaty what the whole government is interdicted from doing in any way. 4. And also to except those subjects of legislation in which it gave a participation to the House of Representatives. This last exception is denied by some, on the ground that it would leave very little matter for the treaty power to work on. The less the better, say others. The Constitution thought it wise to restrain the Executive and Senate from entangling and embroiling our affairs with those of Europe. Besides, as the negotiations are carried on by the Executive alone, the subjecting to the ratification of the Representatives such articles as are within their participation, is no more inconvenient than to the Senate. But the ground of this exemption is denied as unfounded. For examine, e.g., the treaty of commerce with France, and it will be found that out of thirty-one articles, there are not more than small portions of two or three of them which would not still remain as subjects of treaties, untouched by these exceptions.[65]

This passage obviously reflects Jefferson's hostility to treaties,[66] and it would be rash to read it as a general expression of the sentiments of the Senate — or indeed as a general expression of anything other than Jefferson's hostility to treaties. Nonetheless, it contains some important propositions about the treaty power that are worth considering.

Jefferson's first proposed restriction on the treaty power — that treaties must genuinely concern foreign nations — is not as obvious as it may sound. Jefferson was doubtless imagining a putative "treaty" that is in fact simply an attempt to perform an end-run around the Article I legislative process by having a foreign collaborator help construct domestic legislation through the formalities of a treaty. Even many modern advocates of a broad treaty power share some of these concerns about phony treaties.[67] The Constitution only prohibits such arrangements, however, if the collaborative agreement falls outside the boundaries of the term *treaty* as it appears in the Constitution. That is, if an entirely one-sided affair, in which one party simply uses the form of a treaty to alter its domestic law, would not count as a "treaty" for constitutional purposes, then Jefferson was right. Otherwise, it is hard to see why a treaty, if it really is a treaty, is unenforceable simply because it is a bad deal—or even a subterfuge. The Constitution lays down certain formal rules for accomplishing certain ends, and if those formal rules are followed, the procedure is legal *unless* there is some substantive limitation on the scope of the granted power.[68] A properly executed treaty is legally binding unless it is either not a treaty or it exceeds some limitation on the scope of the treaty power that is implicit in the constitutional structure—which brings us to the rest of Jefferson's analysis.

Jefferson's second and fourth limitations—that treaties cannot concern matters that could "otherwise be regulated" or matters in which the Constitution "gave a participation to the House of Representatives"—are closely related; both suggest that treaties cannot serve as substitutes for legislation. According to Jefferson, where the Constitution authorizes regulation by legislation, regulation by treaty is implicitly forbidden. The only sphere of application for treaties, on this understanding, is subjects that cannot be regulated by legislation. That sphere would obviously include the international "lock in" function that cannot be accomplished by legislation. The question is whether the sphere of application could possibly include anything else.

What if certain subjects—for instance, regulation of marriage or local land use—are beyond the enumerated legislative powers of Congress? Obviously, it would not trench upon the prerogatives of Congress or the House to permit treaties to regulate such subjects, because there would be no prerogatives upon which to trench. Just as obviously, it would essentially constitute the federal government as a general government; anything outside the legislative powers of Congress would be within the treaty powers of the President and Senate. That is no doubt why Jefferson added his final limitation on the treaty power: the Constitution "must have meant to except out of these [treaty powers] the rights reserved to the States; surely the President and Senate cannot do by treaty what the whole government is interdicted from doing in any way." That is, treaties cannot reach subjects that are not within some other enumerated federal power. Together, Jefferson's limitations describe a treaty power that is purely *implementational*: it can carry into effect enumerated federal powers by extending them into the international arena in legally binding fashion, but it cannot regulate on its own initiative.

In an 1803 letter to Wilson Cary Nicholas, Jefferson repeated and elaborated this thesis: "If [the Treaty Clause] has bounds they can be no others than the definitions of the powers which that instrument gives. It specifies & delineates the operations permitted to the federal government, and gives all the powers necessary to carry these into execution. Whatever of these enumerated objects is proper for a law, Congress may make the law; whatever is proper to be executed by way of a treaty, the President & Senate may enter into the treaty; whatever is to be done by a judicial sentence, the judges may pass the sentence.[69] That which is "proper to be executed by way of a treaty" is to make domestic law internationally binding or to secure binding commitments from foreign sovereigns. Under a Jeffersonian understanding of treaties, that "lock-in" function is *all* that treaties may properly accomplish. A treaty could, for instance, "execute" a legislated trade agreement by entering into legally binding relations with a foreign government (or by setting up a framework that is triggered by subsequent legislation), but a treaty could not itself establish the terms of trade apart from legislation. Put in terms of a somewhat different modern debate that we have already mentioned: on a Jeffersonian view, treaties are self-executing — that is, take effect without need for further statutory implementation — with respect to the states by virtue of the Supremacy Clause, but they are not necessarily self-executing with respect to federal institutions. Jefferson thus saw the Treaty Clause as an Article II counterpart to the Sweeping Clause of Article I. Both clauses, for Jefferson, grant power to carry into effect other exercises of constitutional power but do not constitute free-standing grants of jurisdiction.

Importantly, the powers implemented by the Treaty Clause need not be Article I powers of Congress. The implementational view permits the treaty power to effectuate *all* powers of *all* federal institutions. Just as the Sweeping Clause permits Congress to pass legislation to implement its own granted powers "and all other Powers vested by this Constitution in the Government of the United States, or in any Department or Officer thereof," the treaty power, on this Jeffersonian understanding, permits treaty makers to carry into execution presidential and judicial powers, as well as powers vested in individual officers (such as the Vice President's power to preside over the Senate or the Chief Justice's power to preside over presidential impeachments).[70]

Although Jefferson's implementational conception of the Treaty Clause has never garnered wide support, it has also proved to be irrepressible. Every half century or so, Jefferson's interpretation of the Treaty Clause finds new life. In 1845, the Senate Committee on Foreign Relations, explicitly invoking the authority of Jefferson, endorsed an implementational theory of the treaty power in a report on the proposed annexation of Texas:

> The committee yield entire assent to this opinion of Mr. Jefferson. . . . [T]he treaty-making power can never have capacity of exertion unless in the cases in which its aid is invoked by some one of the expressed powers to carry out the

purpose which, being of exterior relation, the powers of domestic sphere of operation would be unable for that reason to reach without the aid of this power of exterior operation. The treaty-making power, under this construction, can never be any other than subsidiary — is never a power independent in its vocation, however it is so in its name and structure. It is the handmaid — waits on the occasion of the other powers; and though in no posture to receive orders from them, it never yet moves to its exertion save in subordination to their desires.[71]

In 1898, during the debate over the annexation of the Philippine Islands following the Spanish-American War, Senator George Hoar, without expressly invoking Jefferson, articulated an implementational theory of the power of the United States to acquire territory. Although Senator Hoar derived the power of territorial acquisition from the Article IV Territories Clause rather than from the Treaty Clause, his reasoning would be fully applicable to a power of acquisition by treaty:

> This power . . . to acquire and hold territory or other property, like other constitutional powers, is a power to be exercised only for constitutional purposes.
>
> It is like the power to acquire and dispose of ships or cannon or public buildings or a drove of pack mules or a library, to be exercised in accomplishment of the purposes of the Constitution and not to be exercised where it is not reasonably necessary or convenient for the accomplishment of those purposes. We have no more right to acquire land or hold it, or to dispose of it for an unconstitutional purpose than we have a right to fit out a fleet or to buy a park of artillery for an unconstitutional purpose.[72]

And an implementational conception of the treaty power was implicit in the attempts in the 1950s, led by Senator John Bricker, to amend the Constitution to provide that treaties "shall become effective as internal law in the United States only through legislation which would be valid in the absence of treaty."[73] To the extent that supporters of the amendment thought that they were clarifying rather than changing the Constitution, they were endorsing an implementational view of treaties.

We endorse Jefferson's position, not because another half century has passed since its last appearance, but because we think it is correct. And we think this notwithstanding the fact that the implementational conception of the treaty power is problematic along every dimension that is relevant for constitutional meaning: historical, textual, intratextual, and structural. Historically, although our position was not utterly alien to the founding generation, as Jefferson demonstrates, we certainly do not claim that we were led to our view by the weight of historical evidence. To the contrary, the view is distinctly antihistorical in most important respects. Textually, the Treaty Clause is very stark and does not express any internal limitations. Intratextually, the analogy to the Sweeping Clause raises an immediate objection to our claim: the Sweeping Clause expressly says that it permits only laws that "carry into Execution" other federal powers, while the Treaty Clause contains no such restriction. How could there possibly be stronger intratextual evidence of the absence of any such limitation on the treaty power? Structurally, the Treaty Clause requires consent by two-thirds of the Senate; doesn't that suggest that the Constitution's chosen method for limiting treaties is procedural rather than substantive?

Some of these concerns, such as the textual and intratextual objections, dissolve on close scrutiny. Others are legitimate but ultimately not dispositive. There is no reading of the Treaty Clause that does not generate serious interpretative problems. We maintain only that our "Jeffersonian" implementational reading poses fewer, less serious problems than do any of the available alternatives.[74] A close look at the Constitution's text and structure points, even if somewhat crookedly, to an implementational reading of the Treaty Clause. We must, however, ask for patience during that close look; the argument will take some time to construct.

TAKING TEXT SERIOUSLY

Start with some genuinely incontrovertible facts about the constitutional text. First, the power to make treaties is jointly vested in the President and the Senate: the President can "make Treaties, provided two thirds of the Senators present concur." The treaty-making power is not the only power vested in that particular combination of institutions. The President and Senate also share the power of appointment of principal officers of the United States (and of inferior officers if Congress does not vest their appointment elsewhere).[75] In the case of treaties, however, two-thirds of the Senate must approve, while a majority of the Senate is enough to consent to a presidential appointment. Thus, as with the Article I lawmaking power that is shared among the President, the Senate, and the House, the Constitution commits the treaty power to a combination of actors.

Second, the Constitution specifically denies to the states any treaty-making power: "No State shall enter into any Treaty, Alliance, or Confederation."[76] States may, with the consent of Congress, "enter into an [] agreement or Compact . . . with a foreign Power,"[77] but not even the consent of Congress can authorize a state treaty.

Third, federal treaties, including treaties validly made by the Confederation government, are "the supreme Law of the Land"[78] and accordingly, by the plain terms of the Supremacy Clause, take precedence over state statutes or state constitutions. Under standard conflict-of-laws doctrine, they are also held to take precedence over prior inconsistent federal statutes, though that conclusion is subject to serious question as a matter of original meaning.[79]

Fourth, the First Amendment does not apply to the Treaty Power. This statement, unlike the prior three statements, is likely to seem jarring to modern eyes, but it is as textually certain as is anything in the Constitution. The First Amendment says that "*Congress shall make no law* respecting an establishment of religion, or prohibiting the free exercise thereof; or abridging the freedom of speech, or of the press; or the right of the people peaceably to assemble, and to petition the Government, for a redress of grievances."[80] The President and Senate are not Congress, and the First Amendment by its unmistakable terms applies only to Congress. If a treaty requires congressional implementation for its full effect, then of course Congress could not enact implementing legislation in violation of the First Amendment, but the treaty itself is simply beyond the terms of the amendment.[81]

Modern law, of course, applies the First Amendment to the President, the courts, and the states,[82] and a fortiori to the federal treaty-making authority, but that is a textually indefensible maneuver. To read the First Amendment to apply to entities other than Congress is simply to abandon the enterprise of textual interpretation.

Of course, there may be constitutional provisions that apply to noncongressional actors that have much the same *effect* as the First Amendment, but that is a matter to be explored case by case. For instance, it is possible that the Privileges or Immunities Clause of the Fourteenth Amendment prevents states from (at least discriminatorily) abridging rights of speech, religion, and assembly.[83] One can metaphorically describe this as "applying the First Amendment to the states," but unless the terms of the Privileges or Immunities Clause just happen to track precisely the prohibitions in the First Amendment, the metaphor is misleading. The Fourteenth Amendment may well contain First-Amendment-like proscriptions on state action, but the First Amendment itself does not apply to the states.

Similarly, the First Amendment by its terms does not apply to executive and judicial action. That conclusion is not as striking as it might seem at first glance, for the simple reason that presidents and courts are not in a position to threaten rights of speech, religion, or assembly in the same manner as is Congress. Congress, of course, is not granted any enumerated power to regulate speech, religion, or assembly, and the First Amendment was accordingly simply repeating limits on the lawmaking power that were already contained in the original constitutional structure.[84] Nonetheless, Congress might try to use its authority under the Sweeping Clause to implement federal powers through methods that implicate those rights, such as by banning criticism of import laws in order to maximize their effectiveness. These laws, if enacted, would not be "necessary and proper" for effectuating federal powers, and Congress accordingly never had any enumerated constitutional authority to enact them, but it is easy to understand why people in 1791 might have worried about the prospect. The First Amendment quells concerns about such exercises of congressional power by confirming that Congress has no enumerated power, express or implied, to abridge freedom of speech or religion, regulate the establishment of religion, and such acts, in the course of implementing federal powers. There is no presidential power that poses an equivalent threat to free speech or religion. The President has various executive and war-making powers, but none of those powers remotely would justify presidential action, in the absence of statute, restricting speech or religion in domestic territory. There is accordingly nothing for the First Amendment to clarify with respect to presidential power, because there is no perceptible danger.[85] Courts, of course, can take actions that implicate speech, such as entering libel judgments or issuing protective orders, but no one in 1791 would have imagined that those actions, in the ordinary course of carrying out "[t]he judicial Power," raise any constitutional problems. One can imagine out-of-control judges issuing bizarre orders, but such action would so blatantly exceed "[t]he judicial Power" that no clarifying or confirming amendment was necessary.

The simple fact is that the First Amendment by its terms does not apply to executive or judicial actions, though of course it does limit congressional action that seeks to "carry into Execution" executive or judicial action. That fact may be out of step with modern sensibilities, but it is a fact nonetheless. The same is true of treaties: the First Amendment by its express terms simply does not apply to treaties, though it applies to congressional legislation implementing treaties. If a treaty that commits the United States to restrictions on speech or religion is unconstitutional, it must be unconstitutional for reasons other than the First Amendment.

For identical reasons, at least some of the prohibitions on federal action in Article I, section 9 of the Constitution do not apply to the treaty power. The first, and the most important to an eighteenth-century observer, of those prohibitions states that "[t]he Migration or Importation of such Persons as any of the States now existing shall think proper to admit, shall not be prohibited *by the Congress* prior to the Year one thousand eight hundred and eight."[86] This provision was specifically exempted from the Article V amendment process until its own internal time limit ran its course: "no Amendment which may be made prior to the Year One thousand eight hundred and eight shall in any Manner affect the first and fourth Clauses in the Ninth Section of the first Article."[87] In other words, Congress could not — and unamendably could not — forbid the importation of slaves for twenty years after ratification of the Constitution. The prohibition, however, by its terms applies only to *Congress*. This provision stands in stark contrast to another provision of Article I, section 9, which states that "[n]o Title of Nobility shall be granted *by the United States*."[88] This provision by its terms applies to any action taken on behalf of the United States, which presumably would include treaties.[89] In any event, it is clear that the Slave Trade Clause only restricts Congress.

To pose a question that will loom large later in our story: Does that mean that in 1789, the President and Senate could have entered into a treaty that mutually forbade the importation of slaves into the signatory countries and thus immediately ended the slave trade, despite the fact that Congress could not do so even with the help of explicit constitutional amendments? If the answer is "yes," the Treaty Clause is a more extraordinary provision than anyone, including any of the founding-era opponents of slavery, has thus far noticed. If the answer is "no," it must be by virtue of something in the Constitution other than Article I, section 9.

Fifth, and finally, the Treaty Clause is located in Article II of the Constitution — the article that primarily describes and empowers the federal government's executive institutions. The location of provisions in the Constitution, of course, is not an infallible guide to their characterization. Article I, section 4, clause 3 gives the Vice President power to preside over the Senate and to cast tie-breaking votes in that body, but although the grant appears in Article I, it is not, strictly speaking, a grant of legislative power, for the simple reason that the Constitution itself specifies that "[a]ll legislative Powers herein granted shall be vested in a Congress of the United States, which shall consist of a Senate and House of Representatives."[90] The Senate, in turn, "shall be composed of two Senators from each State," which means that the Vice President is not technically a member of the Senate and therefore cannot share in the Senate's legislative powers.[91] Similarly, even though Article I, section 7 gives the President a vital role in the lawmaking process, the President's presentment power cannot be considered "legislative" for purposes of the Constitution, because the President is not Congress and only Congress can exercise "legislative" power within the meaning of the Constitution. Whether one wants to call these noncongressional Article I powers "quasi-legislative" or some new term invented just for the occasion, such as "legisecutive," is a matter of taste, so long as one does not call them "legislative." For the same reasons, the Senate's roles in the treaty-making and appointment processes do not make senators executive actors for purposes of the Constitution, because the "executive

Power" is vested in the President alone. The Constitution's division of power reflects a real-world political compromise rather than a theoretically pure conception of separated powers; one must take the Constitution's definitions and allocations of power as one finds them without attempting to force them into a prefabricated mold.[92]

Nonetheless, the basic Article I-Article II-Article III/legislative-executive-judicial structure of the Constitution is hard to miss. Indeed, it is perhaps the Constitution's most obvious structural feature. The "legisecutive" lawmaking powers of the President and Vice President no doubt appear in Article I because, although they are not technically legislative powers within the meaning of the Constitution, they more closely resemble legislative powers than they do any of the other three basic categories of governmental action. The Treaty Clause, by contrast, is in Article II. What, if anything, are we to make of this placement?

Of course, once we begin to consider the implications of the Treaty Clause's location in Article II, we quickly leave the realm of incontrovertible textual facts and enter the world of controvertible structural inferences. Structural inference is a legitimate and powerful tool of interpretation. The power of judicial review, for instance, is the product of inference about the scope and character of the "judicial Power" rather than direct textual expression.[93] Perhaps questions about the treaty power find their answers in the same sources.

TAKING STRUCTURE SERIOUSLY

There are two textual features of the Treaty Clause that we omitted from the prior section. First, the Treaty Clause reads like a positive grant of power to the President and Senate, similar to the grants of legislative power in Article I. Second, the Treaty Clause contains no internal limitations on the scope of its granted authority. An informed eighteenth-century audience, after weighing all relevant considerations, would have concluded that both of these features are in fact illusions: the Treaty Clause is not in fact a grant of power to the President and the Senate, and it contains quite significant internal limitations. It will take most of the rest of this chapter fully to explain why the apparent absence of internal textual limitations in the Treaty Clause is an illusion. We can, however, quite readily dispose of the myth that the Treaty Clause is a grant of power to the President and the Senate.

If the Treaty Clause appeared in Article I of the Constitution, there is little doubt that it would constitute an affirmative grant of power to both the President and the Senate. The Treaty Clause, however, appears in Article II. *Enumerations of power in Article II do not serve the same constitutional function as do enumerations of power in Article I.* This basic principle is the key to the meaning of the Treaty Clause.

The first sentence of Article I states: "All legislative Powers herein granted shall be vested in a Congress of the United States, which shall consist of a Senate and House of Representatives."[94] This sentence does not grant any powers to Congress. Instead, it describes the institution — Congress — that must exercise whatever legislative powers are "herein granted" elsewhere in the Constitution. The Article I Vesting Clause designates the holder of certain powers conferred by the Constitution but it does not grant those powers.

The Vesting Clauses that begin Article II and Article III are different.[95] Article II begins by stating that "[t]he executive Power shall be vested in a President of the United States,"[96] and Article III opens by declaring that "[t]he judicial Power of the United States, shall be vested in one supreme Court, and in such inferior Courts as the Congress may from time to time ordain and establish."[97] These clauses do not merely designate the holders of certain offices or powers; they affirmatively grant to the President and the federal courts, respectively, the "executive Power" and the "judicial Power." That point has been demonstrated at length elsewhere, primarily by Steven Calabresi in a series of now-classic articles.[98] One of us has previously summarized the overwhelming arguments for construing the Article II Vesting Clause as a grant of power:

> First, the Vesting Clause does not say that "[t]he *office* of the presidency shall be held by a President of the United States of America." Rather, it says that "[t]he executive *Power* shall be vested in a President of the United States of America." It is very hard to read a clause that speaks of vesting power in a particular actor as doing anything other than vesting power in a particular actor.
>
> Second, as Professor [Steven] Calabresi has pointed out, the plain meaning of the verb "to vest" involves clothing with power or conferring ownership. This conclusion is confirmed by dictionaries from 1755 to the present.
>
> Third, other clauses of the Constitution that use the term "vest" clearly use the term to describe the granting of power. . . .
>
> Fourth, and finally, the Vesting Clause of Article III, which is textually and structurally very similar to the Vesting Clause of Article II, is the only constitutional source of the federal judiciary's power to act. Because the Article III Vesting Clause must be read as a grant of power — the judicial power — to the federal courts, the analogous Article II Vesting Clause should similarly be read as a grant of power — the executive power — to the President.[99]

Of course, if we are wrong about the Article II Vesting Clause constituting a grant of power to the President, our entire argument is misconceived. But we are not wrong about that.

In a portion of the Constitution, such as Article I, in which the Vesting

Clause confers no power, the specific enumerations that follow that clause clearly represent grants of power that define the powers "herein granted" that belong to Congress.[100] Article I enumerations are grants of power.

In portions of the Constitution such as Article II and III, however, in which the first sentence confers a general power, subsequent enumerations serve very different functions. The enumerations of heads of jurisdiction in Article III, section 2, for instance, are *limitations* on the scope of the general judicial power granted by the Article III Vesting Clause; that power "shall extend"[101] only to designated categories of disputes. The federal courts do not draw power from the enumeration of heads of jurisdiction in Article III, section 2. Their power stems from the Vesting Clause. Article III enumerations are limits on that power.

The enumerations of presidential power in sections 2 and 3 of Article II similarly do not constitute sources of presidential power. The President's basic power is the "executive Power" granted by the Vesting Clause. The subsequent enumerations in Article II clarify, qualify, and limit that basic grant of power, but they are not themselves grants of power. Some of those provisions, such as the Commander-in-Chief Clause,[102] prohibit inferences that might otherwise be drawn. In the absence of the Commander-in-Chief Clause, Congress might try to argue that its specific military powers (which do not include a power of troop direction), in conjunction with the Sweeping Clause, give it authority to direct troop movements. That argument would fail on the merits even without the Commander-in-Chief Clause — the "executive Power" granted by the Vesting Clause includes the power to command the nation's armed forces, and none of the granted congressional powers alter this allocation of authority — but the Commander-in-Chief Clause takes away the (plausible) temptation to make the argument and thereby provoke constitutional confrontation. Similarly, the Opinions Clause[103] forecloses any inference that Congress's power to create executive offices under the Sweeping Clause also includes the power to require officers to answer directly to Congress rather than to the President. The Commander-in-Chief and Opinions Clauses clarify and confirm powers that the President possesses by virtue of the Vesting Clause; they do not grant powers that otherwise would not exist.

Other provisions of Article II qualify or limit executive power, most notably with respect to the power to appoint officers of the United States and to convene or adjourn the legislature.[104] Still others impose duties, such as the obligation to make reports on the state of the union and to "take Care that the Laws be faithfully executed."[105] The latter clause also serves as an anti-inference provision by foreclosing any argument, however implausible on its own terms, that the "executive Power" includes a general power to suspend the laws.

The Treaty Clause appears in the middle of Article II. If it follows the general pattern of Article II enumerations, and there is no evident reason for an observer to suppose that it does not, then the Treaty Clause *is not a grant of power to the President.* It is a *limitation,* by way of requiring Senate consent, on a presidential power that is otherwise granted by the Article II Vesting Clause. It grants power to the *Senate* that that body would not otherwise have, but it does not create a federal treaty power that would not exist in the clause's absence. Without the Treaty Clause, the President would have the sole power of making treaties as an aspect of the "executive Power."

This conclusion, while firmly grounded in constitutional structure, is not as straightforward as we have made it out to be. The drafting history of the Treaty Clause does not reveal a conscious consensus to place the clause in the middle of Article II in order to cement its executive pedigree; the drafting process was considerably messier than that.[106] Although the treaty power in the late eighteenth century, consistently with its Article II placement, "would historically have been understood as part of the executive power,"[107] a number of prominent founding-era figures, including some prominent Framers, expressed the view that the treaty-making power was legislative, or at least was not clearly executive.[108] In any event, the proper interpretative inquiry does not focus on concrete historical understandings but on hypothetical historical understandings in light of all potentially relevant factors, so even a strong historical consensus in favor of viewing the treaty power as executive would not be dispositive. Lastly, as David Golove has forcefully argued,[109] the eighteenth-century historical conception of treaty making as an executive function may have rested on a view of executive sovereignty that does not necessarily fit the American Constitution very well. Accordingly, a hypothetical, fully informed eighteenth-century audience may have been quite open to the possibility that the treaty-making power under the American system of government is better viewed as legislative rather than executive.

But while these considerations might be enough to establish that a treaty clause located among legislative powers in Article I should not be regarded as executive, it is very hard to see how they permit a treaty clause located in the middle of Article II to be viewed by an informed public as anything other than executive. As Professor John Norton Moore has elegantly put it, "It is possible to debate theoretically whether the power to make treaties is primarily executive or legislative, as did Hamilton and Madison in the famous 'Pacificus-Helvidius' exchange. Under the Constitution of the United States, however, there can be but one answer. For the treaty power is placed in Article II, under the Executive, with a check in the Senate. It was not placed in Article I, under the Legislative branch, with a check in the Executive. The starting point for analysis under the United States Constitution, then, is that the treaty power is primarily executive in its nature."[110]

Accordingly, one of the "obvious" insights that emerges from a cursory examination of the constitutional text — that the Treaty Clause is a grant of power to the President and Senate — is false, at least as applied to the President.[111] Clauses that speak of granted power do not have the same meaning in Article II that they have in Article I. Article II enumerations of "power" are not grants of power that otherwise would not exist, but instead are clarifications or qualifications of powers that are otherwise part of the "executive Power." The treaty power, as befitting its location in the middle of Article II of the Constitution, is an aspect of the "executive Power," distinguished from other aspects of the executive power by the requirement of consent by two-thirds of the Senate.

Therefore the Treaty Clause, although phrased as an enumeration of power, is in reality a constraint on the President's executive power. Alexander Hamilton thus aptly described the Treaty Clause when he remarked in his defense of the Neutrality Proclamation that "the participation of the senate in the making of Treaties and the power of the Legislature to declare war are exceptions out of the general 'Executive Power' vested in the President."[112] To be sure, Hamilton in *The Federalist*, while he was trying to sell the Constitution to New Yorkers skeptical of broad presidential power, expressly disclaimed the executive character of the treaty power.[113] As has been frequently observed, consistency was not always the Framers' hallmark — which is yet another reason to focus on what the Constitution says rather than on what people said that it says.

The "executive Power," of course, is not boundless. Quite to the contrary, Article II did not need to enumerate the range of cases to which the "executive Power" extends in order to limit that power because *the very nature of the executive power defines its limits*. The essence of the executive power — its "fundamental function," as Sai Prakash has aptly termed it[114] — is to execute, or carry into effect, national laws. These laws include the Constitution, statutes, treaties, judicial judgments, and the common law of the United States to the extent that such a body of law exists, subject to the President's paramount obligation to the Constitution. But the "executive Power," in the course of carrying out its fundamental function, can execute only laws that *already exist independently of the exercise of federal executive power*. That execution, of course, can include interpretation of the laws and hence is not a purely ministerial function. It also includes a strong element of discretion in the selection of the means, forms, and priorities for execution — which collectively we might call the setting of administrative policy. But all of this discretion must be exercised within the confines of ends established by preexisting law. If the laws in question leave too much to the imagination, their "interpretation" would in fact be the *creation* rather than the *execution* of the law and would therefore exceed the President's executive power.[115]

Accordingly, the grant to the President of the "executive Power" is self-limiting. It is a grant of power to carry into effect other law. We can now understand, intratextually, why the Article II Vesting Clause, unlike the Article I Sweeping Clause, does not expressly say, "The executive Power to take all Actions which shall be necessary and proper for carrying into Execution the Laws of the United States shall be vested in a President."[116] The "for carrying into Execution" proviso did not need to be textually specified in the Article II Vesting Clause because it is inherent in the very concept of "executive Power" as the Constitution uses that term. (We will later demonstrate that the "necessary and proper" requirement is also implicit in the grant of the executive power.) It is the nature of the President's "executive Power" to implement existing law, not to create new law. The "executive Power," despite its textually unqualified nature, is an *implementational* power.

We can now understand how the Treaty Clause can be implementational even in the absence of the kind of language found in the Sweeping Clause. The grant to the President of the "executive Power," at least in its fundamental function of executing the laws, carries with it, by its very nature, a requirement that it be used only for carrying into execution federal law. No textual limitation to that effect was necessary. Executive power and legislative power are different enough in character to require different forms of limitation; one would not expect grants of legislative power to be textually limited in precisely the same manner as grants of executive power. To the extent that the treaty power is part of the "executive Power" granted by the Vesting Clause, one similarly would not expect the same kinds of textual limitations that one finds on legislative power.

At least that is true of the "executive Power" in its "fundamental function" of executing the laws of the United States. There is more to the executive power than that. How much more is a matter of considerable controversy, which we cannot hope to discuss, much less resolve, here. It must suffice for now to say that the Constitution's vesting of "all legislative Powers herein granted" in Congress, and its creation of a judiciary department separate from the executive, counsels in favor of a relatively narrow understanding of the scope of the executive power.[117] It is hard to dispute, however, that the Article II Vesting Clause confers, in addition to the power to execute the laws of the United States, a certain core of federative, or foreign affairs, powers that involve a significant degree of policymaking.[118] These powers do not simply carry into effect the ends set by other governmental actors; they constitute an independent head of jurisdiction vested in the President. But they only grant jurisdiction of a limited kind. Most importantly, these general foreign affairs powers typically are not lawmaking powers; they do not permit the President unilaterally to impose rights and obligations on citizens.[119] Rather, these powers concern such matters as communication with foreign nations and the recall of ambassadors.

Some presidential foreign affairs powers, however, do have the potential to affect private rights. To the extent that the President has the "executive Power" to terminate treaties, private rights relating to the terminated treaties can be at stake. And to the extent that the President has the power to employ military force, that action has quite significant consequences for the forces under his command, if not for the country at large. Most significantly for our purposes, as we will discuss at length in a subsequent chapter, the President may act as a lawmaker with respect to occupied foreign territory during wartime. As "legisecutive" powers go, this one is about as "legis" as one can get. It is limited, however, to occupied foreign territory during wartime and provides no basis for exercising jurisdiction over American citizens in American territory. But it is unquestionably a significant grant of power to the President. Thus, while the bulk of the powers granted to the President by the Article II Vesting Clause are limited to the implementation of ends set by other legal actors, some of those powers are best understood as independent heads of jurisdiction.

So, given the dual aspect of the Article II Vesting Clause, which contains both implementational and jurisdiction-granting elements, how would one determine the proper scope of the treaty power? Does the Treaty Clause partake solely of the implementational aspect of the executive power or does it also constitute a unique kind of jurisdiction-extending lawmaking instrument? Before we finalize our answer to that question, we need to flesh out more fully what it means for the treaty power to be implementational. In particular, we need to understand precisely what limitations the implementational view reads into the Treaty Clause by virtue of its Article II location. And that requires a five-hundred-year detour.

TAKING REASONABLENESS SERIOUSLY

We are contending that the Treaty Clause is analogous to the Sweeping Clause: it exists in order to effectuate other enumerated powers of federal institutions. The Sweeping Clause specifically limits its grant of power to laws "for carrying into Execution" federal powers. We have already explained why the absence of such language in the Article II Treaty Clause can be consistent with an implementational view of that clause: if the treaty power is an aspect of the more general Article II "executive Power," its implementational character follows as a matter of course. The Sweeping Clause, however, contains a substantive textual limitation in addition to the requirement that it be used only "for carrying into Execution" constitutionally granted powers. Laws enacted pursuant to the Sweeping Clause must be "necessary and proper" for their implementational purpose. One of us has spent a fair portion of his professional life plumbing the meaning of the word *proper* and has concluded that it requires executory legislation to conform to constitutional principles of federalism, separation of powers, and individual rights.[120] Of course, the better-known term, because of its prominence in *McCulloch v Maryland*, is *necessary*. The term clearly denotes a causal, or telic,[121] relationship between the means employed and the ends served. The debate in *McCulloch* concerned how tightly the means and ends must be linked, with opponents of the bank arguing for a standard of strict necessity and its defenders opting for a standard of helpfulness.[122] Chief Justice Marshall agreed with the latter.[123] There are good intratextual reasons for rejecting the strict necessity standard,[124] though that does not inevitably lead to the latitudinarian position adopted by Chief Justice Marshall. We do not intend to resolve that particular puzzle here. For now, it is enough to say that the word *necessary* is not meaningless. The Sweeping Clause requires a certain degree of "fit" between means and ends. Can one similarly derive some kind of "necessary and proper" requirement for the treaty power from inference?

In order to answer this question, one needs to examine at length some eighteenth-century background principles about delegated power. All of the powers in the Constitution are delegations from the ultimate source of law (whether one considers it the people or the states is irrelevant for this purpose). Many of these grants of power unavoidably involve the exercise of discretion by public officials. It was well understood in eighteenth-century English law that grants from Parliament of discretionary governmental authority carried the implied provision that exercises of discretion had to be reasonable.[125] The principle is often traced back to *Rooke's Case* in 1598.[126] A statute from the reign of Henry VIII in 1531 gave to sewer commissioners the power to determine needed repairs to water-control measures "as case shall require, after your wisdoms and discretions" and the power to assess landowners for the costs of maintenance and repairs as the commissioners "shall deem most convenient to be ordained."[127] The commissioners of sewers under this statute had assessed on one landowner the full costs of a repair to a bank of the Thames, even though "divers other persons had lands to the quantity of 800 acres within the same level, and subject to drowning, if the said bank is not repaired."[128] The court, through Sir Edward Coke, upheld the landowner's challenge to the assessment. An adequate ground for the decision was probably language in the 1427 predecessor to the statute making clear that "no tenants of land or tenements . . . shall in any way be spared in this,"[129] but Lord Coke nonetheless added in dictum: "Notwithstanding the words of the commission give authority to the commissioners to do according to their discretions, yet their proceedings ought to be limited and bound with the rule of reason and law. For discretion is a science or understanding to discern between falsity and truth, between wrong and right, between shadows and substance, between equity and colourable glosses and pretences, and not to do according to their wills and private affections; for as one saith, *talis discretion discretionem confundit.*"[130] This dictum was very influential in the seventeenth and eighteenth centuries. A similar sentiment was oft repeated in seventeenth-century cases,[131] and in 1773 it was restated by the court in *Leader v Moxon.*[132] A statute gave paving commissioners power to pave and repair streets "'in such a manner as the commissioners shall think fit.'" The court nonetheless awarded damages when the commissioners ordered part of a street raised so high that it obstructed the plaintiff's doors and windows, because "the commissioners had grossly exceeded their powers, which must have a reasonable construction. Their discretion is not arbitrary, but must be limited by reason and law."[133] As the court explained, "the act could never intend that any of the householders should pay a rate of 1s. 6d. in the pound in order to have their houses buried under ground, and their windows and doors obstructed. . . . [H]ad Parliament intended to demolish or render useless some houses for the benefit or ornament of the rest, it would have given express powers for that purpose, and given an equivalent for the loss that individuals might have sustained thereby."[134]

In England, the statement from *Rooke's Case* "has lost nothing of its accuracy in over 400 years";[135] the principle of reasonableness remains one of the bedrocks of English administrative law.

The principle of reasonableness in the exercise of delegated discretionary power is a common-law principle that the eighteenth-century colonists would have found very congenial given its rights-protective and antimonarchical character. It was also familiar to American lawyers through William Blackstone, whose *Commentaries on the Laws of England* gave a very powerful statement of the principle of reasonableness and its origins in *Rooke's Case.* (Blackstone was also one of the judges in *Leader v Moxon.*) In discussing the broad statutory power of sewer commissioners, Blackstone explained:

> But their conduct is under the control of the court of king's bench, which will prevent or punish any illegal or tyrannical proceedings [citing *Rooke's Case* in

a footnote]. And yet in the reign of king James I, (8 Nov 1616) the privy council took upon them to order, that no action or complaint should be prosecuted against the commissioners, unless before that board; and committed several to prison who had brought such actions at common law, till they should release the same: and one of the reasons for discharging Sir Edward Coke from his office of lord chief justice was for countenancing those proceedings. The pretence for which arbitrary measures was not other than the tyrant's plea, of the necessity of unlimited powers in words of evident utility to the public, the supreme reason above all reasons, which is "the salvation of the king's lands and people." But now it is clearly held, that this (as well as all the inferior jurisdictions) is subject to the discretionary coercion of his majesty's court of king's bench.[136]

But what could this principle mean operationally in the context of the powers delegated under the American Constitution?

In England before the founding, delegated power effectively meant executive power (which included what we now think of as judicial power). The quintessential case of discretion pertained to the choice of means for carrying out ends established by Parliament. In that context, discretion can be limited from at least three important directions. First, one can say that the delegatee's choice of means must be *measured*, in the sense of reasonably proportionate to the end sought. One does not burn down a village to kill a fox — or, perhaps more to the point, one does not ordinarily fix a road by destroying a house when less destructive alternatives are available. Continental lawyers have raised this notion of proportionality to the level of high principle, refining it and using it to require a relatively precise fit between means and ends that approximates the "least restrictive alternative" analysis familiar to First Amendment lawyers.[137] English law has never recognized this "principle of proportionality" as a distinct legal requirement.[138] It certainly was not a part of English law in the eighteenth century, if only because the principle was developed in Germany in the nineteenth century.[139] Nonetheless, it is not difficult to see elements of proportionality (though not the fully refined Continental principle) in the traditional common-law concept of reasonableness; "the principles of reasonableness and proportionality cover a great deal of common ground."[140] It is very natural to describe a decision as "unreasonable" if the means are grossly disproportionate to the ends, and many English decisions, including *Leader v Moxon*, are consistent with this observation.[141]

A second dimension of unreasonableness is efficacy: a discretionary implementational decision could be thought of as unreasonable if the chosen means are ill-suited to achieve the desired ends; considerations of cause and effect are a basic facet of rational thinking. And third, one might give unreasonableness a purely substantive dimension: a discretionary decision could be seen as unreasonable, however measured and efficacious it might be, if it trenches on substantive rights or represents an inappropriate consideration of manifestly relevant factors.

The most important question, of course, is how far a decision must stray from perfection in order to be "unreasonable." There is a large difference, for example, between requiring an implementational decision to be the least restrictive alternative and requiring it to be plausibly related to the desired end. For now, however, let us leave that critical question aside. It is enough for present purposes to recognize that the abstract principle of reasonableness was a foundational principle of delegated implementational power in eighteenth-century English common law.

One of the great innovations of American constitutionalism is the idea that all governmental power stems from a delegation. All powers of federal actors are delegated powers. Accordingly, it is eminently sensible to suppose that when the Constitution delegated discretionary implementational powers to federal actors in 1788 those delegations carried with them the common-law principle of reasonableness. Consider, for instance, the President's "executive Power" to execute the laws. Could the President, exercising discretion in the selection of forms and means of law enforcement, apprehend a suspect holed up in Concord by leveling the entire town? Could the President, exercising discretion in the forms and means of legal interpretation, interpret laws by channeling the spirit of Elvis? Could the President in 1790, prior to ratification of the Fourth Amendment, exercise discretionary investigative powers by indiscriminately searching an entire region? We think that all of these measures would be, not merely ill-advised, but *unconstitutional*.[142] The Article II Vesting Clause grants the President discretion in law execution, but that discretion is bounded. Not everything done by the President, even in the guise of executing the laws, is an exercise of the "executive Power" delegated through the Constitution.

The same is true of the "judicial Power" granted by the Article III Vesting Clause. Suppose that a federal judge exercises the "judicial Power" to decide a case by flipping a coin. The judge's decision could certainly be reversed on appeal. The judge could certainly be impeached and removed by Congress. But has the judge violated the Constitution? We say yes.[143] The case-deciding power granted by the Constitution's Article III Vesting Clause is not entirely unbounded. There is substantial room within that grant of power for different methodologies, and even substantial room for error, but at some point a judgment falls so far off the map that it simply ceases to be an exercise of the judicial power. Not everything done by a judge, even in the guise of deciding a case, is an exercise of the "judicial Power" within the meaning of Article III. The limits may be broad, but there are limits.

The delegated powers to execute the laws and to decide cases are both implementational, rather than ends-setting, powers. Accordingly, they necessarily carry with them the principle of reasonableness in the exercise of discretionary delegated powers. That principle did not need to be expressly stated in the Constitution because it is part of the very nature of delegations of implementational powers such as the "executive Power" and the "judicial Power" as understood in eighteenth-century common law.

The common-law principle of reasonableness was never applied to Parliament (or, more precisely, to the king or queen in Parliament). It was a principle that applied only to discretionary authority delegated from Parliament, not to supreme legislative authority. Indeed, the law imposed no limits, of reasonableness or otherwise, on the legislative supremacy of Parliament,[144] which stood above the other two governmental departments in the legal hierarchy.

The Congress under the American Constitution, of course, is not Parliament. Congress is not hierarchically superior to the executive or judicial departments. Congress, as do the President and the federal courts, exercises only delegated power, and that power is far from limitless. If the principle of reasonableness derives solely from the existence of delegated discretionary power, then it would follow that the delegated authority of Congress is subject to constraints of proportionality, efficacy, and substantive reasonableness. But would a cautious eighteenth-century lawyer be satisfied with that inference? Could someone plausibly argue that the principle of reasonableness does not apply to Parliament simply because Parliament (at least in its legislative guise) exercises legislative rather than executive or judicial power? If that is the correct basis for refusing to extend the principle of reasonableness to Parliament, it would apply as well to Congress, in which case grants of enumerated power to Congress would not necessarily carry with them a requirement of reasonableness in the exercise of discretion. Accordingly, it makes sense to specify a constitutional constraint on Congress's discretionary powers if such a constraint is desired.

The language of the Sweeping Clause elegantly subjects Congress's implementational legislative powers to the principle of reasonableness. The phrase "necessary and proper for carrying into Execution" is an excellent way to describe requirements of proportionality, efficacy, and substantive reasonableness. A measure is "necessary" if it is proportionate, and it is "proper" if it is well suited to its task (efficacious) and substantively reasonable. It is no accident that when the modern European Court of Justice described the principle of proportionality, it said that the principle, inter alia, requires measures to be "appropriate and necessary in order to achieve the objectives legitimately pursued by the legislation in question."[145]

In sum, there are very good reasons why the federal Constitution would textually specify in the Sweeping Clause that executory laws must be "necessary and proper" but would not use equivalent language in Article II or Article III. Discretionary executive and judicial powers, by their nature, carry with them the principle of reasonableness. Perhaps that is true as well of delegated legislative power (or perhaps at least of delegated implementational legislative power), so that a requirement of reasonableness would exist even in the absence of the "necessary and proper" language in the Sweeping Clause, but the matter is open enough to question to make it prudent to specify the desired limitation on Congress.

The treaty power, we contend, is an implementational, executive power delegated in Article II. Accordingly, it carries the principle of reasonableness by its nature, without need for textual specification. The absence of "necessary and proper" language in the Treaty Clause does not point away from a requirement of a means-ends "fit" for treaties — no more than it does for other delegated Article II and Article III powers. Just as exercises of the law-execution and case-deciding powers must be proportionate, efficacious, and substantively reasonable, the same is true of exercises of the treaty-making power. It remains to be determined, of course, whether the degree of proportionality, efficaciousness, and reasonableness required of treaties is greater, smaller, or the same as the degree required of executory legislation under the Sweeping Clause, exercises of law-enforcement discretion, or exercises of judicial power, but the basic principle of reasonableness applies to treaties.

TAKING HOLISM SERIOUSLY

The implementational view of treaties thus reads the Treaty Clause as an executive power that is, by its nature, subject to a requirement that exercises of the treaty power be "necessary and proper for carrying into Execution" other federal powers. It remains only to demonstrate that the Treaty Clause partakes of the implementational character of the executive power rather than of its jurisdiction-granting element.

That demonstration is already largely completed. The elements of the constitutionally granted "executive Power" that are not purely implementational are quite limited, both in number and in sphere of application. The baseline presumption is that executive powers are implementational. That is an especially reasonable presumption in the case of the treaty power, because tearing it loose from its implementational moorings, and the implicit "necessary and proper for carrying into Execution" requirement that goes with that designation, would leave it without obvious limits. This would be, to say the least, anomalous for an executive power.

The rest of the demonstration looks at the Treaty Clause in relation to the rest of the Constitution. Constitutional clauses do not exist in a vacuum. The actual clauses of the actual Constitution were presented to the public in 1787 as an integrated package. We know, for instance, that the Article II Vesting Clause grants the President the executive power of the United States rather than, say, the executive power of Connecticut because we can read the Vesting Clause in pari materia with the provisions that surround it. A conversation about constitutional meaning, whether in 1787 or today, would only be sensible if it considered how interpretations of various clauses would interact with other clauses.

Consider a treaty in which the President and the Senate agree to make noncitizens eligible for the presidency, in apparent violation of the clause providing that "[n]o Person except a natural born Citizen, or a Citizen of the United States, at the time of the Adoption of this Constitution, shall be eligible to the Office of President."[146] Is that treaty provision domestically enforceable as the supreme law of the land? If the Treaty Clause is read as a jurisdictional grant, there is nothing in the clause to suggest any limitation on the content of treaties. Nonetheless, the treaty provision is clearly inoperative on any plausible understanding of the Treaty Clause. As a matter of domestic law, the Constitution is hierarchically superior to all other forms of law, including statutes and treaties. The same reasoning by inference that led John Marshall correctly to place the Constitution above federal statutes also leads to the conclusion that the Constitution is supreme over treaties. The Eligibility Clause, unlike some provisions such as the First Amendment or the Slave Trade Clause, is framed in sufficiently general terms to apply to *all* federal actions, regardless of their form. It accordingly forbids the treaty provision in question.

If this conclusion seems too obvious for discussion, consider the following variation on the facts: imagine that the United States just decidedly lost a war with Spain. Spanish troops are set to inflict serious damage on the country that will quite probably destroy the United States as a political entity. The Spanish negotiators uncompromisingly demand a noncitizen eligibility provision as a condition of peace. Is it still clear that the treaty power cannot override the Eligibility Clause?[147]

To a dedicated constitutionalist, the answer is straightforward: yes, it is still clear that the treaty power cannot override the Eligibility Clause. That does not mean, as the saying goes, that the Constitution is therefore a suicide pact. The country could satisfy the Spanish demand by the "simple" expedient of amending the Constitution pursuant to Article V. Of course, if the Spanish were not willing to wait for the Article V events to run their course and instead demanded immediate concessions in the treaty, then we would have a problem. But otherwise, the whole point of a limited government is that there may be some potentially useful things that the government is disabled from doing. Whether that is a good idea or a bad idea depends, in the end, on the relative risks of granting too little or too much power in various respects. If the Constitution makes the wrong call on some of these questions, it is perhaps a bad constitution, but that is a matter for political theorists rather than constitutional interpreters.

In any event, the principle that a treaty cannot violate the Constitution seems incontrovertible. It would be interpretative absurdity to claim that the President and Senate hold an all-powerful constitutional trump buried in the middle of Article II. If the limitations imposed on the treaty power by the Constitution prove inconvenient, or even deadly, the constitutional solution is an amendment, not treaty omnipotence.

Once it is acknowledged that treaties cannot violate the Constitution, the trick becomes to determine what counts as a constitutional violation. Surely treaties cannot do what the Constitution expressly forbids to all actors, including the President and Senate, such as granting titles of nobility or withdrawing money from the Treasury without an appropriation. Thus provisions of the Constitution framed as "thou shalt nots" apply to the treaty power whenever their terms encompass the treaty-making authority and not simply a more specific constitutional actor such as Congress.

Another kind of constitutional violation would be an attempt to accomplish actions through forms other than those prescribed by the Constitution. A treaty could not, for instance, permit a revenue measure to originate in the Senate, dispense with the presentment requirement, or permit the delegation of legislative power. And if France took objection to the location of Vermont's capital in the French-sounding city of Montpelier, and accordingly demanded as a condition of a commercial treaty that Vermont be deprived of its voice in the Senate, the federal treaty makers could not agree to that condition.

These propositions about the inability of treaties to alter constitutional form and structure, of course, are not compelled by any specific textual provision. Nor does the Constitution have specific textual provisions stating that the House, Senate, and President under Article I, section 7, the President under the nontreaty powers in Article II, or the federal judiciary in Article III cannot alter basic structural arrangements. No such express provision is necessary because, as Chief Justice Marshall recognized in *Marbury*, it is structurally clear that the Constitution is supreme law. Moreover, the Constitution prescribes a specific amendment process, which by inference creates a very strong presumption against alteration of the Constitution through other means. As a general interpretative principle, power grants to federal actors do not include the power to alter the Constitution unless that power is clearly given.[148]

Hence the seemingly unqualified power to "make Treaties," whatever its scope or nature, is really a power to "make Treaties that are consistent with provisions of the Constitution allocating federal governmental power and that do not violate prohibitory provisions of the Constitution framed broadly enough to apply to the treaty-making authority."

But what about prohibitory provisions that are *not* framed broadly enough to apply to the treaty-making authority? Suppose that in order to secure certain trade concessions with France, a treaty includes a provision demanded by the French that perpetually forbids all Americans from publishing any criticisms of France or the French government. The First Amendment, recall, does not apply to treaties, because they are not acts of Congress. Of course, to the extent that the treaty requires congressional implementation, the First Amendment would pose a problem, but that could be avoided by making the treaty provision self-executing, perhaps by giving the French government power to enforce the prohibition through civil actions for libel. Does the Constitution permit the American treaty makers to refashion state libel law in this manner? And what if the French — in accordance with fears actually voiced at the North Carolina ratifying convention — further added a provision mandating that Catholicism be declared the official religion of the United States?[149] Is that concession within the power of the President and Senate? If the answer is "no," it is not by virtue of anything contained in the First Amendment or any other express provision of the Constitution; it must be by virtue of something internal to the treaty power. Finally, suppose that the French, once again upset by the location of Vermont's capital in the French-sounding city of Montpelier, demand as a condition of a trade agreement that the capital be moved to an Anglo-sounding city such as Burlington. Congress clearly has no enumerated power to alter state capitals, but does anything prevent the treaty-making authorities from agreeing to the deal, which then becomes "the supreme Law of the Land"?

Most significantly, consider the effect of the Slave Trade Clause, which as we noted earlier does not, by its terms, apply to the treaty power. This clause protected regulation of the slave trade for the nation's first twenty years against (1) a majority of both houses of Congress plus the President and (2) a two-thirds majority in both houses without the President. Article V, without any special provision for the Slave Trade Clause, would have entrenched that firewall against combined supermajorities in the House, Senate, and the state legislatures: it would have taken a two-thirds majority in each house or a two-thirds majority of the state legislatures to propose an amendment repealing the Slave Trade Clause, and it would then have taken a three-fourths majority of the states to ratify the amendment. Article V, with its special proviso that exempted the Slave Trade Clause from the amendment process, protected the clause even against that unlikely combination. Thus, until 1808, no possible combination—even a unanimous combination—of the President, the Congress, and the state legislatures could have prohibited the slave trade. But if the treaty power is an independent grant of jurisdiction that is not limited to implementing other enumerated powers, then the President plus two-thirds of a quorum of the Senate nonetheless could have abolished the slave trade by treaty if only the thought had occurred to them. Such a treaty would not have violated any specific prohibition in the Constitution or altered any structural form of action specified in the Constitution. It simply would have done what no other possible combination of constitutional actors, including the amending authorities, had the enumerated power to do. A Constitution that permitted pre-1808 abolition of the slave trade would, of course, have been a *good* Constitution. The question for interpreters, however, is whether it is a *plausible* Constitution.[150]

If the Treaty Clause does give the President and the Senate power to alter state capitals, disestablish state religions, or end the slave trade before 1808, then the entire federal structure, apart from a few fortuitously worded prohibitions on federal action in Article I, section 9, is a President and two-thirds of a quorum of senators (and perhaps a bona fide demand from a foreign government) away from destruction. That is, of course, not an impossible circumstance. Some antifederalists desperately feared it, even if they did not articulate their concerns in precisely the manner that we have done.[151] But in light of the overarching structure and themes of the Constitution, that is a conclusion that one ought to reach only with some hesitation. The potential existence of a "back door" that would permit federal treaty makers to declare a national religion, dictate the location of state capitals, and abolish the slave trade in 1789 is intriguing enough to warrant a bit more interpretative energy with respect to the treaty power.

One could, of course, suggest that the Treaty Clause's requirement of two-thirds consent by the Senate, the body initially selected by the states themselves and in which each state has equal representation, is the only safeguard provided against misuse of the treaty power.[152] Structurally, however, the provision for a supermajority Senate approval does not support any strong inferences about the scope of the treaty power. As John McGinnis and Michael Rappaport have pointed out in a powerful article, most of the Constitution is supermajoritarian.[153] Ordinary legislation must pass through two different branches of the legislature that are (at least under the original constitutional design) selected by different majorities.[154] It must then be presented to the President, who represents yet a different majority. Passage through all three legislative units thus requires approval by three separate majorities, which is a pretty fair description of a supermajority requirement. And if the President vetoes a bill, it can become law only with a two-thirds majority of both the House and the Senate. Article V requires either two-thirds majorities in both houses of Congress or a convention called by two-thirds of the state legislatures for the proposal of constitutional amendments and ratification by three-quarters of the states for the adoption of such amendments. In light of the Constitution's pervasive supermajoritarian theme, a requirement of approval by the President and by two-thirds of the Senate for treaties is not a small matter by any means, but it is not so extraordinary that it short-circuits an inquiry into substantive limits on the treaty power.

In the end, the power to make *implementational* law by carrying other enumerated powers into effect in the international arena makes sense across all fronts. It fulfills the purpose of treaties to permit the United States to enter into and acquire binding commitments from foreign nations. It acknowledges the lawmaking character of the treaty power while still grounding it in the larger structure of Article II. And, most importantly, it prevents the Treaty Clause from unraveling the rest of the constitutional scheme. If the Treaty Clause is read as jurisdiction-extending, one must either figure out some way to limit it, the difficulty of which is demonstrated by two centuries of debates, or maintain that the middle of Article II contains a constitutional joker. To put it bluntly, an authorization to implement other grants of jurisdiction makes sense in the overall context of the Constitution, while a grant of jurisdiction to pursue independent ends does not.

There is no a priori requirement that the Constitution make sense, but if one is trying to project how a fully informed eighteenth-century audience, knowing all that there is to know about the Constitution and the surrounding world, would have understood the power to "make Treaties," the implementational view looks pretty good. To read the Treaty Clause as an end-setting provision, with no direct connection to the otherwise careful enumerations of federal powers, simply does too much damage to the rest of the Constitution to be a plausible reading of a brief clause in Article II, section 2. On that point, at least, Jefferson was right.

We must still determine in precisely what fashion Jefferson was right. There is an ambiguity in the notion of an "implementational" treaty power. On the strictest understanding, treaties can only be used to carry into effect powers *already exercised* by other governmental actors. Thus, if Congress tries to regulate foreign commerce in a way that requires the agreement of a foreign sovereign, a treaty could validly implement that prior exercise of the lawmaking power. But on this understanding, a treaty could not regulate foreign commerce without first having an exercise of congressional power to implement. This would directly assimilate the treaty power into the "fundamental function" of the executive power, which carries into effect laws that already exist.

That is not, however, the only sense in which a power can be "implementational." Consider the Sweeping Clause. The Clause is an implementational power in that it grants Congress power only to pass laws "for carrying into Execution" other granted powers. But Congress does not need to wait for those other powers actually to be exercised in order to use its authority under the Sweeping Clause. For instance, Congress could appropriate funds and authorize the appointment of officers for the negotiation of a particular treaty, even if the President ultimately chooses not to negotiate the treaty at all. Indeed, because all appropriations come from acts of Congress pursuant to the Sweeping Clause, such legislation often *must* be enacted *before* the power that Congress seeks to implement is exercised. On this understanding of an "implementational" power, the power can "pave the way" for the exercise of powers elsewhere granted to institutions of the national government without awaiting the actual exercise of those powers.

There is yet a third possibility to consider. In his September 7, 1803, letter to Wilson Cary Nicholas expressing his view of the treaty power, Jefferson said that the Constitution "specifies & delineates the operations permitted to the federal government, and gives all the powers necessary to carry these into execution. Whatever of these enumerated objects is proper for a law, Congress may make the law; whatever is proper to be executed by way of a treaty, the President & Senate may enter into the treaty." If one emphasizes the phrase "enumerated objects," one can come up with a "hybrid" conception of the treaty power that permits it, on some occasions, to function as a stand-alone power. The Constitution's power-granting provisions can be viewed as the specification of ends or goals that the national government may permissibly pursue. Thus the Commerce Clause specifies the permissible end or goal of regulating foreign commerce. A treaty, on this hybrid understanding, can be used to pursue this otherwise-specified end, but it need not be tied in any way to an exercise of congressional power. That is, the President and the Senate would have an independent jurisdiction to enter into treaties regulating foreign commerce, even if Congress has not acted,[155] but they could exercise this independent power only in connection with ends specified in some provision of the Constitution other than the Treaty Clause.

This was not, of course, Jefferson's own position. Jefferson, we should re-call, believed that treaties cannot concern matters that could "otherwise be regulated" or matters in which the Constitution "gave a participation to the House of Representatives." In other words, where the Constitution specified a particular form for action, Jefferson regarded that form as exclusive. The person to whom Jefferson wrote on September 7, 1803, however, articulated a position fairly close to this hybrid view. In a letter to Jefferson of September 3, 1803, Wilson Cary Nicholas, then a Virginia senator, tried to dissuade Jeffer-son from expressing doubts about the constitutionality of the Louisiana Pur-chase or from articulating an unduly narrow conception of the treaty power. He explained that he did not "see anything in the constitution that limits the treaty power, except the general limitation of the power given to the govern-ment, and the evident object for which the government was instituted."[156] By "the general limitation of the power given to the government," one can easily mean "the ends and objects that institutions of the federal government may permissibly pursue under their enumerated powers." This understanding is consistent with the views expressed by George Nicholas at the Virginia ratify-ing convention, in which he said that no treaty could be made "which shall be repugnant to the spirit of the Constitution, or inconsistent with the delegated powers."[157]

This hybrid position has the typical virtues and vices of a compromise. Its primary virtue is that it gives wide effect to the arguably "legis" aspect of the treaty power while providing clearly marked boundaries for the exercise of the power. Its primary, and fatal, vice is that it misunderstands the Constitution. The Constitution does not specify permissible ends for the national govern-ment to pursue. Rather, it grants specific powers to specific institutions of the national government. In that sense, it specifies permissible ends, as well as permissible means, but they are not ends and means for "the national govern-ment" as a unitary entity. The hybrid view amounts to saying that every power granted to any institution of the national government is also independently granted to the President and the Senate: Congress (and the President) can regulate foreign commerce by statute, so the President and Senate can regulate foreign commerce by treaty. But changing the example shows the deep flaw in this approach: Congress and the state legislatures can amend the Constitution; so can the President and Senate amend the Constitution by treaty? No, no, one immediately objects. When Article V confers the amendment power, it confers it on *specific institutions* to be exercised in a *specific form*. It does not simply specify an abstract end of amending the Constitution; it also designates the proper institution and form for pursuing that end. That is true, but it is as true of the foreign commerce power as it is of Article V.

This means that compromise is not possible. Either the Treaty Clause is an independent grant of subject-matter jurisdiction to the President and Senate or it is a power to carry into effect (whether prospectively or after the fact) valid exercises of power by other federal governmental actors. For the reasons that we have already given, the latter view makes the most sense in light of the Constitution's architecture. The remaining question is whether the treaty power is "triggered" only by prior exercises of constitutional authority or may also be used, à la the Sweeping Clause, to facilitate anticipated exercises of authority. For our purposes, nothing of consequence turns on this question, though the latter view makes more sense in view of the general character of implementational authority. All things considered, the best way to integrate the treaty power into the constitutional structure is to treat it as an implementing mechanism for all federal powers.

TAKING CONSEQUENCES SERIOUSLY

An important component of our argument for the Jeffersonian view of the treaty power is reasoning from paradigm cases: A treaty power that is not limited to implementing the national government's enumerated powers could end the slave trade before 1808, and a treaty power that is limited to implementing Congress's Article I powers would not permit treaties of peace. We have inferred from these consequences that an eighteenth-century observer would accordingly have hesitated to construe the Treaty Clause in either of these fashions. It is, of course, always dangerous to reason from conclusions to interpretations. Unless one fully equates the meaning of a provision with its intended results, which we do not, one must acknowledge the possibility that the Constitution might fail to achieve at least some of the ends that were expected of it. We therefore are not claiming that odd results can overcome a clear contextual meaning. But as we have endeavored to show, the case for reading the Treaty Clause as an independent head of jurisdiction is far from contextually clear. The stark language of the Treaty Clause does not, as some have claimed, settle that question. Rather, it requires us to determine how a fully informed eighteenth-century observer would have understood the Constitution's power to "make Treaties." Paradigm cases, particularly paradigm cases as extreme as the ones that we have invoked, are relevant to that inquiry. If an interpretation of the Treaty Clause is available that avoids the kinds of major sinkholes into which other interpretations get sucked, that is a point, albeit not a conclusive one, in its favor.

Once we make that move, however, we must identify the breadth and depth of the sinkholes to which our own interpretation is vulnerable. What kinds of treaty provisions that an eighteenth-century observer would have regarded as unproblematic would the Jeffersonian implementational interpretation call into question?

Treaties of peace are no problem for the Jeffersonian view. Although Congress cannot terminate a war, and the Treaty Clause therefore cannot be used to implement any such congressional power, the President can terminate a war.[158] Peace treaties can then formalize and set the terms of — in other words, can implement — the state of peace created by the President, which is precisely what the implementational theory of the Treaty Clause contemplates. Because the treaty power is implementational, the treaty could not end the war without concomitant presidential action, but because the treaty itself cannot exist without presidential action to put it before the Senate, that is a matter of no moment.

The more interesting question is what kinds of concessions can be made in peace treaties. To say that the President and Senate can execute a peace treaty is not to say that they can do so on any terms whatsoever. On the implementational view, any provision in a peace treaty, as in any other treaty, must carry into effect some constitutional power of some federal actor. Recognition of a state of peace effectuates the President's peacemaking powers, but peace treaties often do much more than declare peace. In particular, peace treaties, and other treaties as well, are often occasions for the exchange of territory. We will shortly explore the extent to which treaties permit the United States to acquire territory from foreign sovereigns, which of course was the question that initially propelled this entire inquiry into the scope of the treaty power. For now, in order to assess the plausibility of the reading of the Treaty Clause that we will bring to bear on that ultimate question, let us consider the extent to which treaties permit foreign sovereigns to acquire territory from the United States.

Vasan Kesavan has recently demonstrated, at great length, that the general understanding at the time of the framing was that treaties permitted the cession of American territory, including territory that was part of a state, without the consent of the state in which the territory was located. We accept the proposition that a fully informed eighteenth-century audience would have been startled to discover that the federal government had no power to cede territory, even as part of a peace settlement. The implementational view of the Treaty Clause is consistent with this expectation — up to a point.

There is no problem at all with treaties ceding territory that belongs exclusively to the United States. Congress can cede that property by ordinary legislation through its power under the Property Clause to "dispose of . . . Territory or other Property belonging to the United States," and there is accordingly no issue about implementing that power through treaty. The Property Clause, however, does not authorize Congress to dispose of territory belonging to a state. What if the requested price for peace, or even for a particularly attractive commercial treaty, is Maine, Vermont, and New Hampshire?

Our answer is that state territory can be ceded away as part of a peace settlement but not otherwise. Once the treaty power is seen as wholly implementational, there is no arguable power in any federal actor to alienate state territory during peacetime and therefore nothing for the treaty power to implement. During wartime, however, the President has the power to "cede" state territory by refusing to defend it (or by defending it and losing). Once territory is occupied by an invading foreign sovereign, the invader, pursuant to international law, gets to govern the territory in accordance with its own political institutions. A treaty of peace that formally cedes the conquered territory thereby implements the presidential decision to sacrifice part of the country during wartime in order to save the rest.

The joker in the deck is, of course, the Guarantee Clause, which provides that "[t]he United States shall guarantee to every State in this Union a Republican Form of Government, *and shall protect each of them against Invasion.*"[159] Does this clause forbid the President, either as commander-in-chief or as treaty maker, from making a tactical decision to sacrifice one state to save another by imposing a duty to protect "each" of the states against invasion?

There are two ways to understand this clause. First, it might impose on the President a duty to defend in good faith every part of the country with equal vigor. This understanding would satisfy the concern that the President might neglect invasions in disfavored areas or play geographical favorites in the event of a large-scale invasion.[160] It would also permit the President to surrender state territory in a good-faith exercise of tactical judgment, and accordingly would permit the formal transfer of such territory in peace treaties. Alternatively, the Guarantee Clause might be read as an absolute prohibition on the surrender of any state territory under any circumstances. This would mean that if any part of the Union fell to foreign invasion, the entire Union must fight to the death until the invader is repelled or the Union ceases to exist as a viable political entity. This understanding would, of course, forbid treaties of cession — but it would do so even on a much broader understanding of the scope of the Treaty Clause. The Guarantee Clause, after all, is phrased as a duty imposed on "[t]he United States" and accordingly extends to the treaty-making authority. Even if the Treaty Clause were an independent head of jurisdiction for the national government, it would be limited by the duties imposed by the Guarantee Clause, including any putative duty to refuse to surrender state territory. Thus, if the federal government is forbidden from surrendering state territory, it is not because of anything peculiar to the implementational view of the treaty power, but because of the supervening force of the Guarantee Clause.

The implementational view does, however, limit the circumstances under which state territory can be ceded. State territory can be ceded as part of a peace settlement, but not as part of ordinary commercial relations. Northern New England could not be traded away for fishing rights in the Gulf of Mexico or favorable tariff status for cotton. We do not believe that a fully informed eighteenth-century audience would have been scandalized by this outcome.

Treaties of commerce are among the most common types of treaties. Such treaties can fix the terms of trade, set tariff levels, or grant navigational rights. A treaty power that did not include the ability to enter into such agreements would be as peculiar as a treaty power that did not authorize treaties of peace.

Such treaties are permissible as vehicles for implementing the congressional powers to "lay and collect Taxes, Duties, Imposts and Excises" and to "regulate Commerce with foreign Nations." The implementational character of the treaty power does mean, however, that treaties cannot unilaterally set tariff rates or trade rules without congressional action. They can carry into effect statutes that already exist. They can establish frameworks that are triggered by subsequent statutes. But they cannot create free-standing regulatory regimes.

This understanding is contrary to established practice, but not so contrary to eighteenth-century expectations that it takes the implementational view of treaties off the table. Under conventional understandings of the treaty power, in which treaties can fix tariff levels or terms of trade, those treaties "bind" the United States as a matter of international law, but not as a matter of domestic law. Subsequent congressional statutes that violate the terms of the treaty are perfectly valid as a matter of domestic law. They may embroil the United States in international problems, but they are not, in any meaningful sense, "unconstitutional." Full effectiveness of a treaty always requires the collaboration of Congress, if only through inaction, even if one views treaties as self-executing (that is, as taking effect without legislative implementation). Our view is not all that different in substance. Under an implementational theory of treaties, treaties of commerce always require the collaboration of Congress through affirmative action: Congress must either enact a statute for the treaty to implement or, if no such statute yet exists, the treaty can at most establish a contingent legal framework that is triggered by congressional action. Put in the language of modern debates, treaties are not self-executing with respect to Congress, though they are self-executing with respect to the states by virtue of the Supremacy Clause.

Of course, in the process of "implementing" an exercise of power embodied in a specific statute, a treaty "dis-implements" subsequent exercises of the same power by attaching international legal consequences to the enactment of statutes that are inconsistent with the terms of the treaty. But that is always a possibility with implementational powers. The Property Clause, for instance, is both substantive and implementational: the power to dispose of and regulate federal property is a self-contained authorization of both means and ends. Suppose that Congress exercises the power to "dispose of . . . Property belonging to the United States" by vesting a land title in a private person. That statute "dis-implements" future acts that seek to, for instance, make the property part of a post road. Congress can, in fact, make the land part of a post road even after it has been vested in a private party, but there are legal consequences that attach to that action — namely, an obligation to provide just compensation for the taking of property. More directly, if the executive "implements" a statutory scheme by entering into contracts, those contracts create legal obligations that "dis-implement" future actions, in the sense of attaching legal consequences to future actions that are inconsistent with the original implementing act. Treaties have the same status and effect. The treaty-making authority can bind the United States as a matter of international law in the course of implementing enumerated powers, in the sense of making future legislative action bear legal consequences. That is a significant result, which is why the treaty power is a significant power.

A more vexing problem concerns treaty provisions that address subjects typically within the exclusive jurisdiction of the states, such as private-law rights of tort, contract, property, and descent. It is commonplace to give foreign emissaries broad immunity from local laws and broad powers that states might not otherwise give to aliens. It was also commonplace in the founding era. On July 29, 1789, the Senate ratified a treaty with France that had been negotiated by the Confederation government involving reciprocal privileges of consuls and vice consuls,[161] which "trenched more deeply on state prerogatives than any of the other previous treaties negotiated under the Confederation" by, inter alia, granting "consular officials and employees and consular premises extensive immunities from the operation of state laws (though not compelled to do so by the law of nations)."[162] What power, if any, do treaty provisions of this kind implement?

The only possible power is the President's power under Article II to "receive Ambassadors and other public Ministers."[163] Blackstone understood the English king's power to receive foreign emissaries to include, as a necessary incident, the power to receive them free of the normal constraints of municipal law: "[t]he rights, the powers, the duties, and the privileges of ambassadors are determined by the law of nature and nations, and not by any municipal constitution."[164] If the President's constitutional power to "receive Ambassadors and other public Ministers" includes the right to receive them under similar conditions of immunity,[165] then a treaty could implement that power. Of course, in order to know whether the 1789 Consular Convention was constitutional, one would need to explore whether the power (and perhaps duty) to grant immunity to foreign emissaries extended to consuls[166] and whether it included all of the provisions contained in that treaty. We are less interested in the answer to that question than in the general principle that determines the scope of the treaty power to grant rights and immunities to foreign emissaries.

Foreign *citizens*, as opposed to official foreign *emissaries*, are a different story. One of the most contentious foreign relations issues in early American history was the extent to which treaties, either under the authority of the Articles of Confederation or of the Constitution, could give alien citizens rights to own and dispose of real property contrary to state law, presumably in exchange for similar rights for American citizens in foreign countries. The best-known example is Article 9 of the Jay Treaty of 1795, which declared that "British Subjects who now hold Lands in the Territories of the United States . . . shall continue to hold them according to the nature and Tenures of their respective Estates and Titles therein, and may grant Sell or Devise the same to whom they please, in like manner as if they were Natives."[167] Just where did federal treaty negotiators get the power to dictate state rules of property ownership and descent?

They didn't. An implementational view of the Treaty Clause would not permit provisions of this nature. If that limitation unduly burdened federal treaty makers, they would need a constitutional amendment to authorize reciprocal property ownership provisions and other provisions that involve powers not otherwise allocated to some federal institution. As the founding-era controversies over such provisions demonstrate, a significant portion of the actual eighteenth-century public would have found this conclusion wholly congenial. If the hypothetical fully informed eighteenth-century audience that is the target of our inquiry would have been at all distressed by that conclusion, we suspect that it would be far more surprised by a conclusion that the slave trade could have been ended in 1789 if only the President could have mustered a two-thirds majority of a quorum of the Senate.

TAKING EPISTEMOLOGY SERIOUSLY

Suppose, however, that the reader is not convinced. After all, even if we are right that the textual and structural case for a treaty power that extends to any subject is not, as Professor Golove would have it, "compelling, even overwhelming,"[168] that does not establish that the Jeffersonian interpretation is correct either. If both conceptions of the treaty power — the jurisdiction-extending view and the implementational view — can be advanced plausibly in terms of text and structure, where does one go from there?

As we have elsewhere argued at some length,[169] the default rule for federal power is "when in doubt, don't." In other words, the burden of proof always rests with the proponent of federal governmental power. If someone wants to claim that the federal treaty power includes the power to make treaties on matters that are not within the enumerated powers of any federal institution, that person must overcome a presumption against any such power. That anti-power presumption is not grounded in normative or political concerns. It is grounded in the basic *epistemological* principle that he who asserts the affirmative existence of something must prove it. Because the federal Constitution creates the national government as a government of enumerated powers, the existence of a specific federal power is always a matter for proof. Once that power is established, the existence of an external limitation on that power is a matter for proof, so the epistemological presumption does not always work against governmental power. Quite to the contrary, it works in favor of governmental power when one is discussing constitutional restraints on either the federal or state governments in the form of "thou shalt nots." But for the threshold question of determining the scope of enumerated federal powers, the balance always tilts away from the power.

How strongly the balance tilts depends on the strength of the presumption against grants of federal power. That, in turn, depends on the proper standard of proof for claims of constitutional meaning generally and for claims of federal power in particular. That is a project for another day--and another book. For now, it is enough simply to note that doubts about the scope of the treaty power should, all else being equal, be resolved against an expansive view of the power. On that point as well, Jefferson was right.

To be sure, the Jeffersonian view of the treaty power has significant flaws, not the least of which is its relative dearth of direct historical support. But every other view of the treaty power has its own problems to contend with. To paraphrase Churchill, an implementational theory of the Treaty Clause is the worst available interpretation of that clause except for all of the others.

In other words, we view Jefferson's interpretation of the Treaty Clause through the same epistemological lens as did Jefferson himself. Jefferson's notes of Washington Administration cabinet conferences from 1793 describe a discussion among some of the nation's brightest luminaries about the form and effect of President Washington's forthcoming Neutrality Proclamation. Alexander Hamilton evidently initiated a discussion of the treaty power by declaring that, although the President could not unilaterally foreclose a congressional declaration of war by issuing a proclamation, "the constn having given power to the President and Senate to make treaties, they might make a treaty of neutrality which should take from Congress the right to declare war in that particular case, and that under the form of a treaty they might exercise any powers whatever, even those exclusively given by the constn to the H. of representatives." Edmund Randolph countered that "where they undertook to do acts by treaty (as to settle a tariff of duties,) which were exclusively given to the legislature, . . . an act of the legislature would be necessary to confirm them." Jefferson, for his part, insisted, as he would later do in his parliamentary manual, that "in givg to the Prest & Senate a power to make treaties, the constn meant only to authorize them to carry into effect by way of treaty any powers they might constitutionally exercise. I was sensible of the weak points in this position, but there were still weaker in the other hypothesis, and if it be impossible to discover a rational measure of authority to have been given by this clause, I would rather suppose that the cases which my hypothesis would leave unprovided, were not thought of by the Convention, or if thought of, could not be agreed on, or were thought on and deemed unnecessary to be invested in the government."[170]

Treaties and Acquisitions

We can now assess the constitutional propriety of the Louisiana Purchase. We have previously demonstrated that the power of acquisition cannot be found in inherent governmental powers, a power to pursue the general welfare, a power of acquisition implicit in the District Clause, or a free-standing power to spend. Nor does the Treaty Clause by itself provide authority for acquisitions. A treaty can constitutionally acquire territory only as a means for executing some other enumerated federal power. In this respect, the Treaty Clause and the Sweeping Clause work together: Congress has power under the Sweeping Clause to spend money "for carrying into Execution" other federal powers, and the President and the Senate can enter into treaties for carrying into execution other federal powers. The Treaty Clause cannot appropriate the money for the purchase, and the Sweeping Clause cannot secure the needed agreement of the foreign sovereign to the purchase. But because the Treaty Clause and Sweeping Clause are both implementational powers, there must be some power to implement. What power could the Louisiana Purchase, and the congressional appropriation to complete the purchase, possibly have carried into execution?

ADMISSIONS AGAINST INTEREST

Given that all of the land acquired in the Louisiana Purchase is now part of some state, the obvious answer is the power to admit new states: "New States may be admitted by the Congress into this Union; but no new State shall be formed or erected within the Jurisdiction of any other States; nor any State be formed by the Junction of two or more States, or Parts of States, without the Consent of the Legislatures of the States concerned as well as of the Congress."[171] This Admissions Clause was clearly designed to facilitate admission of states formed out of the Northwest Territory, whose 1787 ordinance anticipated statehood for various component territories when they reached a certain level of population.[172] The Admissions Clause's terms, however, are general: "New States may be admitted by the Congress into this Union."

Despite the Admissions Clause's unqualified language, it was not infrequently argued in the early years of the nation, and specifically during debate over the Louisiana Purchase, that new states could come only from territory that was part of the United States when the Constitution was ratified. Obviously, if Congress has no power to admit states from territory acquired after ratification, then the Treaty Clause cannot implement any such power.

A substantial number of founding-era figures doubted Congress's power to convert acquired property into states. Levi Lincoln, Jefferson's Attorney General during the Louisiana Purchase, floated the idea that the Louisiana territory should be annexed to an existing state because "the Genl Govt when formed, was predicated on the then existing *United* States, and such as could grow out of *them*, & out of *them* only, and . . . its authority, is, constitutionally, limited to the people composing the several political State Societies in that union, & such as might be formed out of them."[173] Gouverneur Morris, the principal drafter of the Territories Clause, which immediately follows the Admissions Clause in Article IV, section 3, clearly believed that Congress could not "admit, as a new State, territory which did not belong to the United States, when the Constitution was made."[174] Morris was not alone in that conviction; the same position was expressed in both the Senate and the House in the discussion of the Louisiana Purchase.[175] Clearly, that position was the minority view — as a brief glance at a map or the flag will demonstrate. But it was forcefully advanced by eminent individuals and, as with all arguments about constitutional meaning, deserves to be considered on its merits.

Notwithstanding its pedigree, this view does not survive serious scrutiny. The language of the Admissions Clause does not even hint at a limitation to then-existing territory. That is especially pertinent because the Articles of

Confederation specifically contemplated the admission of Canada with no further action by the states and the admission of other new colonies ("by which was evidently meant . . . other British colon[ies]")[176] if nine states agreed.[177] If Canada, which was welcome in the Confederation at a time of its own choosing, was to be off limits for admission under the Constitution, one might expect something a bit more expressive than an unqualified grant to Congress of the power to admit new states.

Indeed, given the clear text of the Admissions Clause, it is worth asking why anyone would try to read limitations into the admissions power. There are at least two reasons — one hypothetical and one actually, and quite forcefully, expressed in the founding era.

First, although opponents of a broad view of the Admissions Clause did not expressly frame their views in these terms, if one believes that the Territories Clause of Article IV applies only to territory existing at the time of ratification, then there are good reasons to read the same restriction into the Admissions Clause. The two clauses are next to each other in Article IV, which points toward an in pari materia construction. Furthermore, if the Territories Clause is limited to pre-ratification territory, then the acquisition of new territory for statehood (or otherwise) becomes problematic, because there is then no evident enumerated power to govern the territory prior to its admission. One could try to locate a power of governance as an implicit adjunct to the power of acquisition, but given the compound problems of (1) locating a constitutional power of acquisition and (2) inferring forms of governance from such a power, it is understandable that doubts about the scope of the Territories Clause might also prompt doubts about the scope of the Admissions Clause that appears adjacent to it in the same article.

This limited view of the Territories Clause has received surprising play in the Supreme Court over the years. In *Seré v Pitot* in 1810, the Court affirmed the power of Congress to establish territorial governments, but it was ambivalent about the source of that power: "The power of governing and of legislating for a territory is the inevitable consequence of the right to acquire and to hold territory. Could this position be contested, the constitution of the United States declares that 'congress shall have power to dispose of and make all needful rules and regulations respecting the territory or other property belonging to the United States.' "[178] This passage reflects uncertainty about whether the power to govern territories comes from the Territories Clause or as an inference from the power of acquisition (whose constitutional source, we have seen, is not obvious). In 1840, the Court in dictum appeared to ground the power to govern territories squarely in Article IV.[179] Less than twenty years later, however, in *Dred Scott v Sandford*, a plurality of the Court in dictum grounded the power to govern territories acquired after ratification of the Constitution solely in an inference from the right of acquisition, concluding that the Territories Clause applied only to the territory held in common by the states immediately prior to ratification.[180] That resolution, if it could ever have been called that, did not last long. In 1880, the Court summed up the debate by announcing, "It is certainly now too late to doubt the power of Congress to govern the Territories. There have been some differences of opinion as to the particular clause of the Constitution from which the power is derived, but that it exists has always been conceded."[181]

In the end, there is no plausible way to limit the Territories Clause to territory existing at the time of ratification. Albert Gallatin pointed out the fatal flaw in this position in 1803 in his response to Levi Lincoln's proposal to annex Louisiana to Georgia. The Territories Clause is in fact the "Territory or other Property Clause." The clause grants Congress power to "dispose of and make all needful Rules and Regulations respecting the Territory or other Property belonging to the United States." Nothing in this clause suggests that Congress's power over territory is different from its power over "other Property," such as wagons, ink, or muskets. Gallatin drew the obvious conclusion: "as the words 'other property' follow, and must be embraced by the same construction which will apply to the territory, it would result from Mr. L's opinion, that the United States could not, after the Constitution, either acquire or dispose of any personal property."[182] To be sure, this does not prove that the Admissions Clause extends to territory acquired after ratification, but it does prove that the case for limiting the Admissions Clause to pre-ratification territory cannot be supported by anything in the Territories Clause. And there is little else in the Constitution from which such support could be drawn.

A second, and more profound, reason to seek limitations on the power of admission was strongly advanced during the debates over Louisiana. A small but vocal group of northeastern Federalists argued that the Constitution was a compact among the original states whose character could be changed only by unanimous consent of the original parties to the compact. Senator Uriah Tracy from Connecticut, who endorsed a limited construction of the Admissions Clause during the Louisiana Purchase debate, explained that "[t]he principles of our Government, the original ideas and rights of the partners to the compact, forbid such a measure [admitting a foreign territory as a state]; and without the consent of all the partners, no such thing can be done."[183] Representative Thatcher from Massachusetts, though reserving judgment on the full scope of the Admissions Clause, also opined that "[t]he Confederation under which we now live is a partnership of States, and it is not competent to it to admit a new partner but with the consent of all the partners."[184] Perhaps the fullest statement of this position during the Louisiana Purchase debate came from Rep. Roger Griswold from Connecticut, who summed up a lengthy discussion by claiming: "The Government of the United States was not formed for the purpose of distributing its principles and advantages to foreign nations. It was formed with the sole view of securing those blessings to ourselves and our posterity. It follows from these principles that no power can reside in any public functionary to contract any engagement, or to pursue any measure which shall change the Union of the States. Nor was it necessary that any restrictive clause should have been inserted in the Constitution to restrain the public agents from exercising these extraordinary powers, because the restriction grows out of the nature of the Government."[185]

Undergirding this theoretical position were some very concrete concerns, which Senator Tracy voiced:

> Suppose Louisiana contain ten millions of inhabitants; or, for the sake of argument, let it be supposed that we had a President inclined to monarchical principles, and he lived in the northern part of the Union, say in Connecticut or Massachusetts, and that two-thirds of the Senate were with him in sentiment, and that the four northern provinces of Great Britain contained ten millions of inhabitants, and were all determined monarchists, would the parties of the Union say it was competent and Constitutional for the President and Senate to introduce these ten millions of monarchists, who could at once out vote us all . . . ?
>
> . . .
>
> The principle of admission, in the case of Louisiana, is the same as if it contained ten millions of inhabitants; and the principles of these people are probably as hostile to our Government, in its true construction, as they can be, and the relative strength which this admission, gives to a Southern and Western interest, is contradictory to the principles of our original Union.[186]

Senator Tracy's geopolitical concerns were quite plausible; the Louisiana Purchase was not going to result in additional states on the New England seaboard. In resistance to this perceived shift in power, northeastern Federalists wound up endorsing a "compact" theory of the Constitution that would find very different expression, in very different sources, a few short years later.

As applied to acquisitions of territory, this "compact" theory has implications that range far beyond a construction of the Admissions Clause. It would forbid admission of a state from previously foreign territory *even by constitutional amendment.* Article V permits approval of constitutional amendments by three-quarters, meaning less than all, of the states, but under the compact theory, only the unanimous approval of the states could approve a change in the composition of the Union. Senator Tracy acknowledged this point by saying that "no subsequent act of legislation, or even ordinary amendment to our Constitution, can legalize such measures."[187] Senator Timothy Pickering from Massachusetts similarly declared that an amendment for admission of newly acquired territory "could not be made in the ordinary mode by the concurrence of two-thirds of both Houses of Congress, and the ratification by the Legislatures of three-fourths of the several States. He believed the assent of each individual State to be necessary for the admission of a foreign country as an associate in the Union."[188] Under Representative Griswold's version of the theory, it is not obvious that even the unanimous agreement of the states could so alter the Union, though perhaps it could be done by reconstituting the entire Union through a new constitutional convention.

There is no ground for reading such a sweeping principle into the federal Constitution. The Constitution is very clear about the subjects that are beyond the Article V amendment power,[189] and this is not one of them. The addition of previously foreign territory is inconsistent with the original compact only if the original compact forbids it. An alteration in the voting rules of the House (or, less hypothetically, in the selection procedure for the Senate) would likely change the character of the original compact more than would the admission of a new state, but these are clearly not beyond the amendment process. And if the "no alteration of the compact" theory is false, it provides no basis for reading unstated restrictions into the Admissions Clause.

Robert Knowles has recently advanced a variation on the "compact" argument. Although he rejects the strong form of the compact theory, with its requirement of unanimous consent of the states to new admissions, Mr. Knowles maintains that the Louisiana Purchase was nonetheless unconstitutional because it so disrupted the preexisting balance among the states that it required a constitutional amendment. In essence, Mr. Knowles insists that the Admissions Clause must be limited to territory that was part of the United States in 1787 (or at least must be limited to relatively minor changes in that territory that do not alter preexisting sectional distributions of power) because of a background conception of federalism that presupposed a particular distribution of states at the time of ratification.[190] While Mr. Knowles makes a powerful case for the wisdom of a constitutional amendment in 1803, there are two problems with reading such a limitation into the Admissions Clause. First, and most importantly, the evidence for a background presumption that is sufficiently strong to qualify the Admissions Clause just is not there. In order to limit the clear meaning of the Admissions Clause, the sanctity of the 1787 borders must have been so clear to observers that it constituted an interpretative baseline that all reasonable observers shared (or at least that all fully informed reasonable observers would have shared). The universality of this "balance of forces" conception of federalism simply cannot be demonstrated with the requisite clarity. Many people held it, and many others would likely have held it after full argumentation. But it is very tough to say that it would, even under ideal circumstances, have commanded so much assent that it must be deemed to lurk behind the actual text of the document. Second, if such a background principle did exist, it would presumably inform Article V as well as the Admissions Clause, in which case the advocates of unanimous state consent would have been right all along. It is hard to see how an implicit constitutional rule that forbids major changes in the political balance without state consent could be satisfied by anything other than unanimous state consent.

The Admissions Clause means what it says: Congress can admit new states, whether out of territory held by the United States in 1787 or out of territory acquired by the United States at a subsequent date.

PROMISING DEVELOPMENTS

A correct understanding of the Admissions Clause validates the acquisition of Louisiana. Recall that the Treaty Clause and the Sweeping Clause were both needed to implement the Louisiana Purchase: the President and Senate needed to secure France's agreement to the transfer of land, and Congress (and the President) had to appropriate the consideration for the transfer. Once it is understood that new territory can be admitted into statehood, the Treaty Clause and Sweeping Clause can both be brought into action to carry that power into execution. The President and Senate clearly can make a treaty with a foreign nation for the acquisition of territory if it is pursuant to the power to admit new states.

Article III of the Louisiana Purchase Treaty provided: "The inhabitants of the ceded territory shall be incorporated in the Union of the United States and admitted as soon as possible according to the principles of the federal Constitution to the enjoyment of all these rights, advantages and immunities of citizens of the United States, and in the mean time they shall be maintained and protected in the free enjoyment of their liberty, property and the Religion which they profess."[191] This provision raised more constitutional hackles in 1803 than did the more basic question of the power to acquire Louisiana. Even many who did not doubt a power of acquisition doubted the ability to "incorporate" the inhabitants into the United States, and others who did not doubt that particular power in the abstract doubted that it could be effectuated by the President and Senate through a treaty.[192]

The latter doubt was correct, but the former was not. Certainly, the President and Senate could not, by treaty, admit Louisiana as a state. *Congress* has the power of admission. The treaty-making authority can help implement that power by acquiring territory that will be the subject of admission, but it cannot itself admit. And, of course, the Louisiana Purchase Treaty did not purport to admit Louisiana as a state. The treaty merely promised that "the inhabitants of the ceded territory shall be incorporated in the Union of the United States." The treaty did not define "incorporated." It is possible to read the term as implying a promise of statehood, but it is also possible to read it as promising some other, lesser association with the American polity. The only mention of admission in Article III of the treaty concerned, not the admission of Louisiana as a state, but the admission of the *inhabitants* of the territory to the "rights, advantages and immunities of citizens of the United States." Whether any of this could be accomplished by means short of ultimate statehood was left unsaid.

We will have more to say about the idea of "incorporating" territory in Part II, when we examine problems of territorial governance. Whatever the precise meaning of the term may have been, critics of the treaty were correct to point out that Article III was making very potent promises. To the extent that those promises required implementing legislation, the President and Senate could not, of course, compel the House to enact such legislation. But the failure to follow through on the treaty's promises would leave the United States in breach of the treaty and perhaps would invalidate the transfer of territory.[193] It is worth asking whether the treaty negotiators went too far when they agreed to Article III of the treaty.

The United States eventually delivered on its treaty promises in the strongest possible way by granting statehood to all of the territory acquired in the Louisiana Purchase. But it took a while. Louisiana attained statehood in 1812, a mere nine years after the Louisiana Purchase, but Montana, North Dakota, and South Dakota did not become states until 1889; Wyoming was admitted in 1890, and Oklahoma in 1907. Was it constitutional for Congress to wait a full century before incorporating all of the acquired territory as states? If it was not, did that retroactively invalidate (whatever that might mean operationally) the Louisiana Purchase?

The answer to the first question is yes, so there is no need at this point to address the second. A treaty of acquisition is constitutional if it helps carry into effect the congressional power to admit new states. In order to determine the scope and limits of the power of acquisition, one must therefore understand the scope and limits of the Article IV admissions power.

The congressional power to admit new states is discretionary: "New States *may* be admitted by the Congress into this Union." Of course, the Northwest Ordinance of 1787 guaranteed that between three and five states would eventually be formed out of the Northwest Territory. The promise of statehood in the ordinance did not include a specific timetable. Statehood for the northwestern territories was premised on population: "And, whenever any of the said States shall have sixty thousand free inhabitants therein, such State shall be admitted, by its delegates, into the Congress of the United States, on an equal footing with the original States in all respects whatever . . . ; and, so far as it can be consistent with the general interest of the confederacy, such admission shall be allowed at an earlier period, and when there may be a less number of free inhabitants in the State than sixty thousand."[194] The Northwest Ordinance was reenacted with minor changes by the First Congress.[195] The fulfillment of the promise of statehood for the Northwest Territory was required of the new national government under the Constitution if (as seems clear) the Northwest Ordinance was subject to the Engagements Clause of Article VI, which provides that "[a]ll Debts contracted and Engagements entered into, before the Adoption of this Constitution, shall be as valid against the United States under this Constitution, as under the Confederation."[196] In any event, the new Congress's prompt reenactment of the ordinance obviated the need for any questions about its constitutional status.

The Ordinance of 1787 by its terms extended only to the Northwest Territory; it had no direct application to after-acquired territory, though it was extended (without the provisions forbidding slavery) by Congress to territory acquired by cessions from North Carolina and Georgia after ratification of the Constitution and to additional territories in the ensuing decades.[197] Accordingly, the territory acquired in the Louisiana Purchase did not come with a guarantee, statutory or constitutional, of statehood upon achievement of a certain level of population or any other specific circumstance. So what does it mean in this context for an acquisition of territory to be pursuant to a power to admit new states? Does it require ultimate admission as a state?

One possibility, and the obvious answer, is simply that acquisitions give Congress the raw material over which to exercise its discretionary power of admission under Article IV. If Congress never chooses to exercise that power, that is Congress's business. Thus what is necessary to validate an acquisition is not an actual or implied promise of statehood, but simply the promise of *eligibility* for statehood if and when Congress deems it appropriate. Once it is established that territory acquired from foreign sovereigns after ratification of the Constitution is fair game for statehood, the result is that the Constitution places no limits at all upon the acquisition of territory. Every acquisition affords Congress the opportunity to exercise its discretion concerning statehood, and every acquisition therefore implements the admissions power. If that is the correct understanding of the admissions power, and if Congress's discretion to make admissions decisions is unlimited, then there is nothing more to say about acquisitions of territory by treaty. If Article III of the treaty promised ultimate statehood, it was trenching on the prerogatives of Congress by promising something that Congress would not otherwise be obliged to provide, and the article's critics had a very valid and powerful point.

Another possibility is that Congress's discretion under the Admissions Clause is not absolute. If there are circumstances under which Congress is actually required to admit, or is forbidden from admitting, territory as a state, then those limitations apply as well to acquisitions of territory made pursuant to the admissions power. If such circumstances existed in the case of the Louisiana Purchase and affirmatively required ultimate admission to statehood as a validating condition of the acquisition, then the problem with Article III would not be that it promised too much but that it promised too little. An affirmative guarantee of statehood, or at least of serious consideration for statehood, would have been constitutionally necessary and appropriate; it would have trenched upon Congress's power only if it specified a timetable that was more stringent than Congress's (assumedly limited) discretion required.

Given the stark language of the Admissions Clause, what could possibly motivate an argument that Congress's discretion in admitting states is anything other than absolute? We can best answer that question in a roundabout way by first considering whether any powers other than the admissions power could sustain an acquisition such as the Louisiana Purchase.

DELEGATION, DISCRETION, AND ALTERNATIVES TO STATEHOOD

One can avoid all questions about the constitutional inevitability of statehood for the territory acquired in the Louisiana Purchase if one can find some other enumerated power that the treaty of acquisition might be thought to implement. A clever person might suggest that the acquisition could carry into effect the power "[t]o establish Post Offices and post Roads"[198] if, for instance, Congress wanted to construct a post road from Pennsylvania to Georgia via the Mississippi Basin. In that case, statehood or even eligibility for statehood need not be an ultimate consequence of the acquisition. Or suppose that Congress wanted a naval base at New Orleans as part of its power "[t]o provide and maintain a Navy."[199] Could it acquire land west to the Rockies and north to Canada in pursuance of that end? Or, finally, if the acquisition is a really good deal, could one argue that it improves America's creditworthiness and thus helps implement the power "[t]o borrow Money on the credit of the United States"?[200]

The treaty power, as an aspect of the executive power, must conform to the principle of reasonableness. That principle allows us to assess the plausibility of finding a ground for the acquisition of Louisiana other than the future admission of new states. The Postal Clause obviously will not do the trick; doubling America's land mass in order to build a post road fails even the most generous test of reasonableness. Nor does the Borrowing Clause work, though that is less obvious. To see the problem, focus for a moment on the Sweeping Clause (whose use was necessary to effectuate the Louisiana Purchase in any event). Suppose that some members of Congress conclude, perhaps even rightly, that steel stocks are undervalued. Could Congress therefore nationalize the steel industry, paying just compensation to the stockholders in the process, because it would improve the financial position of the United States and the credit standing of federal bonds? There is no slam-dunk answer to this question, and there is really no way to reach an answer without establishing the *degree* of reasonableness required of various exercises of power, which is a task well beyond our present project. But the best answer seems to be "no," for two reasons. First, if the goal is to improve the government's borrowing capacity, there are surely more measured ways to do it than by taking over the steel industry (or buying a very large chunk of the North American continent). Second, as may arguably be true as well of the incorporation of a national bank, the power to take over and operate an industry "seems more like a subject to be separately enumerated than a vehicle for carrying into execution another enumerated power . . . , although . . . the distinction is difficult to verbalize."[201] And if Congress can't bolster the bond rating by acquisitions of industry under the Sweeping Clause, the President and Senate can't do it by acquisitions of territory under the Treaty Clause; there is a case to be made that the principle of reasonableness should be applied more generously to Congress's legislative powers than to Article II or Article III powers, but there is not much to be said for the reverse.

That leaves the establishment of a naval base in New Orleans or some other port. There is no doubt that the power to raise and maintain a navy would support treaties and appropriations that give the United States rights to maintain bases in foreign countries. The questions are whether it would support a power to acquire territory outright for that purpose and whether one could leverage any such power into a further right to acquire a "buffer zone" for the acquisition that stretches, let us say, to Colorado and North Dakota. We do not have a firm answer to that question, because we do not have a firm view on how tightly the Treaty Clause requires means to be fitted to ends. But using the Navy (or Army) Clause as grounds for acquisition presents many of the same problems as does using the Borrowing Clause. Does the power to provide a navy provide authorization for the nationalization of all industries necessary for shipbuilding (or, for that matter, does the power to establish post roads provide authorization for the nationalization of the construction industry)?

Would that constitute a "necessary and proper" means of implementation? If one is talking about a temporary taking during wartime, quite possibly it would. But if one is talking about a permanent taking during peacetime in order to avoid the potential vagaries of the market on a day-to-day basis, the necessity and propriety of the action is much less apparent. If no such power exists, then it is hard to see how security concerns alone could justify the acquisition of territory, under either the Treaty Clause or the Sweeping Clause, which was not very directly related to the underlying security concerns. There is a difference between Mobile Bay and Fargo.

Under a sufficiently latitudinarian understanding of the means-ends relationships contained in the Constitution, one can construct a case for the acquisition of Louisiana by treaty (and appropriation) that does not raise any questions about subsequent admission of the acquired territory into statehood. But under a sufficiently latitudinarian understanding of the means-ends relationships contained in the Constitution, the entire structure of the Constitution comes unraveled. Whatever the right understandings of those relationships may be, an understanding that would unravel the Constitution is the wrong one. If one gives any respectable significance to the principle of reasonableness, it is at best problematic that the acquisition of Louisiana could be justified as anything other than an effectuation of the power to admit new states.

Acquisitions and the Constitution

We now have a framework for assessing the constitutionality of American acquisitions by treaty. The Constitution permits the United States to acquire new territory by treaty. But the acquisition must be in pursuance of some enumerated power other than the power to make treaties. The most obvious power that would justify the addition of territory is the power to admit new states. As we saw earlier, if that power is wholly discretionary, giving Congress complete freedom (apart from the commitments in the Northwest Ordinance) to admit or not admit states as it sees fit, then all acquisitions by treaty seem to be necessarily constitutional, because they implement the admissions power by affording Congress opportunities to consider new admissions.

The one possible rub is the principle of reasonableness. It is extremely unlikely that the principle of reasonableness exercises much direct constraint over the admissions power even if (and we take no position one way or the other) the principle applies to Congress's legislative powers in the absence of specific constitutional language, such as the "necessary and proper" language in the Sweeping Clause. The principle of reasonableness could have bite in the admissions context only if there are particular circumstances that cut so strongly in favor of or against statehood that Congress, in the face of those circumstances, would impermissibly abuse its discretion by making certain statehood decisions. It is difficult to specify what those circumstances might be. Insufficient population is certainly a reasonable basis for declining to grant statehood, and who is to say what counts as insufficient population? A state, upon admission, gets two Senators, which dilutes the votes of the existing states. Would it be "unreasonable" for Congress to refuse admission to any territory until it achieved a population at least equal to that of the most populous state? And when one considers that the decisions of one Congress to deny statehood do not prevent subsequent Congresses from granting it, the task of giving content to the principle of reasonableness in any fashion that would constitute a real constraint on the admissions power is problematic at best.

But whether or not the principle of reasonableness applies, or applies in a meaningful way, to the admissions power, it clearly applies to the treaty power, including the contexts in which the treaty power is implementing the admissions power. If it is highly doubtful whether certain territory would ever be viewed as a plausible candidate for statehood, then there could be a problem with permitting the acquisition as a means for implementing the admissions power. Suppose, for instance, that a mountain-climbing lobby persuades the President and Senate to arrange a treaty with Nepal for the acquisition of Mount Everest. If the Admissions Clause is as broad as we think it is, it would not be "unconstitutional" for Congress to admit Mount Everest as a state. It is not literally impossible to imagine this eventually happening, especially if one looks at a time horizon measured in centuries of potential Congresses. But it is not very likely that we will ever see two Senators from Mount Everest. If the principle of reasonableness means anything at all, it means that there must be some plausible connection between means and ends. Giving Congress raw material on which to exercise discretion to grant or not grant statehood is one thing; doing so under circumstances in which the outcome is effectively foreordained against statehood is another. It is, for lack of a better term, unreasonable to treat the acquisition of Mount Everest as a means for implementing the admissions power.

As constitutional arguments go, this one is pretty "soft," which is perhaps inevitable when one is dealing with a principle as "soft" as the principle of reasonableness. We are not prepared to claim — yet — that the treaty power cannot be used to obtain territory that has no realistic prospects of statehood (over whatever time frame would be appropriate for that inquiry). We do not yet need to address that question, for as long as there is a plausible prospect of ultimate statehood, the acquisition is constitutional beyond any question. And the Louisiana Purchase clearly does not test whatever limits might exist on the power to acquire territory for potential future admission to statehood. No one ever viewed the acquired territory as somehow "off limits" to future statehood when the population grew to a proper level. The long delays in admission for some of the territory acquired in the Louisiana Purchase was a function of demographics rather than of predetermination against statehood; even many decades after the purchase, those territories did not, and still do not, approach in population density the earlier-admitted states. Louisiana was not Mount Everest.

Even under the assumptions least generous to the powers of Congress, the Louisiana Purchase was easily a constitutional exercise of the treaty power. But it was not easily constitutional simply because of the breadth of the Treaty Clause. The breadth of the Admissions Clause was necessary as well to complete the puzzle. Furthermore, the acquired territory was at least a plausible candidate for statehood at the time of acquisition, which establishes a direct telic link between the implementational treaty power and the admissions power that it was implementing. If Louisiana had been more like Mount Everest, the puzzle would have been more difficult. But that is a story for another chapter.

2

Forms: Trouble with Texas?

The Louisiana Purchase initiated a century of American expansion that brought all of the present continental United States into American possession and created an empire that ranged from the Arctic to East Asia. The forms of acquisition ranged from naked conquest (California, the Southwest, and the insular possessions) to thinly disguised conquest (Florida) to diplomacy (Alaska, and perhaps Oregon) to discovery (the guano islands, and perhaps Oregon) to annexation (Texas and Hawaii). All of these episodes raise important questions of history, morality, and political theory, but only a few, and perhaps an unexpected few, raise serious questions of constitutional law.

In this chapter, we examine American acquisitions through 1846, along with the "acquisition" of the guano islands in the last half of the nineteenth century. Our primary concern is to flesh out the appropriate *forms* of acquisition. As we showed in Chapter 1, a treaty is an appropriate mechanism for acquisitions as long as the acquisition implements a constitutionally granted power, such as the power to admit new states. But other mechanisms are also conceivable. What about acquisition by statute? If a two-thirds majority of the Senate cannot be mustered to ratify a treaty of acquisition, can a majority of both Houses of Congress (plus the President) go around them? And does the United States have the same right to acquire territory by discovery that European nations recognized among themselves in 1788? After a brief look at another instance of acquisition by treaty, we will find our answers.

Filching Florida

The boundaries of the territory acquired in the Louisiana Purchase were unclear.[1] The United States acquired from France the same territory that was acquired by France from Spain in the 1800 Treaty of San Ildefonso, which territory was defined as "the Colony or Province of Louisiana with the Same extent that it now has in the hands of Spain, & that it had when France possessed it."[2] France had last possessed Louisiana in 1762, when it transferred to Spain "all the country known under the name of Louisiana, as well as New Orleans and the island in which that place stands" as compensation for Spain's loss of the Floridas to England.[3] But exactly what was known in 1762 "under the name of Louisiana"?

There was no definitive answer. The French title to Louisiana stemmed from LaSalle's expedition down the Mississippi River in 1682 and the resulting settlements, but the extent of the territory claimed by LaSalle or subsequent settlers was understandably imprecise. A century later, most of the American interior was unsettled, so exact surveys of boundaries were unavailable. Nor had there yet been enough agreements among European nations on the division of North America to provide clear demarcations of the Louisiana Territory, which left substantial room for debate, negotiation, or war. Obviously, the maximum northern limit of Louisiana was Canada and the maximum southern limit was the Gulf of Mexico, but to the west, it could conceivably go to the Pacific Ocean; to the southwest, it could go to Mexico; and to the east, it could imaginably run all the way to present-day Florida.

The uncertainty evidently pleased Napoleon, who resisted any efforts by American negotiators to define the boundaries more precisely with the remark to his advisers that " '[i]f an obscurity did not already exist, it would perhaps be good policy to put one there.' "[4] The American minister to France, Robert Livingston, related the following conversation with French foreign minister Talleyrand concerning the eastern boundaries of Louisiana: "'What are the eastern bounds of Louisiana?' asked Livingston. 'I do not know,' replied Talleyrand; 'you must take it as we received it.' 'But what did you mean to take?' urged Livingston. 'I do not know,' repeated Talleyrand. 'Then you mean that we shall construe it our own way?' 'I can give you no direction. You have made a noble bargain for yourselves, and I suppose that you will make the most of it.' "[5]

The United States indeed made "the most of it" by quickly claiming that the Louisiana Purchase included territory along the Gulf of Mexico to the Perdido River, just east of Mobile. In English and Spanish hands, this territory had been part of West Florida, a territory that the British had defined in 1763, during their rule, as roughly extending along the 31st parallel from the Mississippi River to the Apalachicola River in the Florida panhandle. The United States wanted this land because it provided access to the Gulf of Mexico for rivers in the Mississippi Territory (encompassing most of the present states of Alabama and Mississippi) and because Mobile Bay was an attractive location for a southern naval base. The original charge of Robert Livingston and James Monroe in their negotiating mission to France was to acquire New Orleans and the Floridas; indeed, when Talleyrand first broached the subject of selling the whole Louisiana Territory, Livingston's response was: "I told him no; that our wishes extended only to New Orleans and the Floridas."[6]

Spain never regarded West Florida as part of Louisiana. At the time of the Treaty of San Ildefonso in 1800, Spain's title to West Florida came from a different source than did its title to Louisiana: the former came from a 1783 cession from Great Britain and the latter came from a 1762 cession from France. France did not regard West Florida as part of Louisiana and repeatedly tried to acquire it after regaining Louisiana in 1800. When the French made preparations for taking possession of Louisiana in 1802, they defined the boundaries of their (re)acquired territory to exclude West Florida. Until May 1803, Robert Livingston averred that Louisiana did not include West Florida.

On May 20, 1803, however, less than two weeks after all of the signatures were dry on the Louisiana Purchase, Livingston changed his mind and argued that the United States had acquired territory in West Florida to the Perdido River. The reasoning was that prior to 1762, France had owned a portion of North America that extended to the Perdido River in West Florida. In 1762, the French lands west of the Mississippi River went to Spain and the lands east of the river went to Great Britain, which then transferred them back to Spain in 1783. Because the United States acquired the land which France had reacquired in 1800, and because in 1800 France reacquired Louisiana with the same boundaries "that it had when France possessed it," the United States got in 1803 everything that France had held in 1762, including a portion of West Florida that included Mobile Bay.

This theory had one big problem and one big advantage. The big problem, apart from the fact that it flew in the face of every understanding held by every interested nation between 1762 and 1803, was that the Treaty of San Ildefonso had transferred to France "the Colony or Province of Louisiana with the same extent *that it now has in the hand of Spain*." Accordingly, France got back all of the *Louisiana of 1800* that France had possessed in 1762, but the Louisiana of 1800 did not include West Florida.[7] The theory's big advantage, however, was that Spain in the early nineteenth century was too weak to fight a war over North American colonies. Livingston's theory quickly became official United States policy concerning the limits of Louisiana. That policy received expression in the United States Code on February 24, 1804, when President Jefferson signed legislation extending American laws to the Louisiana Territory. The statute declared that "all the navigable waters, rivers, creeks, bays, and inlets lying within the United States, which empty into the Gulf of Mexico east of the River Mississippi, shall be annexed to the Mississippi District."[8] If West Florida was not a part of the United States in 1804, this statute described an empty set, because all of the waters east of the Mississippi River that emptied into the Gulf of Mexico were part of the Floridas. The statute even went a step further and authorized the President, "whenever he shall deem it expedient, to erect the shores, waters, and inlets of the Bay and River of Mobile, and of the other rivers, creeks, inlets, and bays emptying into the Gulf of Mexico east of the said River Mobile, and west thereof to the Pascagoula, inclusive, into a separate [customs] district."[9] Presumably, it would be most inexpedient to declare a Spanish port an American customs district, so this statute was an unmistakable assertion of American sovereignty over West Florida. The Jefferson Administration, however, averted an immediate crisis by construing the law to be merely contingent legislation that would become operative in the event that the United States acquired West Florida.

That position did not last long. By 1810, American settlers in West Florida had revolted, declared themselves an independent state, and requested annexation by the United States.[10] They got their wish in substance, if not in form, on October 27, 1810, when President Madison declared by proclamation that West Florida had belonged to the United States since 1803 and it was high time to occupy it. The order of occupation did not extend to Mobile, for reasons of security, but American troops took possession of that city on April 15, 1813, completing the American occupation of West Florida. When Mississippi became a state in 1817, it included a portion of West Florida, and the same was true of Alabama upon statehood in 1819.

The West Florida saga presents a wealth of material from the standpoint of political diplomacy, morality, and philosophy, some of which we hope to explore in subsequent works. But as a matter of constitutional law, it is anticlimactic. Ultimately, one must view the West Florida acquisition as an instance of cession by treaty. However implausible the American construction of the Louisiana Purchase may have been, the American claim was vindicated by the ultimate method of international vindication: at the end of the day, American troops were there and Spanish troops were not. More fundamentally, the issue was rendered largely moot by the Adams-Onis Treaty of 1819, in which Spain essentially issued a quitclaim deed to West Florida without conceding the legality of the earlier American occupation. The effective date of American sovereignty mattered primarily in cases involving the legality of Spanish land grants made between 1803 and 1819. When the Supreme Court confronted such a case in 1829, it resolved the case by deferring heavily to the views of Congress and the Executive in the years following the Louisiana Purchase.[11] Of course, if the American interpretation of the Louisiana Purchase was correct, the promises of incorporation of the acquired territories made in 1803 applied to West Florida. That was no problem even under the strongest assumptions about those promises. The West Florida territory was clearly a plausible, and indeed a prime, candidate for statehood — as was proved by its relatively rapid admission as parts of Mississippi (admitted 1817), Alabama (admitted 1819), and Florida (admitted 1845).

The Louisiana Purchase gave America no pretensions, plausible or otherwise, to East Florida. That territory had never belonged to France. It had been Spain's ever since its discovery, except for the two decades from 1762 to 1783 when it belonged to England. As a formal matter, the United States acquired East Florida by treaty. In the Adams-Onis Treaty of 1819, which was signed on February 21, 1819, the king of Spain ceded to the United States "all the territories which belong to him, situated to the eastward of the Mississippi, known by the name of East and West Florida."[12] In addition to transferring East Florida to the United States, this language was sufficient to quiet the American title in West Florida as well. There is thus no doubt that both Floridas were acquired by some treaty, whether it be the Louisiana Purchase or the Adams-Onis Treaty of 1819.

In language similar to that employed in the Louisiana Purchase, the treaty provided that "[t]he inhabitants of the territories . . . shall be incorporated in the Union of the United States, as soon as may be consistent with the principles of the Federal Constitution, and admitted to the enjoyment of all the privileges, rights, and immunities of the citizens of the United States."[13] This provision is consistent with, though short of, a promise of statehood for the new territory, and there was never any doubt that East Florida was an eminently plausible candidate for statehood.

The real story, of course, goes far beyond the formalities of the Adams-Onis Treaty. A full accounting of the acquisition of Florida would have to consider the "patriot" movements that sought to duplicate the (partial) success of the West Florida insurrections in securing annexation to the United States and the

First Seminole War, waged by Andrew Jackson, in which American troops effectively occupied a good portion of Spanish East Florida prior to its formal acquisition.[14] But for purposes of locating a constitutional sanction for the official acquisition of East Florida, the Adams-Onis Treaty is sufficient.

Taking Texas

The acquisition of Texas generated more constitutional objections than did any other acquisition in the nation's first century.[15] Nonetheless, few acquisitions were as constitutionally unproblematic.

There was a nonfrivolous argument that all or part of Texas was included in the Louisiana Purchase: Spain had retroceded to France all of Louisiana west of the Mississippi River, and Texas met at least part of that description. Nonetheless, the big tradeoff in the Adams-Onis Treaty of 1819 was to fix the American/Spanish boundary at the Sabine River, which marks the current Texas/Louisiana border. Whatever claim the United States may have acquired to Texas in 1803 vanished in 1819.

The desire for Texas did not vanish. Indeed, many people thought that trading an amorphous claim to Texas for a solid right to Florida was a decidedly bad deal. Efforts to obtain Texas were persistent, both before and after Mexico (with Texas in tow as a province) broke away from Spain. The prospects for American acquisition of Texas became even more heated after Texas declared independence from Mexico on March 2, 1836, and became the Republic of Texas. In September 1836, the new citizens of Texas overwhelming supported a proposition designed to gauge public sentiment in favor of annexation by the United States.[16] On March 3, 1837, the United States officially recognized the Republic of Texas as a sovereign nation. On August 4, 1837, Texas's minister to the United States formally requested annexation. In the face of American doubts about annexation grounded in concerns about economics, slavery, and relations with Mexico, Texas withdrew its request on October 12, 1838.

This simple time line conceals one of the most intriguing — in the sense both of "interesting" and "full of intrigue" — episodes in American history. America did not win Texas's independence from Mexico, but Americans did. The people who formed the Republic of Texas were essentially transplanted Americans.[17] There is no good reason to think that they were acting in official concert with American authorities, but Texas in 1837 was about as foreign to the United States as was Vermont in 1789. Annexation to the United States could hardly have been an afterthought to the Texan revolutionaries. We plan to explore some of the implications of this episode in a future work. For now, however, we are concerned only with the legal form of the American acquisition of Texas.

Texas resumed its annexation efforts in early 1844. On April 11 of that year, American and Texan diplomats signed an annexation treaty. The treaty was rejected by the Senate on June 8, 1844, by the lopsided vote of 35 to 16. The reasons for the rejection were multifaceted, including strong Northern opposition to a new slave state, concerns about treaty obligations and potential war with Mexico, the politics of the presidential campaign in which James Polk made annexation of Texas a key issue, and the politics of personality, which led such potential treaty supporters as Thomas Benton, Henry Clay, and Martin Van Buren to oppose annexation in 1844 [18]

Apart from the Northern antislavery sentiment, none of these concerns was deep-rooted. After Polk's election in 1844, the annexationists moved again in the final days of President Tyler's administration. Faced with the evident impossibility of mustering a two-thirds majority in the Senate for approval of an annexation treaty, supporters of annexation turned to legislation, which would require a more manageable (at least under the circumstances)[19] simple majority in the House and Senate. On January 25, 1845, the House passed a joint resolution for the annexation of Texas by a vote of 120 to 98. On February 27, 1845, the Senate passed a similar resolution by a 27 to 25 margin. The House accepted the Senate version the next day, and on March 1, 1845, President Tyler signed the resolution.[20] On November 10, 1845, Texas voters overwhelmingly approved annexation.[21] The House and Senate voted by large margins to admit Texas as a state, and on December 29, 1845, Texas officially joined the Union.

Along the way, there were fierce objections in Congress to using a legislative mechanism for annexation. The Senate Committee on Foreign Relations issued a report on the proposal for annexation that vehemently insisted that only the treaty power could annex a foreign country.[22] Numerous members of Congress made the same objections during the debates.[23] These arguments against annexation by legislation, however, were more impressive in volume than in cogency. Those who asserted the exclusivity of the treaty power as a means of annexation were decidedly short on reasons for that position. The case for the constitutionality of annexation by legislation is actually quite simple, as the participants in the debates might have recognized had concerns about the extension of slavery not dwarfed other considerations.

Consider how the United States acquires land from existing states. Suppose, for instance, that North Carolina or Georgia wants to cede land to the United States in order to quell disquiet among sister states and to allow the national government to pay debts. By what mechanism does the United States acquire title to the ceded land? The answer is simple: by legislation, which is exactly how the United States accepted cessions from North Carolina and Georgia in 1790 and 1802.[24] If the ceded territory was immediately going to enter into statehood, the acquisition would be authorized by the Admissions Clause, which says that "[n]ew States may be admitted by the Congress." If, as was actually the case with the North Carolina and Georgia cessions, the territory was not immediately entering into statehood, or if for some reason (which is not evident) the Admissions Clause only operates on territory that already belongs to the United States, then acceptance of the cessions was constitutionally authorized by the Sweeping Clause: it was "necessary and proper for carrying into Execution" the power to admit new states.[25] The treaty power has nothing to do with this kind of transaction, which does not involve any foreign sovereigns.

Now suppose that the United States wants to accept a cession of land from a foreign sovereign like Spain. If Congress passed (and the President signed) ordinary legislation authorizing the annexation of Spanish territory, that legislation would be fully effective as a matter of domestic law. As with cessions from existing states, the legislation could be enacted pursuant to the Admissions Clause if the territory was immediately entering statehood, or pursuant to the Sweeping Clause if it was to be held as a territory for some time (or if, for some reason, acquisition must temporally precede admission). No further constitutional authorization would be necessary in order to validate the receipt of the territory as a matter of domestic law. The only problem would be securing compliance from Spain and recognition of Spain's obligation from the international community. Congressional legislation could not bind Spain. In order to validate the transaction on an international level and create an enforceable obligation against Spain, a treaty would be necessary. But it is important to be clear about the role of the treaty: the treaty would be necessary in order to bind Spain as a matter of international law to deliver the property, not in order to authorize the United States as a matter of domestic law to receive it.

For exactly the same reasons, the annexation of Texas by statute was entirely constitutional. Statutes are always sufficient to authorize acquisition by the United States as long as the acquisition exercises or carries into execution a constitutional power. In the case of annexation of an entire foreign sovereignty, no treaty is necessary if the foreign sovereign accedes to the acquisition, because the foreign sovereign ceases to exist upon annexation and there is accordingly nothing for the treaty to operate upon. There is literally no one left against whom to enforce it. Bruce Ackerman and David Golove got this point precisely right: "In retrospect, it is a little hard to understand what was motivating the constitutional objections of the opponents to the joint resolution—other than hostility to the admission of new slave states. There would have been a need for a treaty of cession had Texas been a part of Mexico. But because Texas was an independent state, what would have been the point of a treaty with a country that was immediately going out of existence when the agreement was executed?"[26] Indeed, the interesting question is not whether a treaty was *required* for the annexation of Texas but whether it would have been *effective* for the annexation of Texas. The terms of the Admissions Clause rather plainly give *Congress* the power to admit new states. If the Treaty Clause is, as we have argued, an implementational clause, it could help carry into effect the legislative power of admission to statehood but could not effect an admission of its own force. The only value of a treaty in the context of acquisition of an entire foreign sovereignty as a state would be to bind the foreign sovereign to future consent to statehood once the American legislative process ran its course. Of course, if the territory was not admitted as a state immediately upon annexation, the territory could be acquired by treaty as a means of implementing the admissions power. It could also be acquired by ordinary legislation under the Sweeping Clause as a means of implementing the admissions power. In any case, annexation by joint resolution poses fewer constitutional questions than does annexation by treaty.

Because Texas was acquired directly as a state, the joint resolution of annexation was constitutionally authorized by the Admissions Clause. Alternatively, if for some reason the Constitution requires a two-step dance of acquisition-plus-admission, the acquisition was "necessary and proper for carrying into Execution" the admissions power. In either case, the constitutionality of the annexation of Texas by joint resolution should have been an easy case.

Occupying Oregon

In 1846, Great Britain relinquished to the United States its claims to the Oregon Territory, which included the present states of Oregon, Washington, and Idaho and pieces of Montana and Wyoming.[27] This completed a series of international agreements that formally established American dominion in the territory: the 1819 Adams-Onis Treaty which ceded Spain's claim to that territory to the United States,[28] the 1824 joint convention with Russia in which the latter agreed not to make any settlements in North America south of Alaska,[29] and ultimately the 1846 Oregon treaty with Great Britain which settled a long-standing boundary dispute between the two countries in the Pacific Northwest by drawing the boundary line (at the 49th parallel) between the United States and Canada.[30]

The latter treaty did not include any stipulations about incorporating persons in the Oregon Territory into the United States. By 1846, however, the territory could reasonably be pegged for ultimate statehood. This would not necessarily have been true in 1818, when England and the United States entered into their first agreement about the territory. Many people at that time, and even later, expected the Oregon Territory to develop into a separate republic independent of both the United States and Great Britain. By the middle of the nineteenth century, however, developments in transportation and communication made the barrier of the Rocky Mountains a bit less imposing, so eventual statehood was a reasonable expectation. In any event, the relevant treaties, implementing the power to admit new states, are sufficient grounds for the ultimate acquisition in 1846.

But much of Oregon was occupied by American citizens before the territory was formally acquired. In particular, the Willamette Valley on the south bank of the Columbia River was peopled by American settlers for years before the treaty of 1846. The United States certainly did not view its claim to the Oregon Territory as stemming from the 1846 treaty, but instead regarded that treaty as *recognizing* (at least part of) what had belonged to the United States for decades. So what claim, if any, did the United States have to any portion of the Oregon Territory before 1846? The question is academic in the purest sense of the term, because the United States, despite repeated requests from citizens in Oregon, never enacted legislation for the Oregon Territory until after the treaty of 1846.[31] The Americans in the Willamette Valley organized their own provisional government in the face of this inaction.[32] Accordingly, the Oregon episode prior to 1846 presents no concrete question of American governmental authority over the territory. Nonetheless, as a matter of first principles, it is worth knowing whether and how the United States had any legitimate claims to Oregon for which it was evidently prepared to fight.[33]

A number of prominent figures, including Thomas Jefferson, James Monroe, Thomas Benton, and John Calhoun, argued at various times that the Oregon Territory up to the 49th parallel was included as part of the Louisiana Purchase.[34] This argument rested on the mistaken belief that the boundary at the 49th parallel had been settled by England and France in the Treaty of Utrecht in 1713.[35] There is no evidence that such an agreement was ever made. Once this error is corrected, there is nothing to support a claim that the Louisiana Purchase extended at all beyond the Rocky Mountains.

The American claims during the decades of negotiations with England over the Oregon boundaries were based primarily on the inaptly named doctrine of discovery. *Discovery* is a word with multiple meanings. Within the confines of Anglo-American property law, it can be used as a synonym for first possession of a tangible item: the first possessor of an otherwise unclaimed item has good title to it against all subsequent possessors.[36] As a matter of international law, the doctrine of discovery is a bit more complex.

The doctrine of discovery originated as a tacit convention among European nations for recognizing their respective claims to non-Christian lands.[37] The first country to "discover" a non-Christian territory would acquire the rights to possess (and colonize) it against all other nations in the European Christian community. The big question for the European nations was what it meant to "discover" land. What kinds of acts were necessary to constitute discovery and over what extent of territory did those acts extend the sovereignty of the discovering nation? (The heathens in the "discovered" lands, of course, had their own set of questions about the doctrine.)

The contours of the discovery doctrine were never precise, which left much room for diplomatic negotiation, papal mediation, and the discharge of gunpowder. Nor was the doctrine necessarily consistent over time. Spain and Portugal were the first nations in the European Christian community to land in the Western Hemisphere: did that place the whole hemisphere off limits to England, France, and Holland? The latter nations, and their collective stores of gunpowder, said no. If discovery alone had ever been internationally recognized as a sufficient basis for a claim to new territory, it was not sufficient by the eighteenth century. In order to become a recognized claim to territory, discovery had to be coupled with acts of possession—either symbolic acts, such as hoisting a flag or planting a cross, or actual acts, such as establishing settlements and/or garrisons. [38] One still needed to determine the physical extent of the claims generated by these acts, which is a problem to which there is no theoretical answer, as centuries of boundary conflicts amply demonstrate. Fortunately, we can pass over many of the niceties of the doctrine of discovery here; we need concern ourselves with the doctrine only to the extent that it bears on American and English claims to the Oregon Territory.

Neither the United States nor England was the first Christian nation to discover the Pacific Northwest. Spanish ships got there in the sixteenth century, but that discovery was not followed up by sufficient acts of settlement to generate a claim to anything more than fishing or navigational rights north of California. Accordingly, although the United States acquired Spain's rights to the Pacific Northwest in the Adams-Onis Treaty of 1819, those rights did not amount to a significant territorial claim.[39]

As between the British and the Americans, the British were the first to reach the coast. Captain James Cook of the HMS *Resolution* landed in central Oregon in 1778, but no settlement was established. In the spring of 1792, Captain George Vancouver of the HMS *Discovery* (along with the *Chatham*) sailed along the Pacific Northwest coast on an official mission of exploration, diplomacy, and discovery. On April 27, 1792, Vancouver passed by a promontory and bay that potentially signaled the mouth of a river. A trader in 1788 had failed to find such a river at that location and had accordingly labeled the promontory and bay, respectively, "Cape Disappointment" and "Deception Bay." In light of this prior report, the evident inaccessibility of the bay, and a desire to take advantage of a favorable wind for exploration farther north, Captain Vancouver continued along the coast without attempting to find and enter the river. He extensively explored and charted the Pacific Coast, the Strait of Juan de Fuca, which separates Washington from Canada, and Puget Sound.

While the British were the first to reach the coast, an American was the first to reach the Columbia River. On May 11, 1792, two weeks after Captain Vancouver left Cape Disappointment and Deception Bay, Captain Robert Gray, an American trader in command of the ship *Columbia*, spotted the opening and decided to explore for a river. He found the river that now bears the name of his ship. Under accepted principles of discovery, the discovery of a river carries with it claims to the basin drained by the river. So if getting there first is the key to the discovery doctrine, the important question for Oregon would have been what counts as "getting there."

Under late-eighteenth-century norms of discovery, however, getting there first was not enough to sustain a claim. "Discovery" for purposes of territorial acquisition required discovery plus some undefined amount of settlement. The American claim to Oregon accordingly rested on subsequent events. Most notably, in 1804, President Jefferson sent Meriwether Lewis and William Clark on a westward expedition through the Rocky Mountains. During their two-year sojourn, they explored much of the Columbia River system, emerging at its mouth in November 1805. In 1811 and 1812, another American, John Jacob Astor, established some trading posts along the Columbia River, as well as a settlement named Astoria.[40] The combination of Lewis and Clark's explorations and Astor's settlements gave the United States a very plausible claim under the early-nineteenth-century law of discovery to the Columbia basin, or at least to the Willamette Valley. Or, rather, they would have sufficed if the United States was capable of acquiring territory by virtue of discovery. That is not a small "if."

The doctrine of discovery was a convention among European Christian nations. The United States was not European, but it was sufficiently Christian to be regarded by the European nations as part of the international law community. At least, during the negotiations over Oregon, England never objected that the United States was incapable of exercising rights under the doctrine of discovery. That settles the American right to discover territory under international law. But what about under domestic American law? The treaty power obviously does not validate discoveries, and there is no "Discovery Clause" to fill in the gap. If the United States can acquire territory by discovery, from what constitutional source does that power stem?

Consider the problem from a slightly different angle. Imagine a volcanic island over which no European nation claims any rights. A private American citizen, acting on his or her own initiative, discovers the island, finds a sizable deposit of guano, and markets the guano as fertilizer. Under domestic American property law, the discoverer, as the first possessor, has a better claim to the island than does any subsequent possessor. The island is now private property. But how do the actions of private persons in claiming new territory affect the rights and obligations of the government of the United States? Under eighteenth-century understandings, the power of governments to extend their influence beyond their borders was strictly limited,[41] and there is nothing in the federal Constitution that suggests a power to go beyond then-prevailing international norms of extraterritoriality. So to what extent does private discovery have public consequences? If the United States wants to put a naval base on the island, can it condemn the land under the power of eminent domain (as it certainly cannot with respect to an American's property in, for example, Belgium)? Can Congress promulgate a civil or criminal code for the island?

These very real questions emerged in the 1850s when such uninhabited guano islands became serious sources of fertilizer. Foreign governments sometimes seized the islands from American developers, which induced the United States government to define the status of these islands. The result was the Guano Act of 1856, which remains on the statute books.[42] The statute states that "[w]henever any citizen of the United States discovers a deposit of guano on any island, rock, or key, not within the lawful jurisdiction of any other government, and not occupied by the citizens of any other government, and takes peaceable possession thereof, and occupies the same, such island, rock, or key may, at the discretion of the President, be considered as appertaining to the United States." The statute extends to those islands the federal criminal laws applicable to the high seas and authorizes the President to use military force to protect American interests in the islands.[43]

The statute does not define what "appertaining to the United States" means; "appertaining" is not a term of art with a prior, well-accepted understanding. It is clear from the statute, however, that Congress regards the term as justifying the extension of the maritime criminal laws to guano islands. That extension cannot be an exercise of the constitutional power to "define and punish

Piracies and Felonies committed on the high Seas,"[44] for the simple reason that islands are dry land. Nor can it be an exercise of the power to "make all needful Rules and Regulations respecting the Territory or other Property belonging to the United States,"[45] unless one has first established that the territory in question belongs to the United States in a constitutionally relevant sense. So what is the precise legal effect of a presidential proclamation under the statute that territory "appertains" to the United States?

The Supreme Court faced this problem in 1890 in *Jones v United States*.[46] A worker on one of the guano islands that had been proclaimed as "appertaining to the United States" was convicted of murder under the statute extending the laws concerning murder on the high seas to guano islands. The Court made clear that this statute "does not . . . assume to extend the admiralty jurisdiction over land; but, in the exercise of the power of the United States to preserve peace and punish crime in all regions over which they exercise jurisdiction, it unequivocally extends the provisions of the statutes of the United States for the punishment of offenses committed upon the high seas to like offenses committed upon guano islands which have been determined by the president to appertain to the United States."[47] That, however, simply pushes the inquiry back one step: on what basis does the United States acquire jurisdiction over that region? What clause of the Constitution permits Congress to authorize the President to extend American criminal jurisdiction by proclamation?

The Supreme Court's answer was:

> By the law of nations, recognized by all civilized states, dominion of new territory may be acquired by discovery and occupation as well as by cession or conquest; and when citizens or subjects of one nation, in its name, and by its authority, or with its assent, take and hold actual, continuous, and useful possession . . . of territory unoccupied by any other government or its citizens, the nation to which they belong may exercise such jurisdiction and for such period as it sees fit over territory so acquired. This principle affords ample warrant for the legislation of congress concerning guano islands [citing various international law sources, including Vattel, Wheaton, and Halleck]. Who is the sovereign, *de jure* or *de facto*, of a territory, is not a judicial, but a political question, the determination of which by the legislative and executive departments of any government conclusively binds the judges, as well as all other officers, citizens, and subjects of that government. This principle has always been upheld by this court, and has been affirmed under a great variety of circumstances [including *Foster v Neilson*].[48]

This passage makes two distinct points. The second point is a principle of judicial power, which asserts that courts must accept legislative and executive determinations concerning sovereignty regardless of the Court's own views of the matter: "my country, right or wrong." The first point is a substantive assertion that in this particular case, the exercise of American jurisdiction was constitutionally proper: "my country is right, not wrong." Because we are seeking the meaning of the Constitution rather than a theory of judicial role, our only concern here is the first point. And on that score the Court in *Jones* was singularly unpersuasive. It did a fine job of demonstrating that assertion of American jurisdiction over guano islands did not violate any principle of international law. The real question, however, is whether it violated any principle of constitutional law. By relying on general understandings about governmental power drawn from the law of nations, the Court committed the same fallacy that some members of Congress committed when discussing the power of acquisition during debates on the Louisiana Purchase. The United States government is defined by the federal Constitution, not by the law of nations. There may well be some powers that every other government in the world possesses simply by virtue of being a government, but which the federal Constitution denies to the United States government. It does not follow that because every other government can acquire territory through the discovery of its citizens, so can the United States.

According to the same principles that justify annexation of existing sovereignties or receipt of cessions from states, Congress could certainly purchase a guano island from an American citizen if the purchase was pursuant to some constitutional power, such as the power to maintain a navy. Perhaps Congress could even condemn such an island under the power of eminent domain in order to implement a constitutional power. In the context of the Guano Act, however, the more pertinent question is whether Congress can extend domestic laws to a guano island without taking title to the island. In the language of the Constitution: is an extension of American laws to an island, owned by an American citizen, to which the United States does not have title "necessary and proper for carrying into Execution" a constitutionally granted power?

The answer depends, first, on the strength of the eighteenth-century background norms against extraterritoriality and, second, on the ability to find some power that an extension of laws would implement. Were the norms against extraterritoriality so strong that they call into question whether such extensions of American law could ever be "necessary and proper"? We do not know, though if the norms against extraterritoriality were based purely on considerations of international comity, and there was no sovereign competing for a particular guano island, then there is probably no insuperable obstacle to extending American laws to terra nullius. And if Congress can extend American laws to such territory, Congress can also, as the Guano Act in fact does, allow the President to make the factual determination whether any foreign powers lay claims to the islands that might interfere with the application of American laws. Indeed, a pretty good definition of what the Guano Act means by "appertaining to the United States" is probably something like "determined by the President not to be subject to any claims by foreign sovereigns and to be of more than marginal interest to the American government"; it does not seem to be an impermissible delegation of legislative power to let the President determine the existence vel non of that kind of contingency. Finding a power that statutes extending American jurisdiction can plausibly be said to implement might be a more difficult problem; the answer may well vary with the particular circumstances of each island. In sum, the Guano Act is not constitutional beyond question in all of its applications, but neither is it an easy kill.

All of this assumes that the United States has not actually taken title to the islands in question. If it has, then the islands are territory "belonging to the United States," and the Territory and Property Clause provides straightforward authorization for promulgation of a full civil and criminal code if Congress wants to promulgate it. Of course, for the United States to acquire title from a private citizen, the acquisition must carry into execution some other enumerated power, but once that hurdle is cleared, American jurisdiction is no problem.

Suppose, however, that the island is discovered by an American naval officer on an official mission of exploration. Can the United States take title by virtue of the discovery of one of its agents? That was not the case with Oregon: the United States specifically denied that its claim was based on any official governmental status held by Captain Gray. Interestingly, the private or governmental status of the discoverer does not have as much effect on the power of the United States to acquire territory through discovery as one might suspect. The United States can acquire property (through methods other than the taxing mechanisms specifically identified in the Constitution) only if Congress has authorized such acquisition through a statute that is "necessary and proper for carrying into Execution" some other power. The United States can require its employees to assign their discoveries to the employer if that is what Congress wishes to do. But all acquisitions are ultimately traceable to statutory authorizations, however implicit, and therefore must conform to the requirements of the Sweeping Clause. Put in constitutional language, Congress can (expressly or implicitly) require federal agents to assign discovery claims to the United States if the assignment and the subsequent assumption of title are "necessary and proper for carrying into Execution" some federal power.

It is far more doubtful whether the President could legitimate such discoveries without congressional authorization. European kings certainly could license private parties to make discoveries on behalf of their nations, but the

President is not a European king. It is conceivable that the "executive Power" vested in the President by Article II includes the power to extend American jurisdiction through discovery, but that is a tough sell.

If Captain Gray had discovered an uninhabited island piled high with guano, everything that we have just said about discovery would apply to him (and to the United States). But if Captain Gray discovered anything, it was land that was already inhabited by natives. Lewis and Clark similarly explored and mapped inhabited land, and Astoria was plunked down right in the middle of Indian territory. Basic principles of Anglo-American property law permit acquisition of unowned items, but they do not permit acquisition of previously occupied land. In order to dispossess the Indians, one needed the international doctrine of discovery, which authorized the discovering Christian sovereign to exercise dominion over non-Christian lands. And the doctrine of discovery, as a principle of international law, only operated at the level of sovereigns. Perhaps that is why Captain Gray claimed ownership of the Columbia basin on behalf of the United States rather than for his own account. Under the doctrine of discovery, if he was not acting on behalf of the United States, he could not acquire occupied territory. Of course, another perfectly good reason for not asserting an individual claim to such territory was the problem of defending the claim against the British, the Spaniards, the Russians, and the Native Americans; it helps in such matters to have an army and a navy, which Captain Gray notoriously lacked. So Captain Gray, acting as a private citizen, could acquire a property right in a guano island, but he had no grounds for claiming ownership of an already-occupied Oregon. Only a properly authorized government agent, acting on behalf of a Christian sovereign, could do so.

In the final analysis, the United States' claim to Oregon by discovery was potentially strong in theory, but was missing one very important component in practice: a statute that authorized an American agent to take title to the territory. Without such a statute, the United States had no constitutional claim. But the British didn't need to know that.

3

Limits: Conquest and Colonialism

By 1854, the United States had completed its acquisition of the American mainland by conquering California and the American Southwest from Mexico. Half a century later, America had expanded south into the Caribbean, north to Alaska, and west all the way to the Philippines. The forms of these acquisitions were all familiar: treaty and annexation. Two things, however, were different from the previous acquisitions. First, much of this territory was acquired as spoils of war. Second, all of the territories acquired after 1854 were ethnically, culturally, and geographically distant enough from the mainland to raise doubts about their suitability as future states. The events of the last half of the nineteenth century pose more than their fair share of questions concerning political morality, but did these events raise equally serious questions of constitutional law? In this chapter, we apply the lessons of Chapters 1 and 2 to assess the constitutionality of America's acquisition of an overseas empire.

Conquering California

On May 12, 1846, the United States declared war on Mexico. The stated ground for the declaration was a border incident in which Mexican troops, allegedly, on American territory, killed and captured an American patrol. The war was one-sided, and two years later, on May 30, 1848, ratifications were exchanged in the Treaty of Guadalupe Hidalgo that transferred to the United States territory encompassing California, Nevada, Utah, and portions of Wyoming, Colorado, Arizona, and New Mexico.[1] Six years later, the Gadsden Purchase Treaty transferred to the United States the rest of the present states of Arizona and New Mexico.[2]

Historians can debate whether the transfer of territory, and in particular of California, was the result of the war or its purpose. We will have much more to say about the Mexican-American War and its aftermath in Part II, but for now our concern is merely with the constitutionality of the American territorial acquisitions. Both acquisitions from Mexico are straightforward cases of acquisition by treaty. Article IX of the Treaty of Guadalupe Hidalgo contained the now-standard promise that the people remaining in California "shall be incorporated into the Union of the United States and be admitted at the proper time (to be judged of by the Congress of the United States) to the enjoyment of all the rights of citizens of the United States, according to the principles of the Constitution."[3] Article V of the Gadsden Purchase Treaty specified that this incorporation provision applied as well to people in the territory ceded by that treaty.[4] As with the Louisiana and Florida treaties, this stipulation was consistent with an expectation of ultimate statehood. And although statehood for places like Arizona and New Mexico was decades away, there was no general understanding that these territories were, by their nature, unsuitable for eventual statehood.

The only remaining legal question is whether the federal Constitution permits acquisition through aggressive wars of conquest, if indeed that serves as the best account of the Mexican-American War. There is no evident reason, however, why acquisition as a result of conquest is any more problematic than acquisition as a result of peaceful cession. Although there were suggestions during the Mexican-American War that acquisition by conquest was contrary to constitutional principles because the conquered people did not consent to become subject to American jurisdiction,[5] this does not actually distinguish conquest from purchase. No one formally asked the inhabitants of the Louisiana Territory whether they wanted to become part of the United States; from the standpoint of the people in the new territory, one transfer was much like the other. Indeed, the Treaty of Guadalupe Hidalgo specifically gave inhabitants of the transferred territory the opportunity to remain Mexican nationals.[6] The Treaty of Guadalupe Hidalgo seems every bit as constitutional as the Louisiana Purchase.

Acquiring Alaska

In 1867, the United States acquired Mount McKinley, along with 586,000 square miles of land that surrounds it. Was Mount McKinley the constitutional equivalent of Mount Everest?

In 1741, a Russian expedition led by Vitus Bering made the first "discovery" of Alaska — then called Russian America — by a Christian European power. Subsequent explorations extended Russian claims as far south as the coast of present-day Washington, where they collided with claims of Great Britain, Spain, and the United States. Russia eventually backed off of all its claims beyond Alaska's present boundaries, which were initially defined by an April 1824 joint convention between Russia and the United States[7] and by an 1825 agreement between Russia and Great Britain settling the boundaries between Alaska and British Columbia.[8]

As with Louisiana, Alaska was acquired by a treaty in which the territory was exchanged for money — in the case of Alaska a total of $7,200,000. As with Louisiana, the seller, who needed money as a result of wartime expenditures, was divesting itself of a colony whose costs of upkeep exceeded its likely benefits. And as with Louisiana, the seller preferred to see the territory in American rather than British hands and viewed eventual American occupation as inevitable.[9]

The agreement of sale was reached with relatively little public notice or fanfare. The treaty of acquisition sailed through the Senate on April 9, 1867, by a vote of thirty-seven to two, and ratifications were exchanged on June 20, 1867. The agreement provided for American possession even before payment was made.[10] There were some objections in the House to the appropriation on the ground that it was a bad deal,[11] and there were subsequent allegations of corruption,[12] but the appropriation bill eventually passed the House by a substantial margin on July 14, 1868, and on July 27, 1868, the deal was finalized.

Alaska was admitted as a state on January 3, 1959, ninety years after its acquisition. If "better late than never" suffices as a constitutional maxim, then Alaska's eventual statehood conclusively proves that the acquisition was a legitimate exercise of the treaty power as a vehicle for implementing the admissions power. But when the constitutionality of federal action depends on assessments of suitability for specific purposes, as is true of federal implementing acts such as treaties or executory legislation, those assessments must be made at the time of the action rather than in hindsight. And there are serious questions whether the acquisition of Alaska in 1867 passed muster as a means for implementing the admissions power.

Article 3 of the treaty of acquisition declared that the territorial inhabitants "shall be admitted to the enjoyment of all the rights, advantages, and immunities of citizens of the United States; and shall be maintained and protected in the free enjoyment of their liberty, property and religion,"[13] but as with the Oregon treaty, there was no mention of incorporating the territory into the United States. We have found nothing in the contemporaneous legislative debates that directly addresses the future prospects of statehood for Alaska, but there are reasons to doubt the extent to which Alaska was seen in 1867 as a candidate for future statehood. Alaska was the first acquired territory that was not contiguous with the rest of the United States; it was accessible from America only by sea or through British territory in Canada. Its climate and geography, at least in large segments of its area, were unlike those in any other state. It had no history of prior occupation by Americans or even western Europeans.

In 1900, Max Farrand described the acquisition of Alaska as the initiation of a "new phase" of American territorial dominion: "[W]ith the purchase of Alaska in 1867 the territorial system of the United States entered upon a new phase. The remote situation of Alaska, its inhospitable climate, the difficulty of developing such resources as it might prove to have, and especially the fact that its scanty population was so largely composed of uncivilized Indians, all tended to render it extremely improbable that this region would ever sufficiently develop to be organized as a state and to be admitted into the Union."[14] Farrand noted that even in 1900, Alaska "was not a regularly organized territory but a 'civil district' . . . , meaning by that a part of the public domain (or property of the United States) to which representative institutions are not accorded and which there is no intention of incorporating as a state into the Union, or at least no immediate probability that it will be so incorporated."[15] Edward Bicknell in 1899 expressed identical views of Alaska's initial and (as of the turn of the century) future prospects for statehood:

> Alaska was a country which did not touch our boundaries at any point. Although sparsely inhabited except by the natives, from its geographical location and its climate it offered no inducements for a large emigration of our people or of Europeans. In other words, while every other addition to our territory would, in the ordinary course of growth, become States, this Alaska purchase "offered little or no prospect of ever becoming fit for admission to the Union on an equal footing with the States."
>
> . . . [T]he natural expectation was that Alaska should remain under a territorial form of government or be governed directly by the President and Congress. . . . And, while in all previous cases such a condition of affairs was to be but a temporary expedient, and the form of government adopted in most

cases allowed enough local self-government to familiarize all the people with it and with the principles of the future State government, in Alaska it was expected to be permanent.[16]

Obviously, events proved these predictions wrong. Alaska was made a "full-fledged" territory in 1912 and was admitted as a state in 1959. But if the acquisition of Alaska in 1867 could be justified only by reference to the admissions power — and it hard to see how else one could constitutionally justify the acquisition of hundreds of thousands of square miles of mountains, ice, and tundra — and if there was no reasonable prospect in 1867 of Alaska's ultimate admission, then there was no constitutional warrant for the acquisition in 1867 (though there could have been at some later date).

The constitutionality of the Alaska purchase thus depends on two related and difficult-to-establish facts: exactly how reasonable was the prospect for ultimate statehood in 1867 and exactly how reasonable did it have to be in order to justify an acquisition under the Treaty Clause?

We have thus far studiously avoided addressing the second question with any degree of specificity. We are going to avoid the question again, for the simple reason that it would require a separate book to identify and lay out the degree of "fit" between means and ends required under the treaty power. Quite honestly, we don't know the answer. The best that we can do for the moment is the following: as an implementational power, the Treaty Clause is subject to the principle of reasonableness, including the requirement of an adequate and proportional fit between means and ends. Reasonableness in that sense is very context sensitive. Administrative lawyers have no good theory about when agencies have or have not behaved "reasonably" in various contexts, and there is no reason to think that constitutional lawyers will fare any better when trying to apply similar principles to the treaty power. Judgments about reasonableness are judgments. In that respect, they are not different from many other kinds of judgments that must be made under the Constitution, such as whether a search or seizure is "reasonable" or whether a statute leaves too much discretion to executive or judicial agents. As one of us has said in the latter context, "[w]henever line-drawing involves an element of judgment, one cannot eliminate the need for judgment by a verbal formulation; one can only conceal or obscure it."[17]

One consideration, however, counsels against holding the acquisition of Alaska to a highly stringent means-ends requirement. Times and people change. In 1818, one could easily have viewed the Oregon Territory as an utterly implausible candidate for statehood because of the barrier of the Rocky Mountains. Thirty years later, advances in transportation and communication technology made the Oregon Territory an obvious candidate for future statehood. Those events would have been relatively fresh in people's minds in 1867, which is perhaps why legislators, including legislators who thought that the acquisition was a very bad idea, did not say much about Alaska's unsuitability as a state. Furthermore, as a constitutional matter, a "buy and hold" strategy gains acceptability from the fact that the decision is not irrevocable. If acquired territory turns out to be unsuitable for statehood, one can always turn it loose by granting it independence. Putting together the historically proven possibility of changes in circumstances with the ability to recognize and rectify errors in judgment, even a plausible case for potential statehood seems like enough to satisfy the Constitution. No, we can't prove this in any strong sense of the word *prove*, but we challenge anyone else to do better.

Notwithstanding the doubts of Farrand and Bicknell, the acquisition of Alaska in 1867 probably passes the threshold of plausible candidacy for future statehood. As we have noted, even those legislators who objected to the Alaska purchase did not openly declare that Alaska could never become a state.[18] Nor did that seem to be a prominent theme in the popular press.[19] A number of public figures openly contemplated eventual statehood for Alaska. As early as 1853, William Seward, the Secretary of State who engineered the transaction from the American side, envisioned statehood for the entire North American continent.[20] Senator Charles Sumner, chairman of the Senate Foreign Relations Committee during the Alaska purchase, had a similar vision.[21] One can dismiss these speculations as romantic puffery, but they suggest that the idea of Alaskan statehood was not so absurd in 1867 that it was akin to the prospect of statehood for Mt. Everest. And that is probably enough to satisfy the Constitution.

Handling Hawaii

The United States had been interested in the acquisition of Hawaii since the middle of the nineteenth century.[22] Attempts were made to negotiate a treaty of annexation in the early 1850s, but they perished along with King Kamehameha III in 1854. On July 7, 1898, President McKinley signed a joint resolution passed by both houses of Congress annexing Hawaii to the United States;[23] the annexation became fully effective on August 12, 1898. As was the case with Texas, annexation took place by simple statute because the necessary two-thirds majority in the Senate for ratification of a treaty could not be mustered. Indeed, barely a year before the annexation resolution passed, a treaty between the United States and Hawaii that had been signed and sent to the Senate[24] failed to be ratified owing to pressure from American sugar interests, labor unions, and anti-expansionists. A similar treaty had been sent to the Senate, and then withdrawn without action, by President Cleveland on February 15, 1893.

The only potentially relevant difference between the annexation of Hawaii and the prior annexation of Texas was that Texas entered the United States as a state, while Hawaii entered as a territory. That is not a difference of constitutional dimension. As a matter of domestic American law, ordinary legislation is always sufficient for the acquisition of property as long as the acquisition carries into effect a constitutionally granted power, such as the admissions power. A treaty could secure the consent of the foreign sovereign to annexation, but as soon as the annexation is complete, the treaty no longer exists because one of the parties to the treaty no longer exists. In any case, the acquisition of Hawaii by legislation was unproblematic as long as Hawaii was a sufficiently realistic candidate for statehood in 1898.

As was true of Alaska, Hawaii was noncontiguous and ethnically non-homogeneous with the rest of the United States. This was enough to raise questions in the late nineteenth century about Hawaii's suitability as a state. In 1893, prominent anti-imperialist Carl Schurz, who served in the Senate from 1869 to 1875 and was Secretary of the Interior under Rutherford Hayes, wrote of Hawaii that "[n]o candid American would ever think of making a State of this Union out of such a group of islands with such a population as it has and is likely to have."[25] This view was shared even by some people who generally favored expansion on the North American continent.[26] In the main, however, Hawaii in 1898 was generally recognized as a prime candidate for statehood. Senator George F. Hoar, who generally opposed overseas expansion, supported the acquisition of Hawaii precisely because he saw Hawaii as a territory "where we can reasonably expect that the people we acquire will, in due time and on suitable conditions, be annexed to the United States as an equal part of a self-governing Republic."[27] At least one opponent of annexation grounded opposition on the expectation that Hawaii would become a state (and therefore be entitled to two senators).[28] There were good reasons for this expectation in 1898. By that time, the development of steam power, electricity, and telegraph meant that distance and noncontiguity were even less relevant than they had been in 1867. As imperialist advocate Albert J. Beveridge colorfully put it in a famous speech in 1898, "[d]istance and oceans are no arguments.... Hawaii and the Philippines not contiguous! Our navy will make them contiguous."[29] Moreover, Americans (or at least white people) were largely in control of the Hawaiian economy and, after 1892, the Hawaiian legislature as well. The provisional revolutionary government in 1893 adopted a constitution that effectively concentrated power in the white population. Those who were concerned about absorbing heterogeneous populations into the American empire probably had less cause for concern with Hawaii in 1898 than they did with Alaska in 1867. The case for Hawaiian candidacy for statehood in 1898 was quite strong—certainly stronger than the case for Alaskan candidacy three decades earlier.

The most interesting legal problems concerning the annexation of Hawaii did not involve the power of the American government to acquire the territory, but rather concerned the power of the Hawaiian government to cede it. The government that agreed to annexation was a revolutionary government that had taken over from the reigning monarchy in January of 1893. The United States minister in Hawaii, John L. Stevens, recognized the revolutionary government as legitimate under circumstances that were tantamount to lending support to the revolution. That quick recognition, coupled with the presence of American troops in Honolulu (ostensibly to ensure the protection of American citizens and property) were likely a contributing factor in the success of the revolution. In fact, a century after the events, the United States Congress formally apologized for the American role in the overthrow of the then-lawful Hawaiian government in 1893.[30] Can the United States legitimately acquire territory from a revolutionary government that exists only (or at least largely) because the United States helped put it in power?

Fortunately for us, that is a question of international law (or perhaps of political morality) rather than of American constitutional law. A similar question arose with respect to the admission of West Virginia as a state. West Virginia was carved out of the territory of the state of Virginia. The Constitution provides that no state shall be formed "by the Junction of two or more States, or Parts of States, without the Consent of the Legislatures of the States concerned as well as of the Congress." At the time of the admission of West Virginia, the (former?) state of Virginia was in secessionist rebellion. The "legislature" of Virginia whose consent was sought for the admission of West Virginia was a legislature that represented the Unionist, western portion of Virginia, but which was recognized by the Union Congress as the legitimate representatives of the state of Virginia. Was that sufficient "Consent" of the affected state to permit the admission of West Virginia? Vasan Kesavan and Mike Paulsen have persuasively argued "yes" in a lengthy article, on the ground that the Constitution's procedures for admitting states are formal rather than substantive and the appropriate forms were followed.[31] If that is correct, the same analysis would presumably sustain the constitutionality of the acquisition of Hawaii, which also followed appropriate forms of procedure for annexation. The "acquisition" of Hawaii may well have been dirty pool, but it was constitutional dirty pool.

The Philippine Finale

Just a few months before the annexation of Hawaii, the United States declared war on Spain, ostensibly to secure the independence of Cuba.[32] The war was brief and one-sided. American troops quickly occupied Cuba and Puerto Rico,[33] and American naval forces decisively defeated Spanish warships in Manila Bay and Santiago. The surrender of Spanish forces in Manila on August 14, 1898, was anticlimactic; the war had been effectively over for some time. The treaty of peace ceded to the United States Puerto Rico, Guam, and the Philippine Islands. Spain also disclaimed all sovereignty over Cuba, which was occupied by United States troops.[34]

Cuba would in all likelihood have qualified as a candidate for statehood in 1898. Thomas Jefferson said in 1823, "I have ever looked on Cuba as the most interesting addition which could ever be made to our system of States."[35] In 1854, serious efforts were made by Franklin Pierce and Secretary of War Jefferson Davis to acquire Cuba as a slave state, and Cuba was still viewed as an excellent statehood prospect in the late nineteenth century.[36] Cuban independence, however, was one of the principal stated rationales for the Spanish-American War,[37] and so the United States did not assume sovereignty over Cuba, which it recognized as an independent nation on May 20, 1902.

Puerto Rico and Guam were acquired as spoils of the war, and both acquisitions were clearly constitutional. Guam was never, and is not now, seen as a potential future state, but its acquisition was a permissible incident of the power to provide and maintain a navy. Its location made it a convenient naval base and coaling station in 1898, and while it would have been problematic to seize half a continent in order to secure a naval base at Mobile Bay, it is far less difficult to see occupation of an island the size of Guam[38] as "necessary and proper" for maintaining a naval base. Puerto Rico, because of its hemispheric location, was probably an even better candidate for statehood than was Hawaii.

The problem in 1898 was the Philippine Islands. Although one could find voices suggesting that future statehood for the Philippines was not out of the question,[39] and all of the considerations that warrant a generous view of Alaska's statehood prospects in 1867 also counsel against drawing too hasty conclusions about the Philippines' statehood prospects in 1898, there is very good reason to think that the acquisition of the Philippines was qualitatively different from any other American territorial acquisition. Many contemporary observers certainly thought that the Philippines were different. Former Vice President Adlai E. Stevenson contrasted the acquisition of the Philippines with all prior acquisitions of territory that were "the fit abode for men of our own race," had "passed under the rule of the Anglo-Saxon," and were "acquired with the intention at the proper time — when population and conditions would justify — of carving it into States."[40] The inhabitants of the Philippines, he said, "know no rule but that of force," and as far as statehood is concerned, "[i]n view of the degraded character of the population, their total unfitness for self-government, the proposition is monstrous."[41] Senator Alexander Clay, who did not oppose the annexation of Puerto Rico or Cuba, distinguished the Philippines on grounds of policy because "[t]here is no hope of American communities being built up in this territory capable of statehood."[42] Senator John McLaurin repeated that "[i]t is idle to speak of Americanizing a tropical country 8,000 miles away. Our people will never consent for the people of that far-off land to ever have a voice in the affairs of our country."[43] Similar expressions can be found in other sources.[44] As Richard Hofstadter has put it:

> The taking of the Philippine Islands from Spain in 1899 marked a major historical departure for the American people. It was a breach in their traditions and a shock to their established values. To be sure, from their national beginnings they had constantly engaged in expansion, but almost entirely into contiguous territory. Now they were extending themselves to distant extra-hemispheric colonies; they were abandoning a strategy of defense hitherto limited to the continent and its appurtenances, in favor of a major strategic commitment in the Far East; and they were now supplementing the spread of a relatively homogenous population into territories destined from the beginning for self-government with a far different procedure in which control was imposed by force on millions of ethnic aliens. The acquisition of the islands, therefore, was understood by contemporaries on both sides of the debate, as it is readily understood today, to be a turning-point in our history.[45]

Of course, if the acquisition of the Philippines could be justified as incidental to some power other than the admissions power, the Philippines' prospects for statehood would be constitutionally irrelevant. Certainly, one could have justified acquisition of Manila Bay and Subic Bay as necessary and proper for maintaining a navy. President McKinley seriously considered taking only Manila at the conclusion of the war, and that option would have posed no constitutional problems. Strategically, however, it seemed awkward to maintain a base that far from the American mainland with no surrounding buffer. This concern probably would have justified retaining control over the entire area surrounding Manila. It is less clear whether it would have justified retention of the entire island of Luzon, which was also seriously considered as a realistic alternative in 1898. After all, Luzon is not Guam.[46] Nonetheless, there is something to be said for the proposition that control of the entire island was strategically necessary to preserve the integrity of Manila Harbor; at the very least, we are in no position to contest the military judgment of those who expressed this view in 1898. It is, however, approaching the inconceivable to say that concerns about naval bases could justify annexation of the entirety of the Philippines—no more than it could justify the annexation of Indonesia, Southeast Asia, China, and Australia in the bargain. Admittedly, the line between Luzon and Mindanao, or even between Manila and Mindanao, is not crisp. That is a necessary consequence of the decidedly judgment-driven exercise mandated by the means-ends principles built into the Constitution. But anyone who wants to claim that the annexation of the Philippines was a necessary and proper incident to maintaining a navy needs to make the argument.

That leaves the admissions power as the obvious justification for the acquisition of the Philippines. We have seen that the Philippines were widely regarded as qualitatively different from all other acquisitions, including island acquisitions that were somewhat closer to the mainland United States in terms of geography, culture, and/or demographics. The case for a reasonable prospect of statehood is clearly much weaker for the Philippines than for any other acquisition. But were the Philippines the constitutional equivalent of Mount Everest?

We do not know. Our instinct is that the acquisition of the Philippines was unconstitutional, but we cannot prove that claim to our own satisfaction without a more precise theory of the means-ends relationship required by the treaty power. It is significant, however, that the acquisition of the Philippines was not defended in 1898 as the acquisition of a potential future state, even in the face of explicit arguments that without a prospect for statehood, the acquisition was unconstitutional. Senator George Vest threw down the gauntlet with particular vigor:

> I have not controverted, and do not propose to controvert, the power of the Federal Government to acquire and govern territory, but I do deny that territory can be acquired to be held as colonies, peopled by millions of subjects not citizens, with no hope or prospect of its ever becoming a State of the Union. I may be answered by the statement that this is not a practical question, because Congress has exclusive jurisdiction as to the admission of States, and it may hold this territory indefinitely without any idea of its ever coming into the Union; in other words, establish under cover and by a fraud upon the Constitution the colonial system which the Constitution never contemplated.
>
> I will not insult my brother Senators by supposing that they would thus evade the spirit and letter of the Constitution, and when believing that the colonial system is not possible in this country, would vote to take in vast tracts of land inhabited by barbarians, intending never to allow this territory to

come in as a State, but to hold it for commercial advantages alone, in violation of the fundamental law of the land. Whenever the Congress of the United States becomes so degraded as to do this, it matters little what occurs in the future. It is simply a question of time when the disastrous end will come.[47]

No one answered Senator Vest by challenging his assumptions about the Philippines' prospects for statehood. That does not prove that no such argument could have been constructed had the need for the argument been strongly felt, but it does suggest that Professor Hofstadter was right when he remarked on the revolutionary character of the Philippine acquisition. That acquisition did indeed mark a departure, of real but unspecifiable dimension, from the practice of acquiring territory for potential future statehood. Accordingly, it also marked a departure from the Constitution.

So what should the United States have done in 1898? It had three choices, assuming that it permissibly wanted to keep some part of the Philippines (whether that part encompassed Manila or all of Luzon is irrelevant to this purpose). The United States could have left the remainder of the Philippines with Spain, it could have insisted on a transfer of the Philippines to a third party, or it could have insisted on independence for the Philippines, as it did with Cuba. President McKinley's account of his consideration of these alternatives is among the most famous statements to emerge from the Spanish-American War:

> I walked the floor of the White House night after night until midnight, and I am not ashamed to tell you, gentlemen, that I went down on my knees and prayed Almighty God for light and guidance more than one night. And one night late it came to me this way — I don't know how it was, but it came: (1) That we could not give them back to Spain — that would be cowardly and dishonorable; (2) that we could not turn them over to France or Germany — our commercial rivals in the Orient — that would be bad business and discreditable; (3) that we could not leave them to themselves — they were unfit for self-government — and they would soon have anarchy and misrule over there worse than Spain's was; and (4) that there was nothing left for us to do but to take them all, and to educate the Filipinos, and uplift and civilize and Christianize them, and by God's grace do the very best we could by them, as our fellow-men for whom Christ also died.[48]

It is notoriously easy to make fun of President McKinley's ruminations, and indeed we will not be able to resist the temptation even within this paragraph. But there may be more to some of President McKinley's concerns than his short speech lets on. Leaving Spain in control might not have been merely "cowardly and dishonorable"; it may also have been genuinely disastrous.

"The machinery of Spanish colonial government had collapsed. Isolated Spanish garrisons were helpless as the insurgent rebellion spread across Luzon and to neighboring islands. What held the Philippines together now was a consuming hatred of Spain, and continued Spanish proprietorship would merely stimulate the rebellion — a sure invitation to foreign intervention."[49] Foreign intervention would have meant substitution of one colonial master for another, which is perhaps a more weighty reason to reject the second alternative of transferring the Philippines to another foreign power than was McKinley's stated concerns about what would be "bad business and discreditable." Concerns about Filipino self-rule also cannot be dismissed lightly. "Self-rule" is a metaphor. In the Philippines in 1898, *self-rule* really meant, at least in the short term, rule by the rebel forces. The long term was more difficult to project, but human history did not afford grounds for optimism. Perhaps domestic tyranny is always better than foreign tyranny, but that is not a self-evident proposition.

In the end, however, none of these concerns are constitutionally relevant. Even if American acquisition of the Philippines was, in some normative sense, "better" than the other alternatives in 1898, it was not a legally permissible option. The Constitution permits only acquisitions that carry into effect enumerated powers, and there is no enumerated power to Christianize the Filipinos.

If the acquisition of the Philippines could have been constitutional only if made in contemplation of eventual statehood, then one must determine the consequences of the illegal acquisition. If the United States had no constitutional power to acquire the Philippines, it also had no constitutional power to govern it. Does that mean that the American officials in the Philippines, acting pursuant to unconstitutional directives, were tortfeasors, or even criminals? The answer to that question must await Chapter 6; the Philippines were hardly the first location in which this problem of governance without authority arose.

Possessions and Protectorates

The Treaty of Peace of 1898 did not mark the end of American territorial acquisitions. For the next half century, the United States continued to acquire a widely dispersed array of territories, many of which are still part of the extended American empire.[50] Some of these acquisitions were straightforward exercises of the treaty power, but others present novel and difficult problems of form.

The next acquisition after the Spanish-American War was American Samoa, which, as the name suggests, continues to be associated with the United States as a territory. In the late nineteenth century, the United States, Germany, and Great Britain all sought interests in the Samoan Islands—the United States because of its suitability as a naval base and coaling station. On December 2, 1899, in an agreement among the three powers, Great Britain renounced any claims to the islands, and the United States and Germany divided up Samoa into exclusive spheres of influence.[51] Shortly thereafter, the United States secured from the native chiefs cessions of the islands to which it had obtained exclusive rights from the European powers.[52] The cessions were confirmed and accepted by congressional statute.

The United States is fully capable of accepting cessions of foreign territory by legislation, and the acquisition of the Samoan Islands was surely a legitimate implementation of the naval power. The only problem is that Congress did not get around to accepting the Samoan cessions until February 20, 1929.[53] The cessions of 1900 and 1904 were "accepted" by American naval officers. Congress could have authorized those officers by statute to act as American agents for purposes of accepting the cessions, but that did not happen. If the original cessions were valid, it must be because the President's "executive Power" includes the power to add territory to the United States in the absence of statute. That conclusion is not completely unthinkable, but if there is any support for it in any relevant source of constitutional meaning, we have not seen it. Accordingly, the Samoan Islands were legitimately acquired in 1929. As for what, if anything, justified American governance of the islands until that date—as with the governance of the Philippines between its (unconstitutional) acquisition by the United States and its independence, that is a topic for Part II.

In 1903, the United States acquired the rights to construct and operate a canal in the Republic of Panama within a ten-mile-wide strip of land known as the Panama Canal Zone.[54] In 1977, the United States agreed to turn over the canal and all properties within the Panama Canal Zone to the Republic of Panama; that transfer became effective on October 1, 1979. In 1903, acquisition of the Panama Canal Zone was clearly permissible pursuant to the naval power.[55] The only issues with respect to the Panama Canal Zone concerned the circumstances and terms of the acquisition. As with Hawaii, the Panamanian government that signed the treaty of 1903 was arguably in power as a result of American influence,[56] which may raise problems of international law and political morality, but does not affect the constitutionality of the acquisition. As for the terms of the acquisition, the United States specifically disclaimed sovereignty over the Panama Canal Zone and instead acquired "all the rights, power and authority . . . which the United States would possess and exercise if it were the sovereign."[57] How this differs from full sovereignty is a question that does not affect the constitutionality of the acquisition. The United States, as with any private entity, can acquire leasehold interests, fee simple title, or anything in between, as long as the acquisition carries into execution a national power.

The United States acquired other islands with an eye toward naval bases. In 1917, the United States purchased the Virgin Islands from Denmark[58] in order to control entry into the Gulf of Mexico. In 1976, the people of the Northern Mariana Islands voted to affiliate themselves with the United States as a commonwealth — a status that was first granted to Puerto Rico in 1952 and that Congress extended to the Northern Mariana Islands in 1981. The Federated States of Micronesia, the Marshall Islands, and Palau are all affiliated with the United States through a compact of free association.

For present purposes, the differences, if any, among affiliation with the United States as a territory, a commonwealth, or a free association state are not important.[59] Our present concern is with the constitutionality of the initial acquisitions. The Northern Mariana Islands and the three free association states came under United States control after World War II under the auspices of the United Nations. Driven by concerns that certain territories that had been subject to Axis occupation were not yet ready for self-governance, the United Nations established a system of trust territories, in which major nations were given power and responsibility to administer territories until they could achieve self-determination. The United States assumed a "strategic trust" over the island territories, which permitted the United States to maintain a military presence in the islands, subject to oversight by the United Nations Security Council. Congress agreed to the arrangement on July 18, 1947,[60] and there is no doubt of the United States' power to acquire territory on the limited terms of the trust. The more interesting question concerns the power of the United Nations to determine the fate of the Trust Territories, but that is a story for international scholars to tell.

Finally, the United States maintains control over many islands in the Pacific Ocean that have no permanent population, including such strategic islands as Midway and Wake. The constitutional rules for acquisition of those islands track those for the guano islands, which we have previously discussed at length.

In many ways the most mysterious American territorial acquisition is one of the least discussed: the American-occupied portion of Berlin following World War II. The details of that occupation are interesting but incidental to our discussion here.[61] In the years immediately following the war, American occupation can be justified as an outgrowth of the war. Once the war was officially terminated and a West German government was established in 1955, however, it is hard to see for what constitutional purpose the United States received any interest in Berlin. Perhaps the answer is as simple as the maintenance of an air base. Otherwise, Berlin may truly have been, as Gerald Neuman has put it in another context, an anomalous zone.[62]

One opponent of the annexation of Alaska in 1867 declared, "[W]e are furnishing an example for the annexation of territory not contiguous, by which we may be led on to buy remote islands and to annex distant nations with populations that we cannot control by our own institutions, and to govern whom will only be preparing ourselves for the overthrow of a republican and the introduction of a despotic government."[63] He was certainly prophetic about the future course of American territorial expansion. Was he equally prophetic about the future course of American territorial governance? That is the story of Part II, to which we now turn.

PART **II**

Governing Territory

4

Constitutional Architecture I:
Territorial Legislatures and Executives

Once territory is acquired by the federal government, it must be governed until it becomes part of an American state or an independent nation. Constitutional questions about territorial governance have been at the heart of some of the most famous and contentious episodes in American constitutional history. It is easy to forget that *Marbury v Madison* involved the appointment of a territorial official. Marbury's commission was as a justice of the peace for the District of Columbia, and the constitutional status of territorial judges was prominently in the case's background. Half a century later, *Dred Scott v Sandford* caused problems by holding (correctly) that the Due Process Clause applied to territorial legislation and by holding (incorrectly) that Congress violated that provision by forbidding slavery in federal territories. And another half-century later, in *The Insular Cases*, the fate of American imperialism largely turned on the Supreme Court's willingness to look the other way if Congress tried to govern territories without such constitutional staples as jury trials. Indeed, on at least the latter two occasions, the role of the Constitution in territorial governance was "the premier constitutional question facing the Supreme Court, if interest in both legal circles and the general public is taken as a measure."[1]

Even apart from these well-known episodes, the subject of territorial governance has an important historical dimension. A close examination of the

Constitution's governance structure for territories takes us on a long and arduous, but richly rewarding, journey through some long-forgotten crevasses of constitutional history. Although the question of the proper relationship between territories and the Constitution has largely disappeared from the scene in modern times, it occupied much of the energy of the courts in the nineteenth and early twentieth centuries. The lessons of this oft-ignored chapter of American constitutional history are consistently enlightening, often discomfiting, and more than occasionally entertaining.

The Constitution contains two clauses that specifically address problems of territorial governance. The first provision, in Article I, gives Congress power "[t]o exercise exclusive Legislation in all Cases whatsoever, over such District (not exceeding ten Miles square) as may, by Cession of particular States, and the Acceptance of Congress, become the Seat of the Government of the United States, and to exercise like Authority over all Places purchased by the Consent of the Legislature of the State in which the Same shall be, for the Erection of Forts, Magazines, Arsenals, dock-Yards, and other needful Buildings."[2] A second provision, in Article IV, states that "[t]he Congress shall have Power to dispose of and make all needful Rules and Regulations respecting the Territory or other Property belonging to the United States; and nothing in this Constitution shall be so construed as to Prejudice any Claims of the United States, or of any particular State."[3] Together, these provisions seem to cover the field. The first provision grants Congress general legislative power — that is, legislative power that is not limited to the subjects enumerated elsewhere in the Constitution but instead is as jurisdictionally broad as the legislative power of a state — over the national capital and federal enclaves located within states. The clause contains no internal limitations on the scope of this power. The second provision grants Congress a similar general power, limited only by the modest requirement that laws be "needful," over all other federal territory that is not within the jurisdiction of a state. Congress's authority over federal territories is "general and plenary," and Congress has "full and complete legislative authority over the people of the territories and all the departments of the territorial government."[4]

There is, however, a category of territory that is not encompassed by these provisions. Suppose that during wartime, American troops occupy some portion of a foreign country. While the war is still in progress, the occupied land, whose boundaries may shift from moment to moment, is not "Territory . . . belonging to the United States." The land is still part of the foreign country until such time as it is ceded to the United States or a third nation or becomes an independent state. Nonetheless, the United States has the right (and duty) to govern that territory during the period of occupation. The right to govern occupied territory is part of the international laws of war. The American government acquires that right, not through either of the clauses granting Congress power of territorial governance, but through the President's power as chief executive to wage war in accordance with international norms. During the period of occupation, the conqueror is permitted to substitute its own political institutions in place of the indigenous government, even to the point of levying tariffs on imported goods, though relations of private right remain intact unless altered in accordance with international practice. These principles were all well established as international law in the late eighteenth century, and they received early and consistent recognition from the Supreme Court.[5]

Thus there are in fact three clauses of the Constitution that speak to the question of territorial governance, two of which grant powers to Congress and one of which grants powers to the President. Each clause has its own sphere of application: the District Clause applies to the nation's capital and federal enclaves within states, the Territories Clause applies to federal territories that have been acquired by the United States, and the Article II Vesting Clause applies to territory that is under American military occupation but which has not been formally acquired.

This simple, and even obvious, division of constitutional authority has had little bearing on the actual conduct of American territorial governance. As we will later discuss at length, the Supreme Court has been almost pathologically unwilling to locate congressional power to govern territories in the clauses that, for lack of a better phrase, enumerate a congressional power to govern territories, and the President's power of governance has extended far beyond the wartime limits inherent in the grant of the executive power. Our principal concern, however, is with the structure of governance set forth in the Constitution, not with the actual practices over the past two centuries. In the course of this part, we test those practices against the original meaning of the Constitution.

In this and the next chapter, we explore the institutions of territorial governance in territory that is (on a proper analysis) subject to the jurisdiction of Congress under the District Clause or the Territories Clause. In Chapter 6, we discuss some of the problems that arise in connection with military governance of occupied foreign territory. In Chapter 7, we consider the extent to which territorial inhabitants are entitled to constitutional protections such as those contained in the Bill of Rights.

A federal territory "has no inherent right to govern itself."[6] Congress can, if it chooses, legislate for a territory as a state legislates for its citizens. To the extent that Congress instead elects to set up institutions of governance within a territory, those institutions are "entirely the creation of Congress."[7] The question is whether the Constitution limits Congress's creativity.

Almost no one, we trust, would be surprised to discover that some of our long-established, long-upheld institutions of territorial governance are inconsistent with the original meaning of the Constitution. What may be surprising is the extent of that inconsistency. From an originalist perspective, serious constitutional problems have pervaded nearly every institution of territorial government since the nation's founding. More pointedly, a persistent, even if not consistent, theme of territorial administration has been to try to afford territories as much opportunity for self-government as Congress deems conditions will permit, either as a prelude to statehood or simply as a reflection of a general commitment to democratic political theory. Those democratic institutions of governance, however, are among the features of our territorial structure that raise the most serious constitutional problems. The rest of this chapter explains why.

Territorial Legislatures

A commitment to democratic self-government has influenced policy concerning the territorial lawmaking power since the nation's founding. The Northwest Ordinance of 1787 provided for a (partially) elective legislative assembly as soon as the territorial population was large enough to make an election practicable,[8] and elected legislatures with broad power over local affairs ever since have been a staple of territorial administration. There have been exceptions: the first legislature of the Louisiana Territory was appointed by the President, the same was true in Florida, and an 1884 statute for Alaska specifically forbade establishment of a territorial legislature.[9] As a general practice, however, Congress has established local legislatures as soon as the population was deemed large enough and informed enough to handle it.[10]

The reasons for this practice are obvious. In territories viewed as candidates for statehood, self-government through an elected legislature helps prepare the population for the responsibilities of statehood and establishes laws and institutions to serve as foundations for the new order upon admission to the Union. In territories with no prospects of achieving statehood, limited self-government can prepare the people for nationhood if the territory is ultimately granted full independence, as happened with the Philippines. Finally, even if self-government serves no further purpose, democratic theory suggests that some measure of self-government through a representative assembly is distinctly preferable to rule by a distant Congress, President, or cabinet secretary.

To a constitutionalist, however, the creation of locally elected legislatures looks at first glance like a raw delegation of legislative power. The enactment of territorial laws, including criminal laws, is clearly the exercise of legislative power. Delegations of legislative power generally offend the Constitution. Is democratic self-governance in the territories — or any form of governance other than congressional legislation — therefore unconstitutional?

The consensus view from the framing generation to the present has been in favor of territorial legislatures. James Madison took it for granted in *The Federalist* that the inhabitants of the District of Columbia would be given the power of local self-government.[11] The example of the District of Columbia is instructive, because Congress's legislative power over the District is specifically designated by the Constitution as "exclusive." If Congress can nonetheless delegate legislative authority to a District of Columbia legislature, there cannot possibly be a valid objection to similar delegations to other territorial governments. Although St. George Tucker, writing in 1803, disputed Madison's assumption that a local legislature for the District of Columbia would not offend the Constitution,[12] his doubts did not gain currency, and Joseph Story was able to dismiss them cavalierly thirty years later.[13]

The question was raised with regard to territories in connection with the Louisiana Purchase. Once the territory had been acquired, it had to be occupied and governed. Congress's first enactment for the territory authorized the President to take possession of the territory and then provided, in section 2: "That, until the expiration of the present session of Congress, unless provision for the temporary government of the said territories be sooner made by Congress, all the military, civil and judicial powers, exercised by the officers of the existing government of the same, shall be vested in such person and persons, and shall be exercised in such manner, as the President of the United States shall direct for maintaining and protecting the inhabitants of Louisiana in the free enjoyment of their liberty, property and religion."[14] Unsurprisingly, this sweeping grant of presidential authority raised some hackles. In discussing an earlier, substantively similar version of this provision, Representative Randolph endorsed it in principle but thought that it gave the President power for too long a time.[15] Representative James Elliott countered that "[h]e would never consent to delegate, for a single moment, such extensive powers to the President, even over a Territory. Such a delegation of power was unconstitutional. If such a provision as that contemplated by the Section were necessary, it became Congress itself to enter upon the task of legislation."[16]

Representative Elliott was not alone in his concerns. Representative Griswold had similar problems with the delegation to the President.[17] Randolph responded by challenging Griswold to "show us any way in which the country may be taken possession of, with security and by which the people may enjoy all the rights and franchises of citizens of the United States immediately."[18] Griswold, in response,

> thought it extraordinary that the gentleman from Virginia [Randolph] should call upon him to propose a plan for avoiding the difficulties that would apparently result from the system proposed by the bill. . . . He confessed that he was unable to offer any. To do it would doubtless require time and deliberation. It was sufficient for him that the bill infringed the Constitution. By the second section it is proposed to transfer to the President of the United States all the powers, civil, military, and judicial, exercised at present in that province. What are those powers? No gentleman is able to inform me. It may be presumed that they are legislative; the President, therefore, is to be made the legislator of that country; that they are judicial; the President, therefore, is to be made judge; that they are executive, and so far they constitutionally devolve on the President. Hence we are about making the President the legislator, the judge, and the executive of this territory. I do not said Mr. G, understand that, according to the Constitution, we have a right to make him legislator, judge, and executive, in any territory belonging to the United States.[19]

Representative John Jackson added, while objecting to the delegation of legislative power to the President even for a moment, "I would prefer an interregnum to doing anything which should militate against the Constitution."[20]

The responses to these arguments were largely repetitions of Randolph's point about necessity, which some representatives were prepared to raise to the level of a constitutional trump.[21] A few substantive arguments in favor of the bill were advanced, but they were either silly or undeveloped.[22] In the end, however, the bill passed easily and became law.

Nor has the Supreme Court been troubled by delegations of legislative power in territories. The first serious constitutional challenge to the authority of a territorial legislature reached the Court in 1904 in *Dorr v United States*.[23] The Philippines at that time were governed by the United States Philippine Commission, a presidentially directed body exercising local legislative authority.[24] The commission had enacted a criminal libel statute under which Dorr was prosecuted and convicted. Dorr's principal constitutional challenge to his conviction was the fact that he had been denied a jury trial, which the Court rejected under the "territorial incorporation" doctrine that we discuss, and criticize, in Chapter 7. Dorr also argued, however, that the libel statute was invalid because Congress could not delegate legislative authority to the Philippine Commission that had enacted it. The Court brushed this claim aside in its concluding paragraph: "The [libel statute] was one of the laws of the Philippine

Commission, passed by that body by virtue of the authority given the President under . . . [the governing organic statute]. The right of Congress to authorize a temporary government of this character is not open to question at this day. The power has been frequently exercised and is too well settled to require further discussion."[25]

The issue surfaced twice more in the twentieth century, in connection with elected rather than appointed legislatures. In *Cincinnati Soap Co. v United States*,[26] soap manufacturers challenged the validity of a tax on domestic processing of coconut oil produced in the Philippines. All funds collected under the tax were to be paid over to the Philippine treasury, with no congressional restrictions on or instructions concerning their use.[27] The soap manufacturers argued that Congress could not delegate its authority to establish spending priorities to the (by that time elective) Philippine legislature. The manufacturers protested, on general nondelegation grounds, the absence of standards to guide the conduct of the delegate, and further argued, albeit without explanation, that even with proper standards the Philippine government could not receive a delegation of the spending power.[28] The Court upheld the tax, flatly denying that Congress is required to provide standards to govern the use of general, lump-sum appropriations. More significantly, the Court declared that even if an appropriation without standards would ordinarily be unlawful, it is permissible when Congress delegates authority to a territorial government. "In dealing with the territories," the Court wrote, "Congress . . . is not subject to the same restrictions which are imposed in respect of laws for the United States considered as a political body of states in union."[29]

The last challenge to a territory's legislative power came in 1953 in *District of Columbia v John R. Thompson Co.*[30] The defendant was criminally prosecuted in the District of Columbia for violating a local ordinance prohibiting racial discrimination by restaurateurs. By 1953, a frontal challenge to the District of Columbia's legislative power clearly would have been futile. As a result, the defendant sought to distinguish between the power to enact municipal and police regulations, which it conceded Congress could delegate to the District, and the power to enact legislation, which the defendant maintained was exclusively vested in Congress.[31] The Court rejected the distinction, holding that Congress could delegate to the District, and to other territories, all lawmaking powers that it could itself exercise.[32]

Neither Madison nor Story nor the Supreme Court ever explained why the creation of territorial legislatures (whether elected or appointed) does not violate the nondelegation doctrine. Nonetheless, we are aware of only one modern scholar who has shared the doubts about this practice voiced by

St. George Tucker and some of the representatives during the debate on the bill for the original government of Louisiana. That scholar is one of the present authors,[33] and he was wrong.

The trick is to understand the proper constitutional source of the non-delegation doctrine. That is a subject for a separate article, which the same one of the present authors has written,[34] but a short statement may suffice here. There is no express "Nondelegation Clause" in the Constitution that forbids Congress from delegating legislative power. Neither, however, is there an express "Delegation Clause" that permits Congress to delegate legislative power. The latter conclusion is more important under the principle of enumerated powers. The President and courts generally cannot exercise legislative powers on their own initiative because they are not granted any such powers by the Constitution; they are granted only the "executive Power" and the "judicial Power," respectively. But what if Congress passes a statute that says, in essence, "the President shall exercise legislative power with respect to X." If the President obeys that command, isn't the President simply executing the law in fine Article II fashion? That would be true if the Constitution authorized Congress to pass the relevant law. Congress, however, generally cannot delegate legislative power for the simple reason that the Constitution does not affirmatively authorize such delegations. The only possible source for a general power to delegate would be the Sweeping Clause, but delegations of legislative power are not "necessary and proper for carrying into Execution" federal powers and therefore are not authorized by the Sweeping Clause.

When Congress legislates for the territories or the District of Columbia, however, it does not need to invoke the Sweeping Clause as an authorization. The Territories Clause and District Clause are self-contained grants of general legislative power. Those clauses do not contain any "necessary and proper" requirement. Accordingly, if Congress passes a statute under the Territories Clause that essentially says to the President, "govern this territory as would a general legislature," that statute is a "needful Rule or Regulation," and the President's executive power permits him to execute that statute according to its terms. The Territories Clause and the District Clause thus both serve as affirmative (if implicit) authorizations to delegate legislative power within a limited sphere. Madison, Story, and the Supreme Court were right about delegations of territorial legislative power, even if they did not actually understand why.

Thus the original Louisiana Territory law that essentially turned President Jefferson of the United States into Emperor Jefferson of Louisiana was not unconstitutional by virtue of its delegation of legislative power to the President. Similarly, territorial legislatures do not violate the nondelegation doctrine. But that does not mean that they are always constitutional regardless of their form. Legislation under the Territories Clause and the District Clause does not have to conform to the internal textual requirements of the Sweeping Clause, but it does have to conform to the textual requirements that apply to all federal legislation, such as Article I, section 7's requirements of bicameralism and presentment. And that can be a problem, as we shall see in the next section.

Territorial Executives

Territorial governments require governors, prosecutors, and others to enforce and execute the laws of the territory and of the United States in the territory. The federal courts have never decided a case that squarely addresses the constitutional status and requirements of territorial executive officials. But in 1985, in *Sakamato v Duty Free Shoppers, Ltd.*,[35] they had their chance.

Guam has been an American possession since it was ceded to the United States by Spain following the Spanish-American War. Since 1950, it has been administered by a civilian territorial government whose power extends "to all rightful subjects of legislation," including specifically the power to impose "royalties for franchises, privileges, and concessions."[36] The territorial government used that power to raise revenues for airport improvements by auctioning off monopolies on the sale and delivery of goods at the Guam International Airport.

In the 1980s, Plaintiff Sakamoto and defendant Duty Free Shoppers, Limited ("DFS") sold gift merchandise in Guam, with Sakamoto's principal product evidently being Hawaiian Host macadamia nut candies. The rival gift merchants competed primarily for the business of Japanese tourists, who customarily purchase gifts to take back home. The Japanese are a finicky clientele who "expect and demand that their gift purchases be delivered to them at the airport so that they will not be inconvenienced during their vacation."[37] Hence the right to deliver goods sold elsewhere on the island to departing passengers at the Guam International Airport Terminal is of great importance to merchants competing for this vital segment of the tourist trade.

In 1975, the airport terminal was placed under the direct control of the Guam Airport Authority ("GAA"), an instrumentality of the territorial government of Guam. In 1978, the GAA publicly sought bids on a fifteen-year exclusive concession for the sale and delivery of gift items at the terminal. DFS demonstrated the importance of airport delivery rights by submitting a winning bid of more than $140,000,000.

Following an impressive series of attempts by Sakamoto to circumvent the exclusive concession, which led to an equally impressive series of warning letters from the GAA,[38] he filed suit against DFS, the GAA, and the government of Guam, seeking invalidation of the franchise provision granting exclusive terminal delivery rights to DFS. When the case reached the Ninth Circuit Court of Appeals, the challenge to the provision was essentially twofold. First, Sakamoto argued that the delivery restriction violated the Dormant Commerce Clause, a claim that was correctly rejected by the Ninth Circuit for reasons that are of only tangential concern here.[39] Second, Sakamoto alleged that the concession agreement violated the federal antitrust laws. The principal defense proffered against this claim was the antitrust immunity typically enjoyed by agencies or instrumentalities of the federal government. And thereby hangs our tale.

It is well settled that the antitrust laws do not apply to federal agencies or instrumentalities.[40] It is also well settled that Congress has "general and plenary" authority over territorial governments, including both the statutory and inherent power to annul legislative acts of the territorial government.[41] In view of this dependence on congressional authorization and acquiescence, the Supreme Court has characterized territorial governments as " 'agencies of the federal government.' "[42] The defendants in *Sakamoto* had no trouble completing the syllogism: If the government of Guam is a federal agency, and if federal agencies are entitled to immunity from the antitrust laws, then the Guamanian government's creation of an exclusive franchise must enjoy antitrust immunity. This syllogism was readily accepted by the district court, the court of appeals, and the United States Solicitor General in an *amicus curiae* brief on the petition for certiorari.[43] The Supreme Court denied certiorari, and the case quietly disappeared.

It took with it a problem of remarkable dimension. The Appointments Clause of the Constitution provides that the President "shall nominate, and by and with the Advice and Consent of the Senate, shall appoint Ambassadors, other public Ministers and Consuls, Judges of the supreme Court, and all other Officers of the United States, whose Appointments are not herein otherwise provided for, and which shall be established by Law: but the Congress may by Law vest the Appointment of such inferior Officers, as they think proper, in the President alone, in the Courts of Law, or in the Heads of Departments."[44] The Constitution does not tell us which of the millions of federal employees rise to the level of "Officers of the United States" whose appointments must conform to this clause. The Supreme Court in *Buckley v Valeo*, however, was surely correct to include as officers "any appointees exercising significant authority pursuant to the laws of the United States."[45] The responsibilities of the territorial governor of Guam include "the faithful execution of the laws of Guam *and the laws of the United States applicable in Guam.*"[46] By any reasonable definition, that makes the governor an "Officer of the United States," who must be appointed in full conformity with the Appointments Clause. The point was recognized by the 1950 Organic Act creating the territorial government of Guam,[47] which originally provided that the governor would be "appointed by the President, by and with the advice and consent of the Senate."[48]

In 1968, however, the Organic Act was amended by the Guam Elective Governor Act,[49] which provided that the office of governor (and the newly created office of lieutenant governor) was to be filled through popular election. This election procedure does not conform to the modes of selection permitted by the Appointments Clause. Thus it seems as though the governor of Guam — and by necessary implication all of the governor's subordinates — were disabled by this statute from executing the laws of the United States. But if no Guamanian executive officials are empowered to execute the laws of the United States, how can the government of Guam be a federal agency? Since the antitrust immunity of the GAA's grant of an exclusive concession was upheld by the court of appeals solely on the strength of an agencies-are-immune-and-Guam-is-an-agency syllogism, the DFS's monopoly on airport macadamia nut candy deliveries squarely raised (even if no one thought to argue) a serious constitutional problem with the structure of the Guamanian government.[50]

Indeed, the constitutional problems with elected territorial executives, such as the Guamanian governor, are straightforward and insurmountable. The language of the Appointments Clause is very specific: anyone who is an officer of the United States must take office through one of the specified modes of appointment. Once one grants (as one must) that the Guamanian governor is an "Officer" within the meaning of the Appointments Clause, the clause remorselessly forbids election, just as it remorselessly forbids congressional selection of officials of the Federal Election Commission. It does not matter whether the Guamanian governor is an "inferior" officer or a principal officer; in neither case does the Constitution permit appointment by election. The Appointments Clause imposes a structural requirement that is independent of the "necessary and proper" requirements of executory legislation under the Sweeping Clause, so the general jurisdictional grants of the Territories Clause and District Clause do not save the scheme. Congress can no more avoid the Appointments Clause when legislating for the territories than it can avoid the Presentment Clause.

Of course not all persons playing a significant role in the enforcement of federal statutes must necessarily be officers of the United States. From the time of the nation's founding, state officials have often been called upon to implement federal statutes,[51] but those officials are not by virtue of that fact subject to the Appointments Clause. State officials, however, draw their powers from an independent sovereign entity within a system of dual governmental sovereignty; their authority is part of the background against which all federal authority is exercised. Just as state judges can adjudicate federal causes of action without becoming constitutional "Judges . . . of . . . inferior Courts," state officials can execute federal law without becoming "Officers of the United States." Not so with territorial officials, who owe their existence to and derive all their powers from federal law. Territorial officials appear unmistakably to be officers of the United States, who must be appointed in accordance with the terms of the Appointments Clause.

For whatever it is worth (and we do not think it worth very much), the First Congress appears to have shared this understanding of the Appointments Clause in the territories. The Northwest Ordinance of 1787 provided for appointment and removal by Congress of various territorial officials, including a governor.[52] One of the first acts of Congress following ratification of the Constitution was to amend the Northwest Ordinance "so as to adapt the same to the present Constitution of the United States."[53] Among these adaptations was a provision declaring that "the President shall nominate, and by and with the advice and consent of the Senate, shall appoint all officers which by the said ordinance were to have been appointed by the United States in Congress assembled."[54] Thus the First Congress evidently felt the need to ensure that the appointment of territorial officials complied with the commands of the Appointments Clause in order to "adapt" the Northwest Ordinance to the Constitution.

This construction of the Appointments Clause reigned for more than 150 years in practice and has never been explicitly repudiated in theory. Prior to 1947, every statute creating a territorial government provided for direct control by the executive branch, usually through a presidentially appointed governor.[55] The first clear deviation from this practice was a 1947 amendment to the Organic Act of Puerto Rico authorizing popular gubernatorial elections[56] — a practice that was extended by statute in 1968 to Guam and to the Virgin Islands and by administrative order in 1977 to Samoa.[57] None of these amendments was accompanied by explicit discussion — nor, evidently, by congressional recognition — of their constitutional implications for the Appointments Clause.[58]

The only possible way to avoid the application of the Appointments Clause is to say that territorial governments are categorically exempted from all otherwise applicable structural constitutional requirements. And there is ample authority for that proposition. Joseph Story, for example, thought it obvious that "the form of government established in the territories depends exclusively upon the discretion of congress. Having a right to erect a territorial government, they may confer on it such powers, legislative, judicial, and executive, as they may deem best."[59] A unanimous Supreme Court expressed the same view in dictum in 1850, stating that territorial governments are not subject to the Constitution's "complex distribution of the powers of government, as the organic law; but are the creations, exclusively, of the legislative department."[60] And although the majority and dissenting Justices in the *Dred Scott* case could agree on virtually nothing else, they had been united in believing that "[t]he form of government to be established [in acquired territories] necessarily rested in the discretion of Congress."[61] In 1901, a concurring Justice could present as settled law the principle that Congress has essentially a free hand with respect to the structure of the territorial governments it creates:

> The Constitution has undoubtedly conferred on Congress the right to create such municipal organizations as it may deem best for all the territories of the United States whether they have been incorporated or not, to give to the inhabitants as respects the local governments such degree of representation as may be conducive to the public well-being, to deprive such territory of representative government if it is considered just to do so, and to change such local governments at discretion.
>
> The plenitude of the power of Congress as just stated is conceded by both sides to this controversy. It has been manifest from the earliest days and so many examples are afforded of it that to refer to them seems superfluous.[62]

These authorities suggest a simple answer to the problem posed by the facts of *Sakamoto*: If Congress wants to create territorial governments with elected governors, it may do so, since it is a question of governmental structure committed entirely to its discretion. On this reasoning, the fact that all the territories were run by presidentially appointed officials for 150 years was due to legislative choice, not constitutional compulsion. If the First Congress thought otherwise, it was simply mistaken.

It is one thing to say that Congress has discretion to structure territorial governments in any way that it chooses, without regard to structural requirements such as the Appointments Clause. It is another thing altogether to give *reasons* for that position, and on this front Story and the Court fall short. Indeed, they give no reasons. It is true that the structural principle of nondelegation does not apply to territories, but that is because of the central role of the Sweeping Clause in constitutionalizing the nondelegation doctrine. It is also true that territorial judges have long existed in evident violation of Article III (which indeed was the principal authority relied on by Story). As we will explain in the next chapter, that body of law does not so much construe the Constitution as ignore it. If a territorial official is an "Officer" within the meaning of the Appointments Clause, there really isn't anything else to say.

The implications of the applicability of the Appointments Clause to territorial governance are potentially very far-reaching. At a minimum, it means that elected territorial officials cannot execute national laws in the territories. At a maximum, it means that they cannot execute territorial laws in the territories either. Consider the Organic Act of Guam, which charges the governor with the faithful execution of federal laws and "the laws of Guam" enacted by the territorial legislature. Are these two distinct charges, or one? If Guamanian territorial laws are in fact federal laws for constitutional purposes, then even territorial laws of a purely local character, enacted by local legislatures, must be administered by presidential appointees rather than by democratically elected or locally appointed and responsive officials.

The question whether territorial laws are necessarily laws of the United States under Article II is starkly reminiscent of the battle fought over the authority of the second Bank of the United States to sue in federal court, which the Supreme Court resolved in the Bank's favor in the companion cases of *Osborn v Bank of the United States* and *Bank of the United States v Planters' Bank of Georgia*.[63] Congress created the Bank with authority "to sue and be sued . . . in any Circuit Court of the United States."[64] In *Osborn*, the Court concluded that this statute conferred subject matter jurisdiction on the federal courts,[65] even for simple contract actions brought by the Bank. The next question was whether any of the sources of federal jurisdiction specified in Article III could sustain so expansive a statutory grant. The only possible candidate was Article III's extension of federal judicial power to "all Cases, in Law and Equity, arising under . . . the Laws of the United States."[66] Chief Justice Marshall found this source to be adequate, employing reasoning that could be used almost verbatim in connection with territorial governments:

> The [Bank's] charter of incorporation not only creates it, but gives it every faculty which it possesses. The power to acquire rights of any description, to transact business of any description, to make contracts of any description, to sue on those contracts, is given and measured by its charter, and that charter is a law of the United States. This being can acquire no right, make no contract, bring no suit, which is not authorized by a law of the United States. It is not only itself the mere creature of a law, but all its actions and all its rights are dependent on the same law. Can a being, thus constituted, have a case which does not arise literally, as well as substantially, under the law?[67]

Marshall's reasoning, while far from compelling, is nonetheless persuasive, at least when limited to federal instrumentalities. While the text of Article III can sustain a narrower reading,[68] it can also sustain Marshall's, which better fits the text's evident purposes. As *Osborn* itself demonstrates, federal instrumentalities can receive rough treatment at the hands of the states, and in order to protect them it may be necessary to provide a hospitable judicial forum for resolving even the most mundane common law questions.

If all cases involving federal instrumentalities necessarily "arise under" the laws of the United States, so must all cases involving territorial governments. As with the Bank of the United States, territorial governments get all of their power from the relevant organic statutes; they cannot so much as enter into contracts without congressional authorization. It would seem that all their laws — indeed, all of their acts and decisions — arise under the United States.

The *Osborn* Court's interpretation of Article III, if correct, has implications for Article II as well. If cases arising under territorial statutes enacted by local legislatures are within the constitutional jurisdiction of the federal courts under Article III, by implication one could conclude that the execution of those statutes is within the constitutional jurisdiction of the President under Article II. If rules promulgated by federal administrative agencies can be enforced only by appropriately appointed "Officers of the United States," it seems obvious that territorial statutes can be enforced only by properly appointed officers of the United States, not by locally elected or appointed officials.

This issue was raised in the nineteenth century by the facts of *Snow v United States ex rel. Hempstead*,[69] though neither the parties nor the Court directly addressed it. The 1850 Organic Act creating the Utah territorial government directed the President to appoint an attorney for the territory,[70] but did not specify that officer's duties. The statute also created an elected territorial legislature with power over "all rightful subjects of legislation, consistent with the Constitution of the United States and the provisions of the organic act."[71] Pursuant to this authority, the Utah Legislature in 1852 provided for an attorney general for the territory, to be elected by the legislative assembly. The attorney general was given authority, among other things, to prosecute persons accused of crimes "in cases arising under the laws of the Territory."[72] The territorial statute obviously contemplated a division of authority between the presidentially appointed and territorially elected attorneys: the latter would handle purely territorial affairs, such as prosecuting violations of territorial criminal laws; the former would attend to "cases in which the government of the United States is concerned,"[73] such as those involving federal crimes.

This two-tiered prosecutorial system worked without incident for twenty years, as it had in other territories. In 1870, however, Charles Hempstead, the presidentially appointed United States attorney, brought a quo warranto action against Zerubbabel Snow, the territorial attorney general, claiming exclusive authority to prosecute all criminal actions brought in the courts of the territory, whether the actions involved congressional or territorial laws. Snow conceded Hempstead's exclusive prosecutorial authority "in any case wherein the United States of America is a party, or wherein the offence is against the laws of the United States," but he insisted on his "right and . . . duty of conducting the business in the courts in cases where the Territory is a party or is interested."[74] The Utah Supreme Court ruled in favor of Hempstead, for reasons that remain unclear.[75] The United States Supreme Court reversed, construing the organic act to permit locally appointed officials to prosecute local crimes.

Although the opinion in *Snow* contains an offhand reference to the Constitution,[76] it is clear that the Court and the parties thought the case presented only an issue of statutory interpretation.[77] As so often happens in territorial cases, however, the Court danced on the edge of more important questions. The United States represented "that there had been a very common, if not a universal, custom in Territories to create Territorial prosecuting officers to prosecute . . . local offences."[78] The Court accepted that representation, and its reading of the Organic Act was clearly influenced by its perception of a "long usage" of a dual prosecutorial system in the territories.[79] Along the way, it made a striking observation about this tradition: "It must be confessed that this [dual prosecutorial] practice exhibits somewhat of an anomaly. Strictly speaking, there is no sovereignty in a Territory of the United States but that of the United States itself. Crimes committed therein are committed against the government and dignity of the United States. It would seem that indictments and writs should regularly be in the name of the United States, and that the attorney of the United States was the proper officer to prosecute all offences."[80] The obvious conclusion to this passage would be something to the effect of: "Because the United States is the only true sovereign in the territories, the execution of territorial laws must be treated like execution of any other laws of that sovereign, and can therefore be undertaken only by properly appointed officers of the United States." The actual conclusion was: "But the practice has been otherwise, not only in Utah, but in other Territories organized upon the same type."[81] End of discussion.

At a minimum, territorial officials who are selected in any fashion that does not comply with the Appointments Clause cannot execute the laws of the United States. At a maximum, they cannot execute territorial laws, to the extent that the latter are also, for constitutional purposes, laws of the United States.

Formal Problems, Formal Solutions

Elected officials have had important executive functions in the territories for a long time. If one were to conclude that territorial officials cannot be elected but rather must be appointed in accordance with Article II in order constitutionally to exercise their authority, it would be a conclusion of no small moment. Furthermore, the conclusion does not seem to have occurred to any litigants: to the best of our knowledge, the constitutionality of having locally elected or appointed prosecutors enforce territorial laws has never been challenged. Yet if territorial laws are laws of the United States and thus should be executed by persons appointed in conformity with the Appointments Clause, then for many decades persons in the territories have been imprisoned — and even executed — for alleged crimes prosecuted by usurpers,[82] and Congress's perhaps laudable desire to bring some measure of democracy and self-government to the territories through local elections is constitutionally forbidden.

Indeed, the reach of the Appointments Clause goes even farther. We have shown that territorial legislatures do not violate the nondelegation doctrine, but the Appointments Clause presents an entirely different hurdle. When territorial legislatures act, they do so pursuant to congressional organic acts. Thus their "legislative" acts are in reality the execution of federal law. From a constitutional standpoint, territorial legislators are federal executive officials. Any federal officials who execute congressional statutes must be constitutionally appointed officers of the United States. Hence, territorial legislatures cannot constitutionally be elected by the people of their territory. If they can properly exist at all, they must be subject to appointment and direction by appropriate officials of the federal government.[83]

The only potential avenue of escape is to read the Territories Clause as an authorization to delegate legislative power to private persons who are not, for any constitutional purpose, federal officials. That would be a sensible solution but for a small textual problem: the Territories Clause is in reality the "Territory or other Property Clause." The clause gives Congress power to make "all needful Rules and Regulations respecting the Territory or other Property belonging to the United States." The clause does not distinguish between "Territory" and "other Property." If Congress can delegate to private persons legislative power over territories (including, presumably, the power to promulgate criminal laws), does that mean that Congress can also delegate to private persons legislative power over all federal property? Jefferson's imperial Constitution thus poses a bit of a dilemma: either Congress cannot prepare territories for statehood by establishing mechanisms of elective self-governance or

Congress can delegate legislative power to private persons over all federal property, including presumably military bases and other enclaves. Neither conclusion would commend itself to an eighteenth-century audience.

The lesser evil, however, is to conclude that the Constitution forbids the use of elective officials in federal territory. That is because the same Constitution that sets up a formalistic problem also provides a formalistic solution. If Congress really wants to prepare a territory for self-government, it can provide a near-substitute that achieves the goal without violating the Constitution's formal structures. The Constitution may forbid the outright election of territorial governors, but it does not prohibit the President and Senate from announcing, as a matter of policy, that they will appoint as governor whomever the territorial population chooses in a free, albeit formalistically nonbinding, election. Similarly, Congress could agree formally to enact, perhaps under fast-track rules, whatever "laws" of local concern are "enacted" by an elected local legislature. Such legislation would satisfy all of the formal requirements of Article I, which satisfies the letter of the Constitution, Congress's goals, and us.

It is true that these substitute mechanisms place territorial self-governance at the mercy of the national political departments, but that is true in any event: no one maintains that Congress is constitutionally required to allow territories to govern themselves. Thus, while it is possible that Congress could, under a "shadow government" scheme, refuse to adopt particular items of legislation "enacted" by territorial bodies, that situation would not differ radically from the present, in which Congress is always free to nullify territorial legislation. Perhaps there is some symbolic difference between requiring Congress to enact territorial laws and permitting it to repeal them, but we doubt whether an informed eighteenth-century audience would care very much.

5

Constitutional Architecture II: Territorial Courts

The territorial institution best known to legal scholars — and whose de-mise would probably cause the least distress — is the territorial court. Ter-ritorial judges neither "hold their Offices during good Behaviour" nor "receive for their Services, a Compensation, which shall not be diminished during their Continuance in Office," as Article III of the Constitution requires for "Judges, both of the supreme and inferior Courts."[1] For example, Congress has created a District Court of Guam with "the jurisdiction of a district court of the United States . . . and that of a bankruptcy court of the United States."[2] Unlike regular, tenured district judges, the district judge of Guam is appointed for "the term of ten years . . . unless sooner removed by the President for cause."[3] Although the judge's pay is pegged by statute to the salary of Article III district court judges, the federal courts will not recognize any constitutional barrier to a diminution of his salary.[4] The territorial court system is clearly far removed from the Article III model.

The Constitution could not be clearer about the judicial power. Article III vests "the judicial Power of the United States" — all of it — in courts staffed by judges who enjoy tenure during "good Behaviour" and assurances that their compensation "shall not be diminished during their Continuance in Office." One can argue about whether certain governmental functions are exercises of judicial power, executive power, or both, but certain functions, such as the adjudication of guilt at a criminal trial, are judicial by any plausible under-standing of the term. And once an activity is deemed judicial, the Constitution makes unmistakably clear the kinds of officers who must perform it. The story of how the federal courts avoided this seemingly obvious conclusion is among the most mysterious, and intriguing, in American constitutional history.

The Golden Age

The odyssey of territorial tribunals in the federal courts dates back to *Marbury v Madison* in 1803. *Marbury* was a mandamus action to compel Secretary of State James Madison to deliver to William Marbury his signed commission as a justice of the peace for the District of Columbia, an office created by Congress in 1801 pursuant to its authority "to exercise exclusive Legislation in all Cases whatsoever, over the District of Columbia." The stat-ute creating Marbury's office gave the District of Columbia justices of the peace the same judicial powers and duties as their counterparts in Maryland or Virginia, but prescribed that the appointees should only "continue in office five years."[5] Thus, despite their adjudicative functions, the District of Colum-bia justices of the peace were neither regarded nor constituted by Congress as tenured judges of inferior courts within the meaning of Article III.

In the course of opining that Marbury had a vested right to his office and commission, Chief Justice Marshall declared on no fewer than five occasions that Marbury was not removable at the will of the President once Madison had signed and sealed the commission, thus legally appointing him.[6] This dictum on Marbury's tenure was consistent with two propositions of very different breadth. It might simply have reflected the idea that Congress could limit the President's removal power over at least some officers by giving them a fixed term of office, which is pretty clearly what Marshall had in mind. But the President would also be unable to remove Marbury if Marbury was a judicial officer who was constitutionally entitled by Article III to tenure during good behavior, regardless of the terms of the statute creating his office. The latter proposition, if it had been adopted in the nation's formative years as the Supreme Court's holding, could have had a profound influence on the course of American territorial governance.

Less than a year after the Court decided *Marbury*, a holding of precisely such magnitude emerged from a circuit court in *United States v More*.[7] Like Marbury, Benjamin More was appointed a justice of the peace for the District of Columbia. Unlike Marbury, he took office without incident, although the tranquility was short-lived. The 1801 statute creating More's office contained a clause entitling District of Columbia justices of the peace to charge litigants for the performance of judicial services.[8] More was appointed to his office while this fees-for-services provision was in effect. In 1802, however, Congress declared that so much of the 1801 statute "as provides for the compensation to be made to certain justices of the peace thereby created . . . shall be, and is hereby repealed."[9] Seven months after this repealing statute took effect, More was criminally indicted for demanding and receiving a fee of twelve and one-half cents for adjudicating a minor debt action. In a demurrer to the indictment, More contended that the statute purporting to repeal his authority to collect fees was an unconstitutional attempt to reduce the salary of a federal judge and was thus without legal effect.

The Circuit Court of the District of Columbia, in a split decision, agreed with More and dismissed the indictment. Writing for the majority, Judge Cranch rejected out of hand the government's suggestion that Congress, in legislating for the District of Columbia, is not subject to any constitutional limitations. For Judge Cranch, the correct interpretation of the District Clause was that Congress may legislate for the District "in all cases where they are not prohibited by other parts of the constitution."[10] Article III, argued Judge Cranch, was a part of the Constitution. He saw no distinction between provisions such as Article III's guaranty of judicial independence and provisions such as Article I's guaranty of freedom from bills of attainder or ex post facto laws.

Judge Cranch had a similarly easy time deciding whether More was a judge of an inferior court within the meaning of Article III: "It is difficult to conceive how a magistrate can lawfully sit in judgment, exercising judicial powers, and enforcing his judgments by process of law, without holding a court. I consider such a court, thus exercising a part of the judicial power of the United States, as an inferior court, and the justice of the peace as the judge of that court."[11] In a somewhat extravagant (if noble) display of judicial restraint, Judge Cranch noted that it was unnecessary to decide whether More had a constitutional right to hold his office during good behavior, "[b]ut that his compensation shall not be diminished during his continuance in office, seems to follow as a necessary consequence from the provisions of the constitution."[12]

Judge Kilty dissented at some length, in language starkly prescient of the territorial incorporation doctrine that would emerge almost a century later: "[T]he provisions of the constitution, which are applicable particularly to the relative situation of the United States and the several states, are not applicable to this district." Congress, he stated, is prohibited from passing bills of attainder or ex post facto laws in the District of Columbia, but laws concerning the judiciary "cannot be tested by a provision in the constitution, evidently applicable to the judicial power of the whole United States."[13]

John T. Mason, United States Attorney for the District of Columbia, sought review by writ of error in the Supreme Court, where he and More's counsel, Samuel Jones, resumed the argument. Jones defended the judgment below by echoing Judge Cranch's formalistic reasoning: the Constitution guards the salaries of federal judges, and More's federal office was as judicial as they come. Jones also invoked the discussion of judicial tenure in *Marbury v Madison*, in which Chief Justice Marshall declared that District of Columbia justices of the peace did not serve at the pleasure of the President. That discussion was decisive, Jones argued, because Congress has no constitutional power to limit the removal of presidentially appointed officers "unless in the case of a judge under the constitution." Thus, he reasoned, Marshall's statements in *Marbury* that the President could not remove District of Columbia justices of the peace at will must have rested on the understanding that Article III applies fully to those justices, in which case it would also be unconstitutional to diminish More's salary.[14]

In response, Mason advanced the arguments from Judge Kilty's dissenting opinion, and more besides. Judge Kilty thought that at least some provisions of the Constitution, such as the Ex Post Facto Clause, bind Congress in legislating for the District. Mason made no such concession, averring that "Congress are under *no controul* in legislating for the district of Columbia. Their power, in this respect, is *unlimited*." *Marbury*, he argued, was not to the contrary, having determined only that Marbury had held office "during good behaviour for five years under the law; and not generally during good behaviour, under the constitution." Mason also denied that More's exercise of concededly judicial power necessarily brought him within Article III. Mason argued that since the judicial power in the District of Columbia extended to cases not within the various heads of federal jurisdiction set forth in Article III, it was not the judicial power of the United States. In other words, More's power may well have been judicial, but it was *territorial* judicial power, springing not from Article III but from Article I's grant of power to Congress to legislate for the District.[15]

Jones's rebuttal to this last argument speaks for itself:

> The executive power exercised within the district of Columbia is the executive power of the United States. The legislative power exercised in the district is the legislative power of the United States. And what reason can be given why the judicial power exercised in the district should not be the judicial power of the United States? If it be not the judicial power of the United States, of what nation, state or political society is it the judicial power? All the officers in the district are officers of the United States.
>
> By the 2d section of the third article of the constitution, the judicial power

of the United States is to extend to all cases arising under the laws of the United States. All the laws in force in the district are laws of the United States, and no case can arise which is not to be decided by those laws.[16]

Although *More* was concerned with the District of Columbia, it is hard to imagine a case more clearly raising the key issues concerning the constitutional status of territorial tribunals generally; any arguments made concerning Congress's power under Article I to legislate for the District could equally be made concerning Congress's power under Article IV to legislate for the territories. The Supreme Court never reached the merits in *More*, however, because Chief Justice Marshall sua sponte raised a decisive jurisdictional problem.[17] Accordingly, the Court dismissed the writ of error for lack of jurisdiction; More got away scot-free; and a decision on the status of territorial tribunals had to await another day.

Less than a year after the Supreme Court's decision in *United States v More*, the Court decided *Wise v Withers*.[18] Plaintiff-in-error Wise was, once again, a justice of the peace for the District of Columbia, who evidently did not report when called for militia duty. He was fined by a military court-martial, which sent the defendant Withers to collect the fine. Withers entered Wise's home and seized some of his goods, whereupon Wise brought an action for trespass *vi et armis*.

The case turned upon whether Wise, as a justice of the peace, was exempt from service in the militia. The law governing the organization of the militia in the District of Columbia provided for the enrollment of all nonexempt, resident, able-bodied white males between the ages of eighteen and forty-five.[19] Included among the categories of exempt persons were "the officers judicial and executive of the government of the United States."[20] The Court held that Wise was within this exemption. According to Chief Justice Marshall, the Court had already decided, presumably in *Marbury v Madison*, that justices of the peace were "officers." (Marshall indicated that he would also reach that conclusion as an original matter in view of the fact that Wise was appointed by the President subject to Senate confirmation.) Withers had suggested that a distinction be drawn between officers of the United States, within the meaning of the Constitution, and officers "of the *government* of the United States," within the meaning of the exemption statute. Marshall, however, would have none of it. In an intriguing echo of Samuel Jones's formalistic argument in *More* (intriguing because the contrary argument on behalf of Withers was forcefully advanced by none other than Samuel Jones), he held that Wise "must be an officer under the government of the United States. Deriving all his authority from the legislature and President of the United States, he certainly is not the officer of any other government." That left only the question whether Wise's office was either "executive" or "judicial" within the meaning of the exemption statute. Marshall's affirmative answer was that "[i]f a justice of the peace is an officer of the government of the United States, he must be either a judicial or an executive officer."[21] Since the case did not require the Court to assign Wise specifically to the Executive or Judicial Department, but merely to decide that he was necessarily within one of the two, Marshall added only that Wise's powers "seem partly judicial, and partly executive," which was enough to exempt him from military service.

The problems of reconciling territorial courts with Article III got more serious in 1810. *Seré v Pitot*[22] concerned a simple debt action in an Orleans territorial court brought by an alien against a citizen of the Territory of Orleans. The Court, per Chief Justice Marshall, held that Seré's claim was excluded from the territorial court's jurisdiction by statute. In dictum, however, the Court added that *if* the relevant statute had conferred jurisdiction over the suit, it would have been constitutional despite the fact that Article III provides for federal court jurisdiction over controversies between state citizens and foreign subjects but not between territorial citizens and foreign subjects. "[T]he idea," said Marshall, "that the constitution restrains congress from giving the court of the territory jurisdiction over a case brought by or against a citizen of the territory . . . is most clearly not to be sustained." Marshall's reasoning was terse, conclusory, and alarmist:

> Let us inquire what would be the jurisdiction of the [territorial] court, on this restricted construction [limiting its jurisdiction to the nine heads specified in article III]?
>
> It would have no jurisdiction over a suit brought by or against a citizen of the territory, although an alien, or a citizen of another state might be a party.
>
> It would have no jurisdiction over a suit brought by a citizen of one state, against a citizen of another state, because neither party would be a citizen of the "state" in which the court sat. Of what civil causes, then, between private individuals, would it have jurisdiction? Only of suits between an alien and a citizen of another state, who should be found in Orleans.[23]

As was often his wont, Marshall overstated his case. Under the reasoning of *Osborn v Bank of the United States*,[24] which Marshall was to write fourteen years later, the suits that concerned him could all be entertained by Article III courts in the territories whenever the claim is substantively founded on territorial law (as was evidently true of the claim in *Pitot*), since the case would then "arise under" the laws of the United States. A jurisdictional gap is possible only with respect to claims founded on state law.[25] And even in such cases, the territorial court must at least apply a territorial choice of law rule in order to establish that state law governs the claim, which is conceivably enough to satisfy the Constitution's "arising under" language (though that does seem like a bit of a stretch).

One other early decision deserves mention, though it did not address territorial tribunals, as it suggested that territories are a constitutionally integrated part of the American polity, and thus are (or so one could argue) at least presumptively within the scope of the Constitution's structural provisions. In 1815, Congress had imposed a direct tax on the states for general revenue purposes, which it shortly thereafter extended to the District of Columbia.[26] In *Loughborough v Blake*,[27] the Court upheld Congress's power to levy a direct tax on the District, invoking the authority in Article I to "lay and collect Taxes, Duties, Imposts and Excises."[28] Chief Justice Marshall reasoned that because this grant of power was general, it extended to "all places over which the government extends."[29] He reinforced this conclusion by reference to the constitutional requirement in the Taxing Clause that duties, imposts, and excises be "uniform throughout the United States." Since this modification of the taxing power was plainly coextensive with the original grant of power, the taxing power must extend throughout the United States. The question was thus whether "the United States" for constitutional purposes includes the District of Columbia. Marshall thought the answer clear: "The United States is the name given to our great republic, which is composed of states and territories. The district of Columbia, or the territory west of the Missouri, is not less within the United States, than Maryland or Pennsylvania."[30] According to Marshall, Congress therefore had the power to extend a direct tax to the District of Columbia, but the uniformity provision of the Taxing Clause required any such tax to be apportioned in accordance with the census, as was then required of direct taxes imposed in the states. One could then fairly ask: If a structural provision like the Uniformity Clause applies to the territories, why not other structural provisions as well?

Thus, as the first quarter of the nineteenth century closed, originalists could survey the scene with some satisfaction. *United States v More*, the one square holding on the status of territorial tribunals (albeit issuing from a lower court), clearly held that territorial judges were fully federal judges under Article III and were thus entitled to the guarantees of judicial independence found in the Constitution. The reasoning in both *Marbury v Madison* and *Wise v Withers* was consistent with this view. *Loughborough v Blake* suggested, albeit ambiguously, that the territories were at least not wholly beyond the reach of the Constitution's structural provisions. And *Osborn v Bank of the United States*, which held that all activities of a federally created corporation "arise under" federal law for purposes of Article III, smoothed over the period's one rough spot — the suggestion in *Seré v Pitot* that territorial tribunals could hear cases that are not within the ambit of Article III — and seemed in precise harmony with Samuel Jones's argument in *More* that all activity in the District of Columbia, including the exercise of judicial power, was necessarily federal. The conclusion that territorial judges exercised federal judicial power, and were thus entitled to the tenure and salary guarantees of Article III, seemed inescapable.

Formalism Founders

The conclusion escaped. In 1828, the Constitution received a blow from which it has never recovered. In *American Insurance Co. v 356 Bales of Cotton*,[31] the Supreme Court, per Chief Justice Marshall, appeared to uphold the constitutional validity of territorial tribunals not conforming to Article III. We say "appeared" because it is clear upon careful examination of the opinion that its discussion of the status of territorial courts was dictum, responding to an argument advanced by neither party. Moreover, the Court made no attempt to reconcile this dictum with its prior, and at least arguably inconsistent, case law: Marshall's murky opinion did not cite a single prior decision. Most importantly from the perspective of original meaning, the decision's reasoning ranges from obscure to absurd. Nevertheless, the opinion has been a cornerstone of all subsequent case law on territorial governance, and it both deserves and requires close scrutiny.

The case involved the distribution of authority among the territorial courts of Florida in 1825. Congress had vested "the judicial power of the territory of Florida . . . in three superior courts, and in such inferior courts, and justices of the peace as the legislative council of the territory may, from time to time, establish."[32] The superior courts were given broad original and appellate jurisdiction over territorial matters; and "in all cases arising under the laws and Constitution of the United States," they were vested with "the same jurisdiction" that had been vested in the District Court of Kentucky by the Judiciary Act of 1789.[33] The Judiciary Act, in turn, gave federal district courts "exclusive original cognizance of all civil causes of admiralty and maritime jurisdiction,"[34] among other powers.

In 1823, the Florida territorial legislative council responded to the frequent shipwrecks off the Florida coast by creating salvage courts to be administered by local officials inferior to the congressionally created superior court judges. Specifically, the statute provided that whenever wrecked property was brought into the territory, the salvors, owners, or other responsible persons were required to report the fact "to such justice of the Peace, or Notary Public as may reside next adjacent to the place of arrival."[35] The justice or notary[36] would then summon a five-person jury, which would determine the disposition of the salvaged property. All judicial officers of the territory were limited by the Florida Organic Act to four-year terms of office.[37]

Trouble began on February 7, 1825, when the ship *Point à Petre* foundered on a reef off the coast of Florida while carrying a load of cotton, much of which was insured by the American Insurance Company and the Ocean Insurance Company. A portion of the cargo was saved by rescue ships and brought to Key West, where a notary and five jurors held court in accordance with Florida's salvage statute. The jurors awarded 76 percent of the value of the rescued cotton — an unusually large amount — to the salvors. The presiding notary then conducted (and served as auctioneer at) a judicial sale, at which David Canter purchased 356 bales of the salvaged cotton. Canter took the cotton, or at least 300 bales of it, to Charleston, South Carolina,[38] where he sold it to a broker who in turn resold it at auction. The insurance companies, which had acquired by abandonment the original shipper's interest in the cotton, filed a libel (as complaints in admiralty were then called) in the District Court of South Carolina, claiming that the judicial sale in Key West was invalid and had not transferred ownership to Canter. The district judge agreed with the insurance companies that the Key West tribunal was incompetent to adjudicate salvage cases, on the ground that admiralty jurisdiction — which he took to include salvage — could not be exercised by state or territorial courts. But he also ruled that, because the identifying marks on most of the cotton had been obliterated, the insurance companies could only establish ownership of 39 of the 356 bales of cotton. On cross-appeals, Justice William Johnson, sitting on circuit, reversed the judgment, holding the Key West sale valid and awarding all of the cotton to Canter.[39]

The insurance companies appealed to the Supreme Court, advancing two significant arguments.[40] Neither argument questioned the general constitutional validity of territorial tribunals or the ability of territorial tribunals to adjudicate salvage cases. Rather, the insurance companies maintained in both arguments simply that the case had been brought in the wrong territorial court. The first argument was purely statutory. As noted earlier, the Judiciary Act of 1789 had given federal district courts "exclusive original cognizance of all civil causes of admiralty and maritime jurisdiction," and the territorial organic act gave the congressionally created Florida superior courts "the same jurisdiction . . . in all cases arising under the laws and Constitution of the United States" as was vested in the federal District Court of Kentucky. The insurance companies argued that if the jurisdiction of the two courts was "the same," then the admiralty jurisdiction of the superior courts must be "exclusive," and the territorial legislature was not free to confer such jurisdiction on locally created courts. The Supreme Court correctly rejected this argument for reasons that are of little concern here.[41]

Unfortunately for posterity's sake, the insurance companies also had a constitutional argument against the jurisdiction of the Key West salvage court. The Constitution, they said, extends the judicial power of the United States "to all Cases of *admiralty* and *maritime* jurisdiction," and the judicial power is vested "in a Supreme Court, and such inferior Courts *as Congress* may from time to time establish."[42] Thus, they argued, admiralty jurisdiction could be exercised in Florida only by congressionally created courts — namely, the superior courts. To the extent that Congress sought to authorize the territorial legislature to create courts with admiralty jurisdiction, it was prevented from doing so by Article III.

Marshall's response to this argument ranks among the most remarkable passages in the Supreme Court's history:

> [Article III] declares, that "the Judges both of the Supreme and inferior Courts, shall hold their offices during good behaviour." The Judges of the Superior Courts of Florida hold their offices for four years. These Courts, then, are not constitutional Courts, in which the judicial power conferred by the Constitution on the general government, can be deposited. They are incapable of receiving it. They are legislative Courts, created in virtue of the general right of sovereignty which exists in the government, or in virtue of that clause which enables Congress to make all needful rules and regulations, respecting the territory belonging to the United States. The jurisdiction with which they are invested, is not a part of the judicial power which is defined in the 3d article of the Constitution, but is conferred by Congress, in the execution of those general powers which that body possesses over the territories of the United States. Although admiralty jurisdiction can be exercised in the states in those Courts, only, which are established in pursuance of the 3d article of the Constitution; the same limitation does not extend to the territories. In legislating for them, Congress exercises the combined powers of the general, and of a state government.[43]

This discussion extends far beyond the issues raised by the parties. The insurance companies had assumed throughout their argument that a salvage action could have been brought in the territorial superior courts; at no time did they claim that admiralty jurisdiction in the territories could be vested only in federal district courts imbued with tenure and salary guarantees.[44] This was certainly an unwise concession for the insurance companies to have made, for if territorial courts need not conform to all of Article III, it is difficult to explain why they should have to conform to the portions invoked by the insurers. As the parties had framed the case, however, the constitutional validity of the territorial superior courts was simply not at issue, and Marshall's discussion of the point was gratuitous.

It was also rather flagrantly contrary to the clear meaning of the Constitution.[45] Marshall offered no substantial support for his assertion that Congress can create territorial courts that do not conform to Article III. The undenied fact that Congress possesses "the combined powers of the general, and of a state government" when legislating for the territories does not establish that it can exercise those powers without constitutional constraint. State legislatures do not have to follow federal presentment procedures, but that does not mean that Congress can circumvent those procedures when legislating for territories. Similarly, state legislatures can create courts that do not conform to Article III requirements, but Congress cannot do so, whether those courts are created pursuant to the Tribunals Clause, the District Clause, or the Territories Clause. The general jurisdiction conferred on Congress by the District and Territories Clause relieves Congress from the need to tie territorial legislation to one of the enumerated powers elsewhere in the Constitution, but it does not relieve Congress from the need to follow generally applicable constitutional provisions.

Apart from that assertion of congressional power, Marshall's argument amounts to the claim that because the superior court judges were not afforded Article III's tenure guaranty, we might as well let those courts violate Article III's jurisdictional provisions for good measure.

Moreover, as a matter of judicial practice, if Marshall was going to address the constitutional status of the Florida superior courts, he should have given the parties an opportunity to brief the issue. The insurance companies, after all, did not have to concede that the superior courts were constitutionally proper. They would have been delighted by a ruling that neither the Key West court nor any other Florida territorial court had jurisdiction to preside over the sale of their cotton. If alerted to Marshall's plan to address the point, they surely would have resuscitated Samuel Jones's and Judge Cranch's old arguments on the applicability of Article III to territorial tribunals. And if Marshall was worried about the kinds of jurisdictional problems that he had raised in *Seré v Pitot* eighteen years earlier, the insurance companies could have invoked *Osborn* for the proposition that "arising under" jurisdiction would extend to cases brought under territorial laws.[46] Perhaps Marshall would have rejected all of these arguments, but at least he would have had to work for it.

Notwithstanding its analytic defects, *American Insurance Co.* was taken without discussion by the Court nearly half a century later as a general validation of territorial tribunals operating outside the limits of Article III,[47] and the case ever since has wreaked havoc with much of the law of federal jurisdiction. Its culmination came in 1973 in *Palmore v United States*, which held that District of Columbia courts that did not conform to Article III could nonetheless adjudicate criminal cases.[48] That is quite a distance to travel — and entirely in the wrong direction — from the argument and lower court opinion in *United States v More*.

The idea of a federal criminal conviction that results from a trial presided over by a "judge" who does not fit the requirements of Article III is constitutionally bizarre. A territorial official who is not an Article III judge is, by the process of elimination, an executive official. Executive officials can resolve a great many disputes that are also within the purview of the judicial power, but they cannot resolve them all. Some disputes, most notably the dispute between the government and the accused in a criminal trial, are squarely within the constitutional purview of the judicial power, and the text of Article III is very clear about who can exercise that power. Executive officials, of course, can preside over "criminal" trials in occupied territory during wartime, but that is because such proceedings are not really criminal proceedings and they do not take place in territory "belonging to the United States" within the meaning of the Constitution. Rather, they take place in foreign territory pursuant to the laws of war and therefore fall squarely within the executive power's war-making component. But that executive adjudicatory power only operates in occupied foreign territory where the laws of war are in force. The only thing more constitutionally bizarre than executive officials presiding over criminal trials in American territory during peacetime would be *military* executive officials presiding over criminal trials in American territory during peacetime. And that brings us to the next chapter in our story.

6

War and Peace:
Military Occupation and Governance

During wartime, it is possible for the United States to occupy and govern territory that it does not own in any relevant constitutional or international sense. Suppose that during a war with Mexico, American military forces penetrate into Mexican territory. The occupied territory is not "Territory . . . belonging to the United States" within the meaning of the Territories Clause. Congress could not sell or cede the occupied territory to a third country or vest its land in American citizens, at least not until the territory was formally transferred to American sovereignty, usually by a peace treaty after the war. Nonetheless, the United States has both a power and a duty to govern the occupied territory. Military occupation temporarily suspends the political institutions that previously operated within the territory; conquered citizens owe temporary allegiance to their conquerors. The occupying force has an obligation to fill the governmental void left by the (temporary) dissolution of the preexisting political institutions, and it is has the right to deny its enemy any support, material or otherwise, from the occupied area.[1]

Military governance is an aspect of the international laws of war. As a result, the power of the United States to govern occupied territory stems, not from the grants to Congress of power to govern territory that belongs to the United States, but from the provision in Article II granting the President the "executive Power," which includes the power to wage war in accordance with international norms.

The source of the power defines its limits. If the power to govern occupied territory stems from the President's war-making powers, then the termination of war also terminates the power of wartime governance. This principle is simple and basic. And as with many simple and basic constitutional principles, it has had little impact on the actual course of American practice.

That practice is best illustrated by one of the most important cases in American legal history: the Supreme Court's 1854 decision in *Cross v Harrison*.[2] If you have never heard of *Cross v Harrison*, you are in good company. The case is not even cited in the two major treatises on constitutional law.[3] It does not appear in the *Table of Cases* of any of the eight constitutional law casebooks that we surveyed.[4] The relatively few articles that mention *Cross* primarily cite it, often as part of a string-citation, for very general propositions of law.[5] It is fair to describe *Cross v Harrison* as "obscure."

Nonetheless, our assessment of its theoretical significance is not hyperbole. *Cross* involved the constitutionality of the American government in California between May 30, 1848, when the United States acquired the territory, and September 9, 1850, when California was admitted as a state. As we shall see, the facts of the case formally concerned a time period that ended approximately one year before California attained statehood, but the broad issues raised by the case implicate events up to California's admission to the Union. The case raises fundamental questions about the powers of the principal institutions of the national government in times of war and peace — and about the constitutional line between wartime and peacetime governance — that go to the very heart of the American constitutional enterprise. It completes the picture of American territorial governance, and, from an originalist standpoint, the picture is not pretty.

Trouble with Tariffs

Cross v Harrison was a suit brought by Cross, Hobson & Co., a trading firm, against Edward H. Harrison, a federal customs collector in California, for the recovery of tariff duties collected by Harrison between February 3, 1848, and November 12, 1849. The plaintiffs claimed that Harrison had no legal authority to collect the tariffs during all or part of that time. To understand the basis for the suit, one must understand the relevant chronology of events in California and the significance of Harrison's peculiar status.

On May 13, 1846, the United States Congress declared war on Mexico. Shortly thereafter, American forces occupied the area now known as California. By July 1846, American military commanders were proclaiming California as United States territory by virtue of military occupation.[6]

Under universally accepted principles of international law, the successful occupation entitled, and indeed obligated, the United States to set up a provisional military government in California. In early 1847, President Polk instructed the military commanders in California to establish such a government and to collect duties on goods imported into California.[7] It is important to recognize that these "duties" *are not* the kind of duties referenced in Article I, section 8, clause 1 of the Constitution or other constitutional clauses that discuss or limit the power to lay duties.[8] Wartime "duties" imposed in occupied territory are military exactions that are (within the limitations of international law) just as much a part of the war effort as the bombing of enemy positions. Their domestic constitutional authorization does not stem from the congressional taxing power in Article I but from the Article II grant to the President of the war-making power. That power includes the right of the conqueror to impose "duties" on imported goods to help finance its war effort and to maintain its government in the occupied territory.[9] This latter purpose was especially important in California, because the import fees were expected to be the military government's only source of revenue for quite some time.[10] These war tariffs collected by American military personnel in California during the actual hostilities with Mexico were obviously a valid exercise of the President's war powers, and no one in *Cross v Harrison* ever suggested otherwise.

On February 3, 1848, Mexico and the United States signed a treaty of peace that ended the formal hostilities between the nations and also permanently ceded a large territory, including California, to the United States.[11] Ratifications of the treaty were exchanged in Queretaro, Mexico, on May 30, 1848. The military governor of California formally announced the ratification of the peace treaty to the people of the territory on August 7, 1848.[12]

Obviously, there could be no war tariff if there was no war. Any "duties" levied after the end of the war had to be imposed pursuant to the normal peacetime taxing powers of Congress. The military officials in California fully recognized this fact. On August 9, 1848, two days after the formal announcement in California of the peace treaty, the secretary of state of the military government notified Harrison's predecessor as the customs collector in San Francisco that "the tariff of duties for the collection of military contributions will immediately cease, and the revenue laws and tariff of the United States will be substituted in its place."[13] The California government then applied the congressionally enacted, generally applicable tariff schedules to goods imported into California.

Harrison was appointed temporary collector by the governor of California on September 3, 1848. On February 23, 1849, Harrison demanded $105.62 in duties from Cross, Hobson & Co. in order for them to land their goods in San Francisco. The company paid the duties under protest. On March 3, 1849, Congress formally extended its tariff laws to California and authorized the appointment of a customs collector for San Francisco.[14] On November 13, 1849, Harrison was replaced as collector by James Collier. No objection was made to any tariffs collected by Collier on or after November 13, 1849.

During the fall of 1849, a convention was held in California to draft a constitution in anticipation of statehood. The constitution was ratified on December 12, 1849, and the military authorities at that point gave effective control of the territory to the civilian authorities acting under that constitution. On September 9, 1850, Congress admitted California as a state.[15]

In 1851, Cross, Hobson & Co. sued to recover all of the tariffs collected by Mr. Harrison and by his predecessor dating from February 3, 1848, to November 13, 1849, when Collier relieved Harrison as the customs collector.

This simple time line omits some essential embellishments. Most significantly, Harrison was "appointed" as customs collector of San Francisco by Colonel R. B. Mason, who was governor of California during the military occupation. Mason held his position as "Governor" solely by virtue of the President's power to administer occupied territory during wartime.[16] Harrison's "appointment" by Mason took place, however, more than three months after the exchange of treaty ratifications that ended the war. Even if one allows for the slowness of communications in the mid-nineteenth century,[17] Harrison was "appointed" by "Governor" Mason nearly a month after Mason had formally announced to the people of California, by proclamation, the ratifications of the peace treaty. Where did a military commander get the authority to appoint a military customs collector during a time of peace? And where did a military officer get the authority to collect peacetime federal customs duties without congressional authorization?

The constitutional answer would seem pretty clearly to be "nowhere." The constitutional authorization for a military government stems, as we have noted, from the President's executive power as commander-in-chief of the armed forces. Once the war is over, however, the occupied territory, in accordance with the treaty of peace, will either be ceded to the United States or not. If it is not, and the territory has been returned to its previous sovereign or has become an independent state, then the United States has no more power to govern it and to collect tariffs than it would in any foreign country. If the occupied territory is ceded to the United States, then it becomes territory belonging to the United States. At that point, the constitutional rules for governance shift.

Article IV of the Constitution, as we have repeatedly seen, provides that "[t]he *Congress* shall have Power to dispose of and make all needful Rules and Regulations respecting the Territory or other Property belonging to the United States." During peacetime, in other words, the Constitution grants to Congress and not the President the power to govern American territory. Importantly, the normal constitutional rules on delegation of legislative authority do not apply to the power to administer territories, so Congress may choose to exercise its power by legislatively micromanaging territorial affairs, by giving executive officials virtually complete authority in the territory, or (under long-settled, if erroneous, doctrine) by giving territories a substantial measure of self-governance through elected territorial legislatures (assuming that one can finesse the problems with such arrangements posed by the Appointments Clause). But in any case the power to govern, in whomever it is ultimately vested, must originate in a congressional statute enacted pursuant to Article IV. Similarly, the authority to impose customs duties in peacetime lies exclusively with Congress; the President can no more impose a peacetime tariff than he can create a bankruptcy code or admit a state.

Congress, however, never got around to passing a statute for the governance of California — not even a statute that authorized the President to continue in place the wartime military government. On a more mundane doctrinal level, Colonel Mason, as the chief executive of a large federal territory, was surely a principal officer within the meaning of Article II's Appointments Clause, which means that he could validly serve as the civil governor only if he was nominated by the President and confirmed by the Senate for that post. Mason, of course, was never formally nominated by the President and confirmed by the Senate for the post of governor of California.[18] Accordingly, after the termination of hostilities, there would appear to be no authority for "Governor" Mason or any of his subordinates to act as officials of California, and Harrison's appointment as "collector" is therefore equally suspect.[19] Indeed, there would appear to be no constitutional authority for any kind of American-led government in California in the absence of a congressionally enacted organic statute.[20]

Colonel Mason worried about this problem as much as anyone. On August 14, 1848, he wrote a letter to the Department of War which read:

> For the past two years no civil government has existed here, save that controlled by the senior military or naval officer; and no civil officers exist in the country, save the alcades appointed or confirmed by myself. To throw off upon them or the people at large the civil management and control of the country, would most probably lead to endless confusions, if not to absolute anarchy; *and yet what right or authority have I to exercise civil control in time of peace in a Territory of the United States?* . . . Yet . . . I feel compelled to

exercise control over the alcades appointed, and to maintain order, if possible, in the country, until a civil governor arrive, armed with instructions and laws to guide his footsteps.

In like manner, if all customs were withdrawn, and the ports thrown open free to the world, San Francisco would be made the depot of all the foreign goods in the north Pacific, to the injury of our revenue and the interests of our own merchants. To prevent this great influx of foreign goods into the country duty free, I feel it my duty to attempt the collection of duties according to the United States Tariff of 1846. This will render it necessary for me to appoint temporary collectors, &c., in the several ports of entry, for the military force is too much reduced to attend to those duties.

I am fully aware that, in taking these steps, I have no further authority than that the existing government must necessarily continue until some other is organized to take its place, for I have been left without any definite instructions in reference to the existing state of affairs. But the calamities and disorders which would surely follow the absolute withdrawal of even a show of authority, impose on me, in my opinion, the imperative duty to pursue the course I have indicated, until the arrival of despatches from Washington (which I hope are already on their way) relative to the organization of a regular civil government.[21]

On October 7, 1848, the Secretary of State of the United States directly addressed the problem of congressional inaction concerning a government for California. His remarkable comments (of which we will say much more later) deserve to be quoted at length:

The President, in his annual message, at the commencement of the next session, will recommend all these great measures to Congress in the strongest terms, and will use every effort, consistent with his duty, to insure their accomplishment.

In the mean time, the condition of the people of California is anomalous, and will require, on their part, the exercise of great prudence and discretion. By the conclusion of the Treaty of Peace, the military government which was established over them under the laws of war, as recognized by the practice of all civilized nations, has ceased to derive its authority from this source of power. But is there, for this reason, no government in California? Are life, liberty, and property under the protection of no existing authorities? This would be a singular phenomenon in the face of the world, and especially among American citizens, distinguished as they are above all other people for their law-abiding character. Fortunately, they are not reduced to this sad condition. The termination of the war left an existing government, a government *de facto*, in full operation, and this will continue, with the presumed consent of the people, until Congress shall provide for them a territorial government. The great law of necessity justifies this conclusion. The consent of the people is irresistibly inferred from the fact that no civilized community could possibly desire to abrogate an existing government, when the alternative presented would be to place themselves in a state of anarchy, beyond the protection of all laws, and reduce them to the unhappy necessity of submitting to the dominion of the strongest.

This government *de facto* will, of course, exercise no power inconsistent with the provisions of the Constitution of the United States, which is the supreme law of the land. For this reason no import duties can be levied in California on articles the growth, produce, or manufacture of the United States, as no such duties can be imposed in any other part of our Union on the productions of California. Nor can new duties be charged in California upon such foreign productions as have already paid duties in any of our ports of entry, for the obvious reason that California is within the territory of the United States. I shall not enlarge upon this subject, however, as the Secretary of the Treasury will perform that duty.[22]

This was the backdrop of the lawsuit to recover the duties imposed by "Collector" Harrison. The trial court essentially instructed the jury to find for the government, which it did, and the case went to the Supreme Court.

Avoiding Anachronism

The stakes in *Cross v Harrison* ran much higher than a year-and-a-half's worth of customs duties paid by Cross, Hobson & Co. Obviously, if Harrison had no legal authority to act in an official capacity, neither did anyone else in the postwar California "government." If that "government" in fact had no legal authorization under the laws and Constitution of the United States, then all of the actions taken by its "officials" that amounted to ordinary private law violations could give rise to liability and private law remedies, such as damages. In addition, any actions of the military government that affected private rights, such as the adjudication of land titles, would come under a cloud. A holding that, for any relevant period of time, there was no legal authorization for the military government in California would have potentially staggering consequences.

In similar circumstances today, lawyers would immediately hone in on two issues that might well dispose of the case in short order, or at least would severely mitigate the effects of a holding against the legality of the military government: (1) official immunity and (2) various doctrines that are used to legitimate the actions of de facto government officials. These doctrines permit judgment in favor of defendants even when the defendants act without legal authorization. If *Cross* was decided today, the question of the constitutionality vel non of the military regime would clearly take a back seat to these "threshold" issues. Indeed, in all likelihood, the constitutional issues would never be reached.

Such defenses were not decisive in 1854, however, because they did not then exist, at least not in the form in which we are accustomed to them today. In order to understand the issues in *Cross*, one must avoid looking at the case through the lens of modern doctrines that had no applicability in 1854 (or, more to the point for originalists, in 1788).

OFFICIAL IMMUNITY

Cross v Harrison was not a suit against the United States or the territorial government of California. Any suit against the United States or its instrumentalities would have been flatly barred by the doctrine of sovereign immunity, which was well established by 1848. There were no statutes at that time generally waiving sovereign immunity for such claims.[23] Any relief from the government itself would have had to come from a private bill enacted by Congress specifically authorizing payment to the plaintiff.

The plaintiff instead sued Harrison, the customs collector, in his personal capacity. The claim was a straightforward action of assumpsit for the return of moneys improperly collected.[24] If the plaintiff won, the judgment would run against Harrison personally, though the United States would be free, if it so wanted, to indemnify Harrison against damages either before or after the entry of judgment.

Today, the first inquiry in such a case would be whether the defendant, a government official, was entitled to qualified immunity, meaning that liability could be imposed only if the defendant violated a "clearly established" legal norm.[25] Because the constitutionality of a peacetime military government had not been specifically settled before *Cross*, one can imagine a court holding that Mason, Harrison, et al. did not violate a constitutional norm that was "clearly established" in 1848 within the meaning of the qualified immunity doctrine (though one can also imagine a court saying that the unconstitutionality of the military government was so blatant that anyone could see it). The doctrine of official immunity, however, is a distinctly modern phenomenon. In the mid-nineteenth century, official status was no defense at all to a suit for damages. Official status worked as a defense only if the defendant *was in fact validly authorized to take the action in question*. In the absence of actual legal authorization, to be determined by a court and/or jury without deference to the views of the government, the defendant stood before the law as an ordinary person. A good faith belief in legal authorization counted for nothing.[26]

The correctness of that doctrine is a story for another day. For now, all we can say is that official immunity must be viewed in the context of other doctrines that limit or permit recovery for governmental wrongs: a baseline of governmental accountability, which we think can be established on originalist grounds, does not necessarily require any one specific *mechanism* of accountability. A relaxation of the doctrine of sovereign immunity might permit a concomitant tightening up of the doctrine of official immunity. We plan to explore these questions in a subsequent work. In the case of *Cross*, if the issue had arisen, we think that the correct outcome would have been to find no official immunity because there was no other formal mechanism of governmental accountability in place. A private lawsuit against the offending government officer was the proper way — and the only way — to vindicate in court a private-law wrong that resulted from official action. Under that regime, Collector Harrison would have needed to show actual, valid legal authorization for his action. Otherwise, he had committed a simple act of extortion. Harrison's good faith belief in his legal authorization would surely shield him from criminal liability for his conduct, but because the action of assumpsit does not require a bad motive, nothing would shield him from civil liability for monies that he unlawfully took from the plaintiff. Perhaps the United States would indemnify a defendant such as Harrison under those circumstances and perhaps not. But that would not be the concern of the law. Thus Harrison probably did not raise an official immunity defense because there was no such defense to raise in 1854.

DE FACTO OFFICER

Another obvious modern response to the lawsuit in *Cross* would be to say that even if the California government was unconstitutional, it was acting under color of law. People residing in California would reasonably believe that they were obliged to obey the government's officials and were therefore entitled to rely on that obedience. Perhaps the government could, in some formal sense, be declared unconstitutional, but surely that should not undo everything that happened while it was acting with apparent authority. The formal expression for this commonsense view is the de facto officer doctrine.

The de facto officer doctrine has been around for more than five hundred years. In its simplest form, it legally validates the acts of a government official who illegally holds office, provided that the officer "is in fact in the unobstructed possession of an office and discharging its duties in full view of the public, in such manner and under such circumstances as not to present the appearance of being an intruder or usurper."[27] The effect, and purpose, of the doctrine is to prevent technical defects in an officer's title, such as a clerical error or a failure to post a required bond, from having potentially disastrous effects on settled legal rights.[28] For example, in *McDowell v United States*,[29] a circuit judge had designated Augustus S. Seymour, a North Carolina district

judge, to serve temporarily in the district of South Carolina. There were serious questions about the circuit judge's ability to make this designation under
the relevant statutes. The plaintiff was convicted and sentenced by Judge Seymour while the judge was sitting in South Carolina, and the plaintiff challenged those rulings on the ground that Judge Seymour lacked authority to
issue them. The Court held that, regardless of the formal legality of his designation, Judge Seymour was a de facto judge while serving in South Carolina
whose decisions could not be challenged. This de facto officer doctrine seems
tailor made for a case like *Cross v Harrison*, in which persons with questionable authorization acted in the role of government officials.

There are several problems with applying the de facto officer doctrine to
Cross. First, and most obviously, the Supreme Court had not formally recognized the doctrine in 1854. It had applied the doctrine in dictum in 1842,[30] but
the doctrine was not developed in holdings until late in the nineteenth century.

Second, and more fundamentally, even had the doctrine applied in 1854,
Harrison would not have satisfied its formal requirements. The de facto officer
doctrine is designed to address technical defects in officeholding. The problem
with Harrison was not a technical defect in his appointment (such as, for
example, the lack of a quorum during Senate confirmation), but the fact that
his "office" was putatively illegal. There was no statute creating the office of
customs collector in California until November 3, 1849, and there was certainly no statute creating the office of "person who calls himself a customs
collector but who really is collecting military exactions under a military government, albeit one that is operating during peacetime." The real question in
the case concerned the legitimacy of Harrison's office itself, not the specific
qualifications of the officeholder. Indeed, within a few decades of *Cross*, the
Supreme Court was to hold that the de facto officer doctrine cannot be applied
when the statute creating the office in question is unconstitutional: there can
be no de facto officer if there is no office to hold de facto.[31] That holding has
been widely criticized,[32] but those criticisms are based on a conflation of the de
facto officer doctrine with other, related concepts concerning de facto authority. One who seeks to defend Harrison on these general grounds needs to say,
not simply that one can have de facto officers, but that one can also have de
facto offices, which is a very different claim. What is needed to make a case like
Cross v Harrison go away quietly is a doctrine of de facto government.

DE FACTO GOVERNMENT

In his letter of October 7, 1848, Secretary of State James Buchanan
specifically referred to the California military authorities as a "de facto government." Was this label accurate, and did it shield the actions of that government from legal scrutiny?

As an introduction to these questions, it is useful to examine two cases that are sandwiched in time around *Cross*, and whose fame is as great as *Cross*'s obscurity: *Luther v Borden*[33] and *Texas v White*.[34]

Luther v Borden was decided in 1849, just a few years before the argument and decision in *Cross*. The case arose out of a civil war in Rhode Island in 1841–42. Rhode Island had been governed since 1663 by the charter granted by Charles II. In 1841, however, a group of Rhode Island citizens took it upon themselves to hold a constitutional convention and to form a government under their new constitution. They declared the adoption and ratification of the new constitution, elected and appointed officers of the new government, and asked the established charter government to step aside. The charter government instead declared martial law and effectively prevented the new "government" from exercising power. The charter government did, however, sponsor and sanction another constitutional convention in January 1842, which resulted in yet another constitution. In May 1843, the charter government voluntarily disbanded in favor of a government that was formed under the 1842 constitution.

The plaintiff was a supporter of the government that proclaimed itself under the 1841 constitution. During the period of martial law, the defendants, purportedly acting under the authority of the charter government, entered the plaintiff's house without permission and sought to arrest him. The plaintiff sued for trespass. If the charter government had ceased to have any legal authority upon the formation of new government in 1841, then there was no actual authorization for the defendants' actions and there would be no obvious defense to the plaintiff's trespass action. If the charter government continued to have authority, however, then the question would become whether that authority was sufficient to immunize the defendants' actions from civil liability. Thus the Supreme Court was called upon to determine whether the charter government or the 1841 constitutional government was the rightful authority in Rhode Island in 1842.

The Court was acutely aware of the potential stakes in the case:

> For, if this court is authorized to enter upon this inquiry as proposed by the plaintiff, and it should be decided that the charter government had no legal existence during the period of time above mentioned, — if it had been annulled by the adoption of the opposing government, — then the laws passed by its legislature during that time were nullities; its taxes wrongfully collected; its salaries and compensation to its officers illegally paid; its public accounts improperly settled; and the judgments and sentences of its courts in civil and criminal cases null and void, and the officers who carried their decisions into operation answerable as trespassers, if not in some cases as criminals.[35]

The Court sided with the charter government. Everyone agreed that the Rhode Island courts that held office under the May 1843 constitution were legally valid, and those courts had clearly treated the charter government as the valid authority during the period of conflict by, inter alia, upholding convictions of persons who raised as a defense their purported authority under the constitution of 1841. The Court held that the federal courts were bound by the determinations of state courts concerning the legitimacy of their own governments.[36] The Court was, however, worried enough about this question to bolster its primary holding with a variety of other arguments, including perceived evidentiary problems, the awkwardness of potentially differing pronouncements on governmental legitimacy from different courts, and a lengthy dictum on the limited role of courts under Article IV's Guarantee Clause.[37] The Court was obviously uncomfortable deciding the issue of authority, but it reached a decision nonetheless.

How, one might ask, could the Court have done anything other than decide the issue in one way or another? One can imagine, however, the Court issuing the following opinion:

> We frankly don't care whether the charter government or the 1841 constitutional government was the "real" government in 1842. Whether or not the charter government was lawful, it was *at least* a de facto government. It existed, with unquestioned de jure authority, prior to 1842 and it never clearly relinquished power until 1843. Had the 1841 constitutional government succeeded in its attempted overthrow for some period of time, it would be an interesting question whether it could also qualify during that period as a de facto government, but the 1841 constitutional government never had enough raw power to pose that question. In any event, even if the 1841 constitutional government was the de jure government of Rhode Island, the actions of the charter government had enough appearance of authority to clothe its officials with whatever immunity governmental status provides. Our question is now whether that governmental status, under the state of martial law declared by the government, was enough to defeat the plaintiff's trespass action.

Such a holding would have neatly solved all of the problems that the Court in *Luther* found so troubling.[38] Nonetheless, the Court did not adopt any theory of de facto governmental authorization to dispose of the case.

Twenty years later, however, matters were a bit different. Prior to the outbreak of the Civil War, the State of Texas had acquired certain bonds from the United States. The law of Texas at that time required the endorsement of the state governor before the bonds could be negotiated. When the rebel government took control in Texas during the war, it repealed the statute requiring the governor's endorsement and it used the bonds to acquire supplies. After the war, the State of Texas, through the Reconstruction government imposed by Congress and the President, sought recovery of the bonds on the ground that the absence of a proper endorsement from the governor rendered them non-negotiable and voided all transfers, including the initial transfer from the state treasury. The suit was an original bill in the Supreme Court, pursuant to the clauses in Article III extending federal jurisdiction to "controversies . . . between a State and citizens of another State" and granting the Supreme Court original jurisdiction over cases "in which a State shall be a Party."

In *Texas v White*, decided fifteen years after *Cross*, the Court held that Texas was a "State" for purposes of these jurisdictional clauses, notwithstanding its purported secession, its governance by federal officials, and its lack of representation in the Congress and the electoral college.[39] We are not concerned here with whether that holding was correct. Our focus is on the action of the rebel government in purporting to alter the manner in which the bonds could be negotiated. If that statute was valid, then Texas should have lost on the merits. If the act of secession was, as the Court held, illegal, then the legislature of the rebel government was not a de jure legislative body. But could its enactments nonetheless have legal force as the acts of a de facto government? The Court acknowledged that the rebel government of Texas was "[to some extent] a de facto government, and its acts, during the period of its existence as such, would be effectual, and, in almost all respects, valid."[40] The Court in 1869 thus expressly endorsed the concept of a de facto government whose actions could create binding legal rights even without de jure authority.

Well, almost. An unqualified holding to this effect would, as noted, mean that Texas should have lost the case. The Court's next task was to explain why the repealing act was different from all other acts:

> It is not necessary to attempt any exact definitions, within which the acts of such a State government must be treated as valid, or invalid. It may be said, perhaps with sufficient accuracy, that acts necessary to peace and good order among citizens, such for example, as acts sanctioning and protecting marriage and the domestic relations, governing the course of descents, regulating the conveyance and transfer of property, real and personal, and providing remedies for injuries to person and estate, and other similar acts, which would be valid if emanating from a lawful government, must be regarded in general as valid when proceeding from an actual, though unlawful government; and that acts in furtherance or support of rebellion against the United States, or intended to defeat the just rights of citizens, and other acts of like nature, must, in general, be regarded as invalid and void.[41]

In other words, good acts are valid and bad acts are not. Applying this standard, the Court held that allowing the negotiability of the bonds in order to finance the war effort was a bad act and therefore invalid.

Which view is right: the implicit view in *Luther* that only de jure authority will validate a government or the explicit view in *White* that de facto authority is generally (or at least often) good enough? The recognition of de facto authority, especially at the federal level, is very troublesome. The whole point — the revolutionary point — of the federal Constitution was to create a government of limited and enumerated powers. No federal institution is supposed to be able to act without constitutional authorization. That scheme can be seriously undermined by the existence of a "shadow government" that exists without legal authorization but whose acts are nonetheless binding. A "de facto federal authority" is almost a contradiction in terms. Moreover, as *Texas v White* demonstrates, once one lets in the notion of a de facto authority, one must face the unenviable task of figuring exactly how far that authority goes. Does de facto authority legitimate everything that the illegal government does, or perhaps everything that a legitimate government in the place of the illegitimate government would have done? This last alternative raises hopeless conceptual and practical problems. For example, although we have not researched the point, we are confident that the rebel government in Texas altered the tax structure in ways that helped finance the Confederate war effort. Were those laws therefore invalid under the test of *Texas v White* because a loyalist state government would not have enacted them?

On the other hand, the de facto government doctrine conforms to a powerful intuition that says that private rights, at least, should not be thrown into jeopardy because of political disputes beyond the control of most citizens. Should marriages and land titles be held invalid because the only government available to register them was not a legitimate de jure government? Should murderers go free because the judges who sentenced them did not have the proper legal authorization?

A full answer, as is true with many of the themes addressed in this book, would require a separate, lengthy treatment. The key, however, is to place the de facto government doctrine where it belongs: as part of the law of remedies. De facto authorization is not legal authorization no matter how it is analyzed, so the actions of a de facto authority (at least at the federal level) can never count as a valid source of substantive law. The question is what legal consequences to attach to that fact when the absence of real authority affects legal rights. When the relief sought by a party is equitable, there is no conceptual problem with saying that the existence of de facto legal authorization for challenged governmental conduct could and should be relevant to the decision whether to grant relief. Equitable relief, after all, is normally discretionary, and it is natural to make concerns about de facto authorization part of that equitable balance in an appropriate case.[42] The hard questions come when a party seeks damages in an ordinary action at law and the validity vel non of a governmental act is relevant to the claim. No act of discretionary balancing is required for an award of damages. Where, if anywhere, do courts get the remedial power to refuse to award damages because of essentially equitable concerns about reliance on de facto governmental acts?

At the federal level, the question reduces to: does "[t]he judicial Power of the United States" include some power to overlook de jure illegalities in cases seeking damages? Our very hesitant, and somewhat unsatisfying, answer turns on the currently unpopular distinction between public and private rights. Where an action for damages concerns essentially private rights, which the government merely administers, there is much to be said for overlooking technical defects in the administering authority under some circumstances. Where, however, the case involves public rights, which would not exist but for the machinery of government, de facto authority is irrelevant.

The reasons for this distinction would have been clearer to a 1788 observer than to a modern observer. To a fully informed 1788 observer, private rights, such as rights of property and contract, exist independently of the government; the government is there, if at all, only to facilitate and regularize transactions. As long as the governmental activity in question essentially formalizes the kinds of transactions that parties would otherwise engage in, it is not bizarrely counterfactual to presume that matters would have turned out much the same even if the (assumedly) illegal governmental authority had not been in control, which raises questions as to whether the illegality actually "caused" any harm in a legal sense. That presumption could be overcome by showing, for example, that the illegal government changed the legal rules so dramatically that the assumption of a continuous baseline is no longer valid. But in the normal course of events, private rights should not suffer because a de facto authority signs the papers. No harm, no foul.

Where the de facto authority acts in a public capacity and creates rather than enforces the legal rules, however, matters are different. We do not have the time or space here to detail exactly how far this category of public rights extends,[43] nor do we need to do so here. The tariffs collected by Harrison in *Cross v Harrison* are very clearly in this public category. Indeed, they are quintessentially the kind of action that exists only because of the presence of a governmental authority. Thus, even if one was inclined to apply a doctrine of de facto authority in *Cross* — and, judging by its decision in *Luther v Borden* in 1849, the Court in the early 1850s was not so inclined — it would not obviate the need to decide *Cross* on the merits.

One more point bears mention. In order to qualify as a de facto government on any theory, the government in question must be in a position to expect and command obedience from the public. That was clearly true of the rebel government in Texas in 1861. It was probably true of the charter government in Rhode Island in 1842. Whether it was true of the military government in California in 1848 is a different question altogether, which we will later address.

Anarchy, State, and Myopia

The Supreme Court in *Cross* affirmed the lower court's judgment in favor of Harrison, finding that all of the duties were properly collected. Because the case turns on the extent to which changes in events also change the legal status of various actors, it is best analyzed in terms of discrete time periods. The plaintiff broke down the case into two principal time periods: (1) between the date of the signing of the peace treaty between the United States and Mexico (February 3, 1848) and the enactment by Congress of a statute making San Francisco a collection district under the generally applicable tariff laws (March 3, 1849) and (2) between the latter date and the replacement of Harrison as a customs collector (November 13, 1849). This reflected the plaintiff's principal theory of the case: although the plaintiff broadly challenged the power of the military government to collect even statutorily imposed tariffs during peacetime, its principal contention was that tariff laws did not apply to California until Congress specifically extended them by statute. This was not a surprising litigation strategy. If the statutory argument was successful, plaintiff had a sure winner on all tariffs up to March 3, 1849. And the plaintiff was no doubt leery — and justifiably so — of its prospects of prevailing on a broad-based challenge to the authority of the California military government. The plaintiff's breakdown of the case to accommodate its statutory argument, however, obscures some of the most important constitutional issues. Accordingly, the Court broke down the relevant time periods along somewhat different lines, as we do as well. Because this case largely involves the consequences of war and peace, a better temporal breakdown focuses on the events surrounding the conduct and termination of the war.

MAY 13, 1846–MAY 30, 1848: THE WAR IS ON

The Court in *Cross* spent a fair amount of energy establishing the obvious: the war tariffs collected by the military government in California during the period of actual hostilities prior to the signing of the peace treaty on February 3, 1848, were valid.[44] No one ever claimed otherwise, least of all Cross, Hobson & Co. Its complaint only sought the return of tariffs collected after February 3, 1848, which marked the signing of the peace treaty between the United States and Mexico.

The first real question posed by the case was at what point the legal authorization for the wartime tariff ended so that Harrison's exactions could be justified, if at all, only by peacetime tariff laws. As long as the wartime tariff was valid, Cross, Hobson & Co. clearly had no claim. So how long could the war tariff really last?

There are at least five possible answers to that question: the authority for the war tariff might have ended when (1) the treaty of peace was signed on February 3, 1848, (2) when ratifications of the treaty were formally exchanged between the United States and Mexico on May 30, 1848, (3) whenever the treaty itself declared a full end to the war and its legal consequences, (4) when official notification of the ratifications was actually given to American personnel in California,[45] or (5) when official notification of the ratifications should reasonably have been given to American personnel in California given the constraints of communications that existed in 1848.[46]

The plaintiff could prevail for the time period before May 30, 1848, only if the first answer was correct. The Court held that the terms of the peace treaty made clear that that answer was wrong and that authority for the war tariff therefore continued at least until ratifications of the treaty were exchanged on May 30, 1848:

> Nothing is stipulated in that treaty to be binding upon the parties to it, or from the date of the signature of the treaty, but that commissioners should be appointed by the general-in-chief of the forces of the United States, with such as might be appointed by the Mexican government, to make a provisional suspension of hostilities, that, in the places occupied by our arms, constitutional order might be reestablished as regards the political, administrative, and judicial branches in those places, so far as that might be permitted by the circumstances of military occupation. All else was contingent until the ratifications of the treaty were exchanged, which was done on the 30th of May, 1848, at Queretaro.[47]

The Court was entirely correct; the treaty itself stipulated that it would take full effect only upon ratification by both parties.[48] Accordingly, the war tariff remained in effect at least until May 30, 1848, and all "duties" collected before that date were legally valid as military exactions.

MAY 30, 1848–AUGUST 9, 1848: THE WAR IS . . . ?

The time period from May 30, 1848, to the notification to California officials and residents of the peace treaty in August 1848 is more problematic. The obvious answer is that peace means peace, so that the authority of the military government expired immediately upon the formal cessation of the state of war on May 30. That was clearly the magic moment under international law. California became the property of the United States on May 30, 1848, so as far as the world at large was concerned, California was no longer a site on which war was being waged. At that point, the norms of international law concerning government of occupied territory ceased to apply to California, because it was no longer occupied; it was thereafter subject to the full, undivided sovereignty of the United States.

The pertinent question, however, is whether May 30, 1848, was the magic moment under domestic American law. The answer has large consequences. Channels of communication in 1848 were hardly instantaneous. It could take weeks or months for news of the termination (or commencement) of a war to reach across a continent. Even today, with near-instantaneous forms of communication, there will always be some time lag, however modest, between events and knowledge of those events. If the end of a war carries domestic legal consequences, can those consequences really take effect the moment that the war, as a matter of public international law, formally ends? Does it really make sense to say that constitutional authority operates, or disappears, instantaneously across the world, even where it is impossible for news of the relevant events to travel that fast? Put starkly, when did the Mexican-American "War," as a matter of domestic American law, really end?

Nations had faced these problems for centuries before *Cross v Harrison*, and their solutions are instructive. Although it is possible that a war could end, as a matter of international law, without a formal treaty of peace,[49] a treaty is the normal means of formalizing the termination a war. But ending a war via a peace treaty means more than simply signing a piece of paper declaring that fighting should stop. The news of the treaty needs to be sent to the troops that are actually engaged in combat. In the premodern era, this could easily take weeks or months. What happens during that transitional period? Are the soldiers who are still engaged in conflict reduced to the status of vandals and murderers — or at the very least tortfeasors — because their authority to engage in war has formally ended?

In the normal course of events, these matters are handled in the peace treaty. A well-drafted treaty will include realistic timetables for notification and withdrawal of troops and will contain provisions for immunizing the soldiers and their governments from liability for damage inflicted before news of the peace can reach them (and perhaps will also contain provisions for compensation to the citizens and governments that suffer such damage). The end of the "war," in the extended sense that includes the post-treaty period of transition, will thus normally be determined by reference to the treaty.

The Treaty of Guadalupe Hidalgo that terminated (or initiated the termination) of the Mexican-American War paid very close attention to these issues. The treaty was signed by the parties on February 2, 1848, and ratifications were exchanged on May 30, 1848. The treaty was quite specific about the timetable for implementing the peace agreement. Article III of the treaty stipulated that "[i]mmediately" upon the exchange of ratifications,

> orders shall be transmitted to the commanders of [the United States'] land and naval forces, requiring the latter . . . immediately to desist from blockading any Mexican ports; and requiring the former . . . to commence, at the earliest moment practicable, withdrawing all troops of the United States then in the interior of the Mexican Republic, to points that shall be selected by common agreement, at a distance from the seaports not exceeding thirty leagues; and such evacuation of the interior of the Republic shall be completed with the least possible delay; the Mexican Government hereby binding itself to afford every facility in its power for rendering the same convenient to the troops, on their march and in their new positions, and for promoting a good understanding between them and the inhabitants.[50]

Orders were also supposed to go out immediately to all United States personnel in charge of customs houses to return control of the facilities to Mexican authorities and to provide an accounting of all duties collected after May 30, 1848, which (minus the costs of collection) were to be turned over to Mexico.[51] Even more specifically, removal of American troops from the capital of Mexico "shall be completed in one month after the orders there stipulated for shall have been received by the commander of said troops, or sooner if possible."[52] Article IV of the treaty further provided that "immediately after the exchange of ratifications of the present treaty all castles, forts, territories, places, and possessions, which have been taken or occupied by the forces of the United States during the present war, within the limits of the Mexican Republic . . . , shall be definitively restored to the said Republic."[53] Finally, and most significantly, Article IV specified that "[t]he final evacuation of the territory of the Mexican Republic, by the forces of the United States, shall be completed in three months from the said exchange of ratifications, or sooner if possible."[54] The treaty thus specified the time at which the final effects of the war, and therefore the war itself in its broadest sense, shall end: August 30, 1848, or sooner if the United States could get its troops out more quickly. Until that time, one could plausibly say that the state of war, and whatever powers flowed to various agencies of the United States government from that state of affairs, was still in existence.

At least, one could say that with respect to issues concerning American troops in what was to remain Mexico after the treaty. But just as constitutions and statutes can become effective in stages, there is no reason to assume that every provision of a treaty must take effect, or every aspect of a war must end, at the same moment in time. Article V of the treaty ceded to the United States a vast amount of territory, including the territory that now comprises the State of California. The treaty said nothing specific about the timing of the transfer of sovereignty from Mexico to the United States, so the natural assumption is that the transfer was immediate upon completion of the ratifications. That is the standard rule at international law, and the Supreme Court had expressly applied that rule just a few years before *Cross* in *United States v Reynes*,[55] in connection with the series of transfers of Louisiana from Spain to France to the United States in the early 1800s. As the Court explained in refusing to give effect to a purported Spanish land grant within the territory made after the various treaties concerning Louisiana were exchanged: "In the construction of treaties, the same rules which govern other compacts properly apply. They must be considered as binding from the period of their execution; their operation must be understood to take effect from that period, unless it shall, by some condition or stipulation in the compact itself, be postponed."[56] Nothing in the Treaty of Guadalupe Hidalgo suggests any delay in the transfer of sovereignty over California. Quite to the contrary, provisions in the treaty dealing with the status of Mexican residents in the transferred territory and with the United States' obligation to prevent Indian incursions into Mexico[57] seem to assume an immediate transfer. Secretary of State Buchanan flatly declared that "the constitution of the United States, the safeguard of all our civil rights, was extended over California on the 30th May, 1848, the day on which our late treaty with Mexico was finally consummated. From that day its inhabitants became entitled to all the blessings and benefits resulting from the best form of civil government ever established amongst men."[58] The Supreme Court in *Cross* took it for granted that the cession of territory became effective upon the exchange of ratifications.[59] Thus California became the property of the United States on May 30, 1848. The treaty did not have to make provision for the removal of American troops from that territory because the territory no longer belonged to Mexico. Thus the treaty's extension of some measure of American wartime authority into the territory of Mexico did not serve to extend American wartime authority into American territory.

Does that mean that the war ended, as far as California is concerned, on May 30, 1848? If the answer is yes, then the authority for the military tariff in California ended on that date as well, though such authority held by military commanders on the Mexican mainland might well continue for some time, subject to the treaty's requirement that the proceeds from such "tariffs" ultimately go to the Mexican government.

That straightforward answer is hard to avoid. As noted above, the treaty contained careful terms for dealing with certain items beyond the May 30, 1848, exchange of ratifications but made no such time-specific provisions for the transfer of sovereignty of California. The inescapable conclusion is that, as far as California was concerned, the war was over on May 30, 1848.

The Supreme Court escaped the conclusion nonetheless. Its discussion bears quotation in full:

> [A]fter the ratification of the treaty, California became a part of the United States, or a ceded, conquered territory. Our inquiry here is to be, whether or not the cession gave any right to the plaintiffs to have the duties restored to them, which they may have paid between the ratifications and exchange of the treaty and the notification of that fact by our government to the military governor of California. It was not received by him until two months after the ratification, and not then with any instructions or even remote intimation from the President that the civil and military government, which had been instituted during the war, was discontinued. Up to that time, whether such an intimation had or had not been given, duties had been collected under the war tariff, strictly in conformity with the instructions which had been received from Washington.
>
> *It will certainly not be denied that those instructions were binding upon those who administered the civil government in California, until they had notice from their own government that a peace had been finally concluded. Or that those who were locally within its jurisdiction, or who had property there, were not bound to comply with those regulations of the government, which its functionaries were ordered to execute.* Or that any one could claim a right to introduce into the territory of that government foreign merchandise, without the payment of duties which had been originally imposed under belligerent rights, because the territory had been ceded by the original possessor and enemy to the conqueror. . . . The plaintiffs in this case could claim no privilege for the introduction of their goods into San Francisco between the ratifications of the treaty with Mexico and the official annunciation of it to the civil government in California, other than such as that government permitted under the instructions of the government of the United States.[60]

With all due respect, the phrase "It will certainly not be denied" is an unconvincing argument even when it is printed in the pages of the United States Reports. The plaintiff in *Cross* certainly denied it with vigor, and the force of reason seems entirely on the plaintiff's side. It is true that the authorities in California could not possibly have known on May 30, 1848, that their legal authority had just vanished, but, as the saying goes, ignorance of the law is no excuse. And in any event, ignorance of the law cannot create a valid tariff statute; only Congress and the President can do so, pursuant to Article I.

The correct analysis of the law may well expose persons like Harrison to liability that they could not reasonably avoid. Congress, however, could easily have saved the day by passing contingent legislation for the governance of California that took effect immediately upon ratification of the peace treaty, and the President and Senate could have made any constitutionally necessary appointments at the same time. Because the nondelegation doctrine does not apply to territorial legislation, the statute could even have been a simple authorization to the President to maintain the existing institutions of governance along with proper civilian appointments to the necessary offices. Such a statute could have operated from the moment of its enactment even if it took months for news of the statute to reach California. And because the private law liability of government officials depended on actual authorization rather than the officials' belief (or lack of belief) in authorization, this straightforward statutory solution would have neatly dealt with the myriad legal problems posed by the end of the authority for the war government.

The officials in California clearly anticipated such a congressional response. In his August 7, 1848, announcement of the peace treaty to the people of California, Colonel/Governor Mason declared: "The Congress of the United States (to whom alone this power belongs) will soon confer upon the people of this country the constitutional rights of citizens of the United States; and, no doubt, in a few short months we shall have a regularly organized territorial government: indeed, *there is every reason to believe that Congress has already passed the act, and that a civil government is now on its way to this country, to replace that which has been organized under the right of conquest.*"[61] This was a perfectly reasonable assumption given the representations made by government officials in the early days of the war concerning the need for the establishment of institutions of civil government even during wartime.[62] Mason further declared that until there was firm word about congressional action, "the present civil officers of the country will continue in the exercise of their functions as heretofore."[63] Had Congress passed the right kind of legislation, Mason's actions would have been lawful even if he did not know it.

Congress, however, did not oblige. The reasons for Congress's inaction are not mysterious: the issue of slavery in California so deadlocked the Congress that it could not reach agreement on any legislation for the territory.[64] Regardless of the reason, however, the fact remains that the military authorities in California had no statutory authorization for their postwar governance. What, then, if anything, sustained the actions of the military officials once their wartime authority ran out?

Perhaps one can construct an argument that will salvage the government's authority at least with respect to the time period running into early August 1848. Here is the best that we can do (though it is ultimately unsuccessful): The Treaty of Guadalupe Hidalgo made no provision for the removal of Mexican soldiers from American soil because the war was rather one-sided. That does not mean, however, that no Mexican soldiers remained in the territory that was transferred as part of the peace treaty. Such an assumption is unlikely; surely some small number of soldiers remained "behind the lines" even while American troops pressed into the Mexican mainland. We know that about two thousand Mexican nationals who resided in the ceded territories ultimately chose to return to Mexico[65] — the prospect of United States citizenship and potential riches from gold notwithstanding. It is natural to assume, therefore, that some portion of the indigenous California population posed a military threat to the American forces.

The Constitution vests in the President control over the armed forces. This is the domestic constitutional source of power for the operation of a military government. Perhaps one could argue that, even though the international law consequences of a state of war ended with respect to California upon the exchange of ratifications and the cession of territory, the constitutional wartime powers of the President continued for some time even after the treaty became official and the international dispute was formally over. In other words, one can argue that the constitutional grant of power to the President carries a "penumbral force" that takes effect as a matter of domestic law once the cession of territory terminates any presidential authority that derives from the existence of war. This argument does not require any assertion of a generalized executive power to deal with perceived crises. The power of wartime governance in this case was properly called into play by the existence of a war; the question is when the full legal force of that war power expires. Is it absurd to suggest that that power continues, as a matter of domestic constitutional law, for some period of time after the peace treaty has taken effect, at least long enough to ensure the public safety? If not, the next step is to determine how long after the formal entry of peace the effects of the presidential war power continue to linger. A plausible candidate would be: until a reasonable time has passed for notice of the formal peace to reach all of the potential combatants.

This is not an argument that the California government was a legitimate de facto government. This is a claim for de jure authority, as a matter of domestic constitutional law, based on an asserted temporal relationship between physical events and constitutional authority. Under this line of argument, the de jure authority of Governor Mason and his tax collectors to impose military exactions would run until notice of the peace should reasonably have reached

California. The actual period of notice was evidently two months, and from what we have gathered, that was not an unreasonable amount of time in 1848 for a message to travel from Queretaro, Mexico, to Monterey, California.

Thus, let us assume for the moment that August 7, 1848 — the date of Mason's announcement of the peace treaty to the people of California — was the constitutionally appropriate time for notice. On that date, the war tariff, even on the most generous assumptions that one can muster, is on its last legs.

Colonel Mason evidently agreed with this assessment, for on August 9, 1848, H. W. Halleck, the Secretary of State in Mason's military government, wrote to the San Francisco (military) customs collector that "the tariff of duties for the collection of military contributions will immediately cease."[66] If we assume that our penumbral presidential power implicitly allows some time for the news of peace to disseminate once it reaches the California government, perhaps we can validate the military tariffs up to August 9, 1848. After that point, however, ingenuity is exhausted and the war tariffs are finished.

Obviously, although this argument is more persuasive than the Supreme Court's ipse dixit, we do not think it is successful. The President, no less than Congress, can exercise only those powers granted to him by the Constitution. The power to impose and maintain a military government during peacetime is not a small matter. However broadly one might construe "[t]he executive Power," it surely does not stretch that far. The President's war power does include such a power, but the whole problem in *Cross* is that the war power formally ceased to be a source of authority on May 30, 1848. And that formal cessation is the end of the matter. Constitutional powers operate — or fail to operate — from the moment of their effectiveness. Their operation is not delayed while news of their effectiveness travels the world--just as statutes take effect (unless Congress says otherwise) from the moment of enactment, not from the moment when knowledge of that enactment reaches the public. The central premise of this "penumbral" argument is simply false.[67] The President and Senate could, in principle, "preserve" the President's war power for some period of time by drafting the peace treaty to delay the transfer of sovereignty over California, but that was not done. Authority for the military tariffs ended on May 30, 1848.

In any event, at the absolute maximum, under the most generous assumptions, any authority for the California military government expired on August 9, 1848. Even the officials in California agreed that the war tariff must end once they were given notification of the peace treaty. And even the Supreme Court did not contend that the legitimacy of the war tariff "will certainly not be denied" after that date. All of which brings us to a period in which the military government's authority cannot be sustained even by the most extravagant understanding of the Constitution's war powers. How could Cross, Hobson & Co. possibly lose with respect to tariffs collected after August 9, 1848?

AUGUST 9, 1848–NOVEMBER 13, 1849: THE WAR IS OVER

The end of the military tariffs in California on August 9, 1848, did not mean the end of the tariffs. In the same breath in which he instructed the San Francisco customs collector to end the military tariff, Secretary of State Halleck added that "the revenue laws and tariff of the United States will be substituted in its place."[68] Cross, Hobson & Co. sought return of all monies paid up until November 13, 1849, when a civilian collector was constitutionally appointed to administer the tariff laws at the congressionally established collection district in San Francisco. War powers will not sustain any exactions after May 30, 1848, or at the very latest after August 9, 1848. What happened after that date that could possibly justify the actions of the military government? If not from the war powers, then from whence did Colonel Mason and Collector Harrison get the authority to take money from the plaintiff?

One possible argument that would largely avoid the need to address broad constitutional issues for at least part of the postwar time period should be dealt with right away. Congress did not designate San Francisco as a collection district—that is, as a port in which imports may lawfully be landed upon proper payment of duties—until March 3, 1849. The plaintiff sought to argue that this was decisive for the time period up to that point because, in the absence of such a designation, there was no federal authority to collect duties. Strictly speaking, that may have been true, but the argument had a serious potential boomerang effect against the plaintiff. A collection district is simply a congressionally designated port of entry. The specification of certain ports as collection districts reflects a corresponding congressional determination that goods *may not lawfully* be imported into the United States at any other place. Accordingly, the real consequence of the failure to make San Francisco a collection district until March 3, 1849, was that, until that date, it was flatly unlawful for the plaintiff to bring any goods into the United States through that port, with or without the payment of any "duties" to Harrison.

Should that have saved Harrison from liability, at least until March 3, 1849? The Court intimated that it might,[69] but that argument is clearly wrong. The absence of legislation making San Francisco a collection district meant that Harrison or other federal authorities might have been within their rights to refuse to allow the plaintiff to land its goods—not in their capacities as officials of California but as officers of the United States enforcing federal statutory law. (This raises serious questions about the authority of United States military personnel to enforce federal civilian law, but let us assume that one could finagle that problem somehow.) It *did not* mean that the officers could allow the plaintiff to land goods in return for the payment of something that they labeled a "duty." Suppose that Congress authorizes operation of a gift shop in the Capitol Building that sells miniature replicas of the Capitol. Tourists can leave with a replica if they pay the clerk at the desk ten dollars. If someone filches a replica and is caught outside by a police officer, it would not be proper for the officer to say, "Give me the ten dollars and go on your way," even if the officer then turned the money over to the clerk. It simply is not the officer's job to collect money for replicas, though it certainly is the officer's job to arrest shoplifters. In *Cross*, Harrison might have been able to tell the plaintiff, "Go land your goods at a designated port of entry or suffer the consequences of a violation of the customs laws," which would have been forfeiture of the offending ships and goods.[70] But Harrison did not have the legal right to permit the goods to land in return for payment of a sum equal to what would have been required under the federal tariff law.

The officials in California were very well aware of the true state of the law concerning entry of goods into California. On February 9, 1849, Harrison wrote to Secretary of State Halleck requesting guidance on how to handle ships that entered San Francisco. (Less than a month later, Congress would declare San Francisco a collection district, but Harrison and Halleck had no way to know this — and probably did not find out about the designation until the summer or fall of 1849.) On February 24, 1849, Halleck provided the following assessment of the situation:

> In the instructions just received from Washington, it is assumed that, by the treaty of peace with Mexico, California has become a part of the Union; that the constitution of the United States is extended over this Territory, and is in full force throughout its limits.
>
> The position of California, in her commercial relations, both with respect to foreign countries and to other parts of the Union is, therefore, the same as that of any other portion of the territory of the United States. There, however, being as yet no collection districts established by Congress in California, no foreign dutiable goods can be introduced here. Vessels having on board dutiable goods which they wish to land in California, must enter them in some regular port of entry of the United States, and there pay the duties prescribed by law. Any such vessels presenting themselves in a port of California, without having so entered their dutiable goods, ought properly to be warned away

and refused admission; and when the goods are entered at a regular custom-house, they can be brought here only in American bottoms. Such is the course required by a strict interpretation of the law.[71]

Halleck's analysis conforms precisely to the clear state of the law as we describe it above. His letter to Harrison, however, continues with the following remarkable passage: "[B]ut, as this [strict interpretation of the law] would subject such vessels to great inconvenience and expense, the authorities having charge of this matter have resolved to present to them the following alternative: *To pay here all duties and fees, and to execute all papers prescribed by the revenue laws of the United States*; and, upon their doing so, their goods will be admitted."[72] The "authorities having charge of this matter" were, of course, the military officers in California. Indeed, the architect of this makeshift customs scheme appears to have been Brevet Major General Persifor F. Smith, who informed the army's adjutant general on April 5, 1849, "I thought it proper that the parties should be allowed to deposite [*sic*] the amount of duties and land the goods; but, lest this should be construed as giving them a right for the future, and as the President may think proper to put an end even to this indulgence, I have addressed a circular to all our consuls on these seas, warning them of this possibility."[73] This "indulgence" may have been very generous to shippers like Cross, Hobson & Co., who otherwise would have had to enter their goods in ports on the Atlantic side of the continent, with no Panama Canal to ease the journey, and it may have been very important to Californians, who badly needed the goods,[74] but that does not make it lawful. And without any such authority, the sums collected by Harrison should have been returned to the plaintiff[75] — *unless* Harrison, Mason, Halleck, Smith, and other military personnel in California had authority to take the money as officials of the territorial government of California.

The plaintiff regarded enactment of the March 3, 1849, statute that made San Francisco a collection district as a major event. However, until Collier, the properly appointed collector, assumed the duties of his office on November 13, 1849, the statute changed nothing. A collection district is a place in which dutiable goods may be landed upon the proper payment of duties to (and the filing of appropriate documents with) *the proper authorities*. Harrison's "appointment" as customs collector rested solely on his appointment by "Governor" Mason, whose status as governor depended throughout his tenure on the validity of the military government. If that government's authority cannot be sustained as a matter of federal constitutional law, the plaintiff should have gotten back its money.

This brings us to the main event: the Court's validation of the actions of the military government throughout its period of operation. The answers provided by the Court and the Executive Department to the questions arising from the governance of California represent some of the most astounding assertions of constitutional power ever put forth.

The Supreme Court validated the acts of the military government throughout its period of operation in one critical paragraph, which reads in full:

> [Mason's] position was unlike any thing that had preceded it in the history of our country. The view taken of it by himself has been given in the statement in the beginning of this opinion. It was not without its difficulties, both as regards the principle upon which he should act, and the actual state of affairs in California. He knew that the Mexican inhabitants of it had been remitted by the treaty of peace to those municipal laws and usages which prevailed among them before the territory had been ceded to the United States, but that a state of things and population had grown up during the war, and after the treaty of peace, which made some other authority necessary to maintain the rights of the ceded inhabitants and of immigrants, from misrule and violence. He may not have comprehended fully the principle applicable to what he might rightly do in such a case, but he felt rightly, and acted accordingly. He determined, in the absence of all instruction, to maintain the existing government. The territory had been ceded as a conquest, and was to be preserved and governed as such until the sovereignty to which it had passed had legislated for it. That sovereignty was the United States, under the Constitution, by which power had been given to Congress to dispose of and make all needful rules and regulations respecting the territory or other property belonging to the United States, with the power also to admit new States into this Union, with only such limitations as are expressed in the section in which this power is given. The government, of which Colonel Mason was the executive, had its origin in the lawful exercise of a belligerent right over a conquered territory. It had been instituted during the war by the command of the President of the United States. It was the government when the territory was ceded as a conquest, *and it did not cease, as a matter of course, or as a necessary consequence of the restoration of peace. The President might have dissolved it by withdrawing the army and navy officers who administered it, but he did not do so. Congress could have put an end to it, but that was not done. The right inference from the inaction of both is, that it was meant to be continued until it had been legislatively changed.* No presumption of a contrary intention can be made. Whatever may have been the causes of delay, it must be presumed that the delay was consistent with the true policy of the government. And the more so as it was continued until the people of the territory met in convention to form a State government, which was subsequently recognized by Congress under its power to admit new States into the Union.[76]

Therefore, said the Court, "the civil government of California, organized as it was from a right of conquest, did not cease or become defunct in consequence of the signature of the treaty or from its ratification. We think it was continued over a ceded conquest, without any violation of the Constitution or laws of the United States, and that until Congress legislated for it, the duties upon foreign goods imported into San Francisco were legally demanded and lawfully received by Mr. Harrison."[77]

In other words, as long as the President and Congress do not affirmatively stop an illegal act, their inaction will be considered valid legal ratification. At its narrowest, the Court's reasoning is that wartime powers carry over into peacetime as long as the President and Congress do not affirmatively end them. This is an absurd warping of the constitutional scheme of limited government. Constitutionally, the President is a nonplayer in this story after May 30, 1848 (or at the very latest after August 9, 1848), except in his legislative role under Article I, section 7. As the Court itself observes, Congress has the exclusive power of territorial governance during peacetime, so the President's failure to order the troops home is constitutionally irrelevant. As for Congress, it did nothing. This is not even a case of purported legislative ratification of the misconstruction of a statute through a failure to amend, which is enough of a stretch in its own right. Here there was no statute to fail to amend. There was no statute at all. Congress *never* took any action with respect to the governance of California (beyond making San Francisco a collection district, which has nothing to do with the internal governance of the territory). Congress may well have wanted or intended to keep the military government in force, but its collective wishes are not a constitutional substitute for a statute. Congress cannot exercise its Article IV powers of governance by having hopes and wishes, holding a séance, or anything else short of enacting a statute. Congress's Article IV power is a *legislative* power that must be exercised in accordance with Article I's lawmaking procedures, including presentment to the President.

All in all, the Court probably would have been better off simply to say, "It cannot be denied that . . . ."

CROSS'S THEORY IN PRACTICE

The Court's validation of the government in *Cross* has important ramifications. Military governments of occupied territory during wartime operate in accordance with the laws of war. They need not comply with the procedural forms for governmental action prescribed in the Constitution; the courts that they establish during wartime need not conform to the dictates of Article III; and the Bill of Rights does not, for instance, require soldiers in occupied territory to get warrants before they search houses for insurgents. There are, of course, limits to the powers of military governments. As the Court held just two years before *Cross* in *Mitchell v Harmony*,[78] military officials cannot seize private property even during wartime unless they can demonstrate that such seizure is in fact necessary; and (in an era before modern immunity doctrines) the officers would be held personally liable for such seizures if a jury subsequently found that the action was not justified by military necessity. But these limits are far from the limits imposed on civilian government by the Constitution. What happens if one of these wartime governments acquires, through judicial grace, some kind of legitimate existence after the war is over and the occupied territory has been ceded to the United States? Does the ongoing military government retain all of the powers that it had during the war?

If the answer is no, then one has the unwelcome task of determining exactly which constitutional restrictions do and do not bind wartime governments that somehow cross over into peacetime. Although *Cross* has never been taken as far as its reasoning might permit, it has had enough precedential force to make the Supreme Court face some of these questions.

The Insular Cases, which we discuss at more length in the next chapter, were a series of decisions spanning the first quarter of the twentieth century that dealt with the aftermath of the Spanish-American War.[79] That war ended in a treaty of peace whose ratifications were exchanged on April 11, 1899. The treaty ceded to the United States a number of island territories, including the Philippines and Puerto Rico. In the case of Puerto Rico, Congress enacted a statute providing for a civil government for the territory on April 12, 1900, with an effective date of May 1, 1900. For more than a year, therefore, Puerto Rico was an American possession without a statutory government. As happened in California in 1848, the American military government continued in operation until displaced by the statutory civilian authorities. And as happened in California, one of the military government's principal functions was to collect duties on goods imported into Puerto Rico. There was no question that the government had such power until the exchange of ratifications that formally ended the war with Spain, including the power to impose military exactions on goods imported into Puerto Rico from the continental United States. But what happened after Puerto Rico was ceded to the United States?

The Court addressed this question in *Dooley v United States*.[80] After the ratification of the peace treaty, the military government continued to collect exactions on goods imported to Puerto Rico, including goods imported from the continental United States. The Court held, on the authority of *Cross*, that the military government validly continued in operation until the congressionally created civilian government took over on May 1, 1900.[81] But the Court further held that that authority did not include the power to impose exactions, in the guise of tariffs or otherwise, on goods imported from the United States. While the power of a military commander, said the Court, "is necessarily despotic, this must be understood rather in an administrative than in a legislative sense. While in legislating for a conquered country he may disregard the laws of that country, he is not wholly above the laws of his own."[82] The powers of a military government, said the Court, extend only to "the necessities of the case," and those necessities did not (in the Court's judgment) include the need for tariffs on imported American goods. Thus "the authority of the President as Commander-in-Chief to exact duties upon imports from the United States ceased with the ratification of the treaty of peace."[83]

The Court's reasoning is, to say the least, obscure. At one point, the Court seems to infer the absence of presidential power from "the spirit as well as the letter of the tariff laws,"[84] though because those laws are not the source of the power to impose military exactions, it is not clear why they are relevant. At another point, the Court indicates that a tariff on American imports "might have placed Porto Rico in a most embarrassing situation"[85] by damaging its economy, which may well have been true but seems like an odd basis for a constitutional limitation on the presidential war power. The remark that military governments are not always "above the laws" of their own countries is not explained: the rule that private rights can be infringed only if necessary is a principle of the law of war that needs no additional support in domestic law. *Dooley* provides little guidance about the extent to which peace limits what would otherwise be the powers of military government.

The Court further elaborated on the peacetime powers of military governments in *Santiago v Nogueras*.[86] The case again concerned the period in Puerto Rico between the cession to the United States on April 11, 1899, and the establishment of a civilian government on May 1, 1900. On June 27, 1899, the military authorities created the United States Provisional Court. The court's stated purpose was to deal with an increasing stream of business "that does not fall within the jurisdiction of the local insular courts,"[87] but the court's jurisdiction was quite broad. The plaintiffs' land was sold to execute a judgment issued by the Provisional Court and was eventually acquired by the defendant. The plaintiffs sought recovery of the land on the ground that the Provisional Court was a legal nullity and had no power to enter the judgment for which the land was sold. The Supreme Court had no trouble upholding the validity of the Provisional Court. The military government was valid on the authority of *Cross*, and such a government clearly had the power to create courts.[88] The Court intriguingly observed, however, that "[t]he authority of a military government during the period between the cession and the action of

Congress, *like the authority of the same government before the cession*, is of large, though it may not be of unlimited, extent."[89] The suggestion here (though it is not absolutely entailed by the statement) is that there is not much difference between a peacetime military government and a wartime military government (though *Dooley* precluded a holding that there were no differences at all). Because the establishment of courts was an easy case, the Court did not need to plumb the limits of this authority.

An analysis of *The Insular Cases* must await the next chapter. The salient point here is that *Cross* has served as the fundamental precedent for upholding territorial governments by military governments in peacetime. The rationale underlying *Cross* is the rationale for a significant amount of territorial governance over the past 150 years.

MADISON, HAMILTON, JAY . . . AND HOBBES?

If the Supreme Court's assertion in *Cross* of national power to maintain a peacetime military government seems extravagant, it is nothing compared to the claim of power advanced in the case by the executive arm of the United States government.

Colonel/Governor Mason was several months' distance from Washington, D.C. When he received news of the ratification of the Treaty of Guadalupe Hidalgo in August 1848, he had no instructions from anyone concerning the governance of California. He had no way to know whether Congress had passed any statutes, or whether those statutes authorized him or deprived him of authority to govern. Under the then-governing rule of personal liability, that meant that Mason simply had to make his best guess and live with the consequences. He chose to continue to govern, but with no illusions about his formal legal authority:

> I am fully aware that, in taking these steps [to continue the government and collect import duties], I have no further authority than that the existing government must necessarily continue until some other is organized to take its place, for I have been left without any definite instructions in reference to the existing state of affairs. But the calamities and disorders which would surely follow the absolute withdrawal of even a show of authority, impose on me, in my opinion, the imperative duty to pursue the course I have indicated, until the arrival of despatches from Washington (which I hope are already on their way) relative to the organization of a regular civil government.[90]

That letter could be read as a plea from Mason for Congress to bail him out from any problems that his decision may cause in the future. (The Supreme Court's decision in *Cross*, of course, obviated any subsequent need for a private bill.) The executive department in Washington, D.C., however, took a different view of Mason's authority. On October 7, 1848, Secretary of State James Buchanan wrote an astonishing letter concerning the governance of California and New Mexico. Buchanan acknowledged that "[b]y the conclusion of the Treaty of Peace, the military government which was established over [the people of California] under the laws of war, as recognized by the practice of all civilized nations, has ceased to derive its authority from this source of power."[91] Buchanan continued, however, by reasoning:

> But is there, for this reason, no government in California? Are life, liberty, and property under the protection of no existing authorities? This would be a singular phenomenon in the face of the world, and especially among American citizens, distinguished as they are above all other people for their law-abiding character. Fortunately, they are not reduced to this sad condition. The termination of the war left an existing government, a government de facto, in full operation, and this will continue, with the presumed consent of the people, until Congress shall provide for them a territorial government. The great law of necessity justifies this conclusion. The consent of the people is irresistibly inferred from the fact that no civilized community could possibly desire to abrogate an existing government, when the alternative presented would be to place themselves in a state of anarchy, beyond the protection of all laws, and reduce them to the unhappy necessity of submitting to the dominion of the strongest.[92]

Buchanan added that "[t]his government de facto will, of course, exercise no power inconsistent with the provisions of the Constitution of the United States, which is the supreme law of the land," and that accordingly "no import duties can be levied in California on articles the growth, produce, or manufacture of the United States, as no such duties can be imposed in any other part of our Union on the productions of California. Nor can new duties be charged in California upon such foreign productions as have already paid duties in any of our ports of entry, for the obvious reason that California is within the territory of the United States."[93]

President Polk expressly endorsed the substance of Mr. Buchanan's analysis in his state of the union message of December 5, 1848:

> The inhabitants [of California], by the transfer of their country, had become entitled to the benefits of our laws and Constitution, and yet were left without any regularly organized government. Since that time, the very limited power possessed by the Executive has been exercised to preserve and protect them from the inevitable consequences of a state of anarchy. The only government which remained was that established by the military authority during the war. Regarding this to be a *de facto* government, and that by the presumed consent

of the inhabitants it might be continued temporarily, they were advised to conform and submit to it for the short intervening period before Congress would again assemble and could legislate on the subject.[94]

Fairly read, this is a claim, put forward by the President and Secretary of State, that continuation of the military government in California was affirmatively *legal*, as a matter of domestic American law, even in the absence of congressional authorization. The claim raises legal and factual issues.

Let us assume for the moment that every sensible person would choose virtually any organized government over none at all — although many seemingly sensible people, including one of the present authors, emphatically disagree with this claim. What does that mean, as a matter of domestic law, about the powers of the American national government? Does that mean that there is constitutional authorization for the establishment of an American military government anywhere in the world where there is a governmental vacuum? Does it mean that the presumed consent of the people living in a state of governmental interregnum permits the President and military authorities, as a matter of domestic law, to fill the void? The claim is bizarre enough at the level of abstract political theory. It is positively clinical in the context of the American constitutional scheme, under which the national government is an institution of limited and enumerated powers. Perhaps a Hobbesian sovereign would be able to claim the kind of legal authority that Polk and Buchanan attributed to Colonel Mason (and that Colonel Mason never claimed for himself),[95] but neither the United States government nor its territorial arm in California during 1848 meets that description.

The American government's position is even more bizarre when one reflects on its central assumption: that in the absence of American military rule, there would be anarchy, in the sense of no functioning institutions of order. When the United States conquered California during the Mexican-American War, it did not simply occupy a territory that had no prior human inhabitants. Before the President established a military government in 1847, the people of California did not live without government. There were plenty of governmental institutions that operated under the sovereignties of Spain and Mexico. Before the American invasion, California "had a well-defined and relatively effective legal structure based largely on customary law and conflict resolution."[96] Indeed, as is typical in cases of conquest, the vast majority of the indigenous laws remained in force after the occupation; only those laws specifically displaced by the military government ceased to be effective.[97] Had the American military government disappeared on May 30, 1848 (or any later date), the people of California could have fallen back on their pre-occupation system of government.

Those structures may have been inadequate to the changed circumstances of 1848. The American population had been increasing dramatically because of the discovery of gold. The Mexican legal institutions were less formal than Anglo-American institutions, and were therefore unfamiliar and unattractive to American settlers.[98] But that is not the kind of chaos that would, even under Buchanan's Hobbesian premises, justify an otherwise unconstitutional government. The prior institutions could have been adapted or replaced without the intervention of the American military. Many of the American settlers were quite prepared to establish their own independent government. Indeed, barely a month before outbreak of the war, a group of settlers initiated a very small-scale revolution to establish an independent government in California.[99] Throughout the period of military occupation, there was a vigorous movement for self-government within California.[100] It is absurd to suggest that the alternative to American military rule was complete lawlessness — unless, of course, the preexisting Mexican institutions simply did not count, in Mr. Buchanan's eyes, as a government.

This last point suggests a deeper problem with the American government's assertion of power from implied consent. Who, exactly, are the "people of California" whose consent was being implied? Could Polk and Buchanan really have believed that the Mexican inhabitants of California, who had been operating their own institutions of government for some time before the American military took over, tacitly consented to the continued rule of the occupying forces in preference to the reinstitution of their own forms of government? Even many of the American settlers were distinctly, and vocally, unhappy with the military government to which they were being presumed to consent, so the game of implied consent for the nonsettlers is particularly intriguing.[101]

Accordingly, if Buchanan wanted to invoke notions of implied consent, he needed to identify whose consent was being implied. It is very hard to get a handle on exactly who was in California during various times in 1848. In 1846, there were probably between 130,000 and 250,000 Native Americans in California and approximately 10,000 nonnatives, about 7,500 of whom were Latino.[102] Implied consent to an American military government in 1846 did not look promising. By 1848, however, matters had changed. Gold had been discovered in January 1848, and people were flocking to the region, including hordes of white Americans. By the 1850 census, there were approximately 165,000 residents in California.[103] What, if anything, does this mean about the state of affairs in the summer of 1848? That is hard to say, though it is not at all clear that many of the new immigrants to California during the gold rush would have preferred the military government to their own private institutions of justice, much less to the kind of independent government that they were prepared to establish — and indeed that they did eventually establish before statehood.

But, of course, this is all silly speculation. It is doubtful that President Polk and Secretary of State Buchanan were engaging in deep political theory when they sought to justify the California military government during peacetime. No doubt they were simply expressing the "commonsense" view, implicit in the idea of a de facto government, that one should not lightly dissolve an existing mechanism for preserving order without a high degree of confidence that something equivalent or better is about to take its place.

Even on that modest level, however, the postwar government in California does not fare well. The gold rush was under way, and among the rushers were many, if not most, of the soldiers who were supposedly providing order. On August 14, 1848, less than two months before Secretary of State Buchanan sought to derive an extraconstitutional power to govern from the imperative need for a military government to maintain order, Captain (and Assistant Quartermaster) J. L. Folsom described the state of affairs in San Francisco: "The most mortifying state of things prevails here at this time. Government, both civil and military, is abandoned. Offences are committed with impunity; and property, and lives even, are no longer safe. . . . Acts of disgraceful violence occur almost daily on board the shipping, and we have no power to preserve order. Tomorrow morning the volunteers will be mustered out of service, and we shall be utterly without resource for the protection of public property."[104] As for what was happening in the rest of the state, we cannot do better than to quote Colonel Mason, who on November 24, 1848, between Buchanan's and Polk's stirring tributes to the order-preserving power of the military government, reported to his commander: "The war being over, *the soldiers nearly all deserted*, and having now been from the States two years, I respectfully request to be ordered home. I feel the less hesitancy in making this request, as it is the second only that I recollect ever to have made, in more than thirty years' service, to be relieved from any duty upon which I have been placed: the first was asking to be relieved from the recruiting service, in 1832, that I might join my company in the Black Hawk war."[105]

The problem continued into the next year, as was acknowledged by General Persifor F. Smith, who in a March 6, 1849 letter to Mason (who was still saddled with the unwanted duty of governing the territory until April 1849) pointed out that new soldiers "will require some additional inducements beyond their pay to prevent them from deserting." The trick was to "keep them through the mining season"; if that could be done, he hoped, "they will remain next winter; and in the spring circumstances may be altered." [106]

The order that existed in California during the postwar period was not the product of the American military government. It was largely the product of private mechanisms for justice that evolved in mining colonies. As Professor Saunders has observed, "[T]he military government exerted little, if any, control over the mining camps[.] [T]his effectively created a large number of completely independent townships functioning entirely under their own sets of rules, but often utilizing the Spanish-Mexican nomenclature. The local laws developed for protecting gold mine claims in the California mining camps became the foundation of United States mining law."[107]

Under Hobbesian assumptions, the sovereign's authority depends upon its ability to deliver on the promise of order. Even as a Hobbesian constitutional theory, the approach of President Polk and Secretary of State Buchanan fails to establish the authority of the California territorial government.

In the end, there is really nothing to be said in favor of the constitutionality of the postwar California military government. Congress and the President could have avoided most, if not all, of the problems by the simple expedient of enacting a statute converting the military government into a genuine Article IV territorial government (provided that the President and Senate made whatever appointments and confirmations were necessary to complete the governmental structure). But Congress was paralyzed by the debate over slavery. That, however, is not the Constitution's problem. If congressional paralysis is really a mandate for disregarding constitutional commands, then constitutionalism is a bad joke — as it surely was for California from May 30, 1848, until statehood.

7

Bulwark or Façade?
The Rights of Territorial Inhabitants

It is easy to overdraw a distinction between constitutional provisions that protect rights and provisions that pertain to governmental structure. Structures often protect rights, and rights are often meaningful only in the context of particular structures. For example, the constitutional requirement that only tenured judges with salary protections can exercise the federal judicial power is a structural provision that carries a corresponding "right" to certain adjudications — certainly at least adjudications of criminal guilt — by government officials possessing certain structural characteristics. And many of the provisions of the Bill of Rights that are often considered paradigms of "rights-bearing provisions" actually have a great deal to do with governmental structure.[1]

Nonetheless, it is fair to ask to what extent the various "thou shalt not" provisions in the Constitution aimed at federal institutions apply to federal legislative, executive, and judicial conduct in the territories. Historically, this has been the central question of territorial governance. Our relatively brief treatment of the question here reflects our own particular interest in less-developed questions of structure rather than an assessment of the question's importance.

The original Constitution contains one primary set of provisions in the form of "thou shalt nots" directed at various federal actors. Article I, section 9 contains a number of direct limitations on governmental actors: it forbids Congress from ending the slave trade before 1808, passing bills of attainder or ex post facto laws, laying direct taxes that are not apportioned by population (a limitation which has since been superseded by the Sixteenth Amendment), laying taxes or duties on state exports, or giving commercial preferences to the ports of any state.[2] Executive and judicial officials are forbidden from withdrawing money from the treasury without appropriations,[3] and all relevant institutions are forbidden from suspending the writ of habeas corpus except in specified emergencies or from granting titles of nobility.[4] A number of specific power grants also contain their own built-in limitations; the most obvious example is the uniformity requirement in the Article I, section 1 Taxing Clause. Otherwise, the original Constitution limits power through the device of enumeration: "thou shalt nots" only kick into play when there is first a "thou mayest."

The original Constitution, of course, contains no specific prohibition on laws restricting speech, regulating religion, authorizing general warrants, and so forth. Those precepts did not take the form of textual "thou shalt nots" until 1791 when the Bill of Rights was ratified. Does that mean that for the first two years of its existence, the federal government was free to abridge freedom of speech, establish or forbid the establishment of religion, prescribe the use of general warrants, and confiscate private property without compensation?

The general answer is no. If Congress in 1790, for instance, had wanted to establish a religion or prescribe the use of general warrants, it first would have had to find an enumerated power that would authorize the action. Because the Constitution does not contain a "Regulation of Religion Clause" or a "General Warrant Clause," Congress would have to argue that such statutes were justified under the Sweeping Clause as means for implementing other enumerated powers. For instance, it might argue that general warrants help implement the customs laws by making it easier to detect smuggling. But that argument would fail. As one of us has explained at length elsewhere,[5] the Sweeping Clause only authorizes laws that are "necessary and proper for carrying into Execution" other federal powers. Laws that infringed on widely respected liberties, such as freedom of conscience or freedom from general warrants, would not be "necessary and proper" and therefore would not have been constitutional even before ratification of the Bill of Rights. The Bill of Rights, as the Federalists correctly maintained, was essentially declaratory of rights that were already protected by the constitutional structure of enumerated powers.[6]

At least, that was true when Congress had to rely on the Sweeping Clause as the source of its claimed authority. When Congress legislates for the District of Columbia, federal enclaves, or federal territories, it does not need the

Sweeping Clause for any purpose, because the District Clause and the Territories Clause give Congress the legislative jurisdiction of a general government. The sorts of laws that normally must be justified as "necessary and proper for carrying into Execution" enumerated powers only have to be "needful Rules and Regulations" when they concern the territories and only have to fall within Congress's power of "exclusive Legislation in all Cases whatsoever" when they concern the nation's capital or federal enclaves within states. Congress was constrained with respect to the Northwest Territory because the Northwest Ordinance, which contained many guarantees of such things as religious freedom and limited self-government, was binding on the new federal government by virtue of the Engagements Clause of Article VI, but any other federal territory acquired by Congress after ratification of the Constitution but before ratification of the Bill of Rights would have been subject to Congress's general jurisdiction. If Congress wanted to restrict speech, establish religions, or authorize general warrants, it is hard to see what in the Constitution would have stopped it. The only possible constraint on Congress would have been the principle of reasonableness *if* — and it is a large "if" — one could argue that the principle applied to all delegations of discretionary power, including constitutional grants of legislative power to Congress. And even if the principle of reasonableness did apply to Congress, it is not at all clear that it would provide the same kind of constraints on a general legislative power that it places on implementational powers, whether legislative or otherwise.

Of course, prohibitions on national action that do not stem from the Sweeping Clause applied to territorial actions from the start. Before 1791, executive and judicial actors could not exceed the scope of the "executive Power" or the "judicial Power," respectively, even in territories. Nor could Congress grant titles of nobility or pass ex post facto laws in the territories *if* — another big "if" — the prohibitions in Article I, section 9 apply to the territorial legislative authorization in Article IV, section 3. The various prohibitions in Article I, section 9 are framed in a general fashion, but their location immediately after Article I, section 8 could support an inference that they apply only to laws enacted pursuant to the powers enumerated in Article I, section 8. That argument, however, does not withstand close scrutiny. It would also exempt from the Article I limitations any laws pursuant to the Full Faith and Credit Clause and other Article IV authorizations. Furthermore, it would seem to place all of those Article IV enactments outside the Presentment Clause as well; if proximity is enough to limit the scope of legislative provisions, the distance between Article IV and Article I, section 9 is shorter than the distance between Article IV and Article I, section 7. As fond as we are of arguments from the location of various clauses, the location of Article I, section 9 is not enough to limit its application to laws enacted pursuant to Article I, section 8. Nonetheless, the scope of these generally applicable limitations is quite small. Under the original Constitution, territorial inhabitants stand in a very different relationship to the national government than do inhabitants of the states, because the critical protection of the Sweeping Clause does not apply to territorial inhabitants.

Amended Texts; Amended Rights?

In 1791, the Bill of Rights became part of the Constitution. What effect did that have on territorial inhabitants?

The first question is whether the Bill of Rights applies to the territories at all. That is not a trivial question, but the answer is yes. The wording of Amendments 1–9 is completely general. Of course, that general language must be read in context. As a straightforward textual matter, there is even a plausible case that those amendments (other than the First Amendment, which refers specifically to Congress) applied to the states in 1791. Nonetheless, Chief Justice Marshall was correct in *Barron v Baltimore*[7] to hold that the Bill of Rights does not directly apply to the states. That holding is correct for the same reason that Article II does not make the President the chief executive of Connecticut, even though Article III's Vesting Clause specifically vests the "judicial Power of the United States" in federal courts, while Article II's Vesting Clause merely vests the "executive Power," with no further qualification, in the President. The background rule for the federal Constitution is that it speaks only to the federal government that is created by the Constitution unless it specifically says otherwise.

There is no comparable background principle that would prevent the Bill of Rights from applying to legislation for the territories. The fact that (at least in the case of territories, though not the case of the District of Columbia or federal enclaves) such legislation stems from Article IV rather than from Article I is not significant. The Bill of Rights does not limit its application to Article I, and it is hard to see how any such limitation could be inferred. Indeed, some of the provisions of the Bill of Rights quite plainly apply to Articles II and III, and some (the Fourth Amendment is the most obvious example) clearly apply to powers granted by Articles I, II, and III. There is nothing constitutionally magical about Article IV. Congress could not enforce the Full Faith and Credit Clause in a fashion that violates the First Amendment, and the same is true of the Territories Clause. Such legislation is federal legislation, and that is enough to bring it within the compass of the Bill of Rights.

Many of the provisions in the Bill of Rights clarify limitations on executive or judicial action. Those provisions clearly apply to territories, because executive and judicial officials have no different status in the territories than in the states. The Territories Clause gives Congress a power that it does not acquire from Article I, but it vests no power in the President or federal judges. Those actors must draw their authority from the vesting clauses in Article II and Article III, and those grants of power do not distinguish states from territories.

The strongest argument against application of the Bill of Rights to territories stems from the Federalists' understanding of the role of the Bill of Rights. They saw the amendments essentially as confirming, or declaring, limitations on federal actors that were already implicit in the constitutional structure. The provisions in the amendments dealing with Congress were basically restatements of limitations contained in the requirement that executory laws be "necessary and proper." If the Bill of Rights exhausts its force by clarifying the Sweeping Clause, then it has no application to the territories.

But to call the Bill of Rights declaratory is somewhat to misunderstand its character (and it is a misunderstanding to which one of us has fallen prey at times). The Bill of Rights is not so much *declaratory* as *redundant*. The various amendments express limitations that would, in large measure, exist even in the absence of the Bill of Rights. That does not, however, mean that they are merely declaratory. A simple example will illustrate the point. Prior to enactment of the Seventh Amendment, the Sweeping Clause would clearly have required the use of civil juries in many cases, but would the "necessary and proper" requirement of the Sweeping Clause have been read to contain a requirement as specific as the provision for civil jury trials "where the value in controversy shall exceed twenty dollars"?[8] The text of the Bill of Rights shapes the norm to some degree even if it does not literally introduce the norm into the Constitution. Even though every substantive limitation in the Bill of Rights was already implicit in the Sweeping Clause or the Article II and Article III Vesting Clauses, their expression in the Bill of Rights elaborated upon them in some ways. The Bill of Rights may have been largely superfluous, but that is not the same thing as being legally ineffective.

Once one recognizes that the Bill of Rights has real legal (even if almost entirely redundant) effect, and that there is no background principle that would exclude Article IV or the District Clause from its reach, the best conclusion is that the Bill of Rights extends at least some of the limitations on Congress that are built into the Sweeping Clause to the territories. Accordingly, although the proposition is not beyond question, the Bill of Rights did have some bite — indeed, perhaps its most significant bite, given its otherwise essentially redundant character — in federal territories. Limitations on congressional power found in the first eight amendments apply to the territories just as do the limitations in Article I, section 9.

A somewhat more interesting question is whether those limitations apply to actions of territorial legislatures created by Congress. If Congress directly passed a law establishing a religion in a federal territory, such a law would plainly run afoul of the First Amendment. Suppose, however, that Congress instead passes a statute granting general jurisdiction over local matters to a territorial legislature, and that territorial legislature then proceeds to establish a religion in the territory. Does the fact that the ordinance was enacted by the territorial legislature rather than by Congress grant it validity? Put another way, can Congress delegate to a territorial legislature power that Congress could not itself exercise? As a general principle of agency law, the answer is clearly no, and that is probably enough to carry the day. Territorial legislatures are constitutionally permissible (at least if the legislators are presidential appointees) because the Territories Clause is best read to contain an implicit authorization for such delegations. It would be tough to read in as well the kind of extraordinary authority to delegate that would be necessary to validate territorial laws that could not be enacted by Congress.[9]

The Tenth Amendment obviously has no bite in the territories, as the District Clause and the Territories Clause are clear delegations of power to federal authorities. The territorial bite, if any, of the Ninth Amendment is a more complicated story that we will not enter into here. The short answer is that if one reads the Ninth Amendment as a guarantee of substantive rights that had the same status (whatever that might mean) in 1791 as did the rights specifically enumerated elsewhere in the Constitution, then the limitations on legislative power entailed by those rights would apply to territorial legislation. If, however, the Ninth Amendment is an interpretative rule that simply precludes using the enumerations in the Bill of Rights as a means of unduly limiting the meaning of the phrase "necessary and proper" in the Sweeping Clause, then the Ninth Amendment has no effect in the territories, because the Sweeping Clause has no effect in the territories.

We do not intend to engage here in the debate over the correct interpretation of the Ninth Amendment. For our purposes, it does not matter which view is right. The important point for now is that the Constitution, as originally written and amended, places some restrictions on the ability of Congress to legislate for the territories. Limitations contained in Article I, section 9 and the first eight amendments provide some measure of protection for territorial inhabitants. Those protections do not on their face go as far as the protections against federal action afforded to state inhabitants, but it is possible that they place territorial inhabitants in an even *better* position than some state

inhabitants. That is because territorial inhabitants are not subject to the jurisdiction of any state; the only source of governing authority is the federal
government. Because states are not constrained by the Constitution in the
same fashion as is the federal government, it is entirely possible that the federal
government's general legislative power over the territories, as limited by the
Constitution, is more constrained than is a state's general legislative power
over its inhabitants.

Wrong about Rights

Anyone who is at all familiar with the history of territorial governance
knows that anything resembling the constitutional analysis described above
sank to the bottom of Manila Bay along with the Spanish fleet in 1898. After
1898, territorial inhabitants do not necessarily get the benefit of constitutional
provisions that seem, by their terms, to apply to them. For those who are not
familiar with the history of territorial governance, it is a bit difficult to explain
how this came about. The modern doctrine makes no sense on its face, and it
makes even less sense the deeper one digs into it.

As was true in *Cross v Harrison*, the law emerged from a dispute over tariffs.
To make a long story at least a bit shorter,[10] present doctrine concerning the
applicability of the Constitution to territories grew out of a series of cases
precipitated by America's acquisition of far-flung, noncontiguous island territories during and shortly after the Spanish-American War of 1898. These so-
called "Insular Tariff Cases," decided in 1901, concerned duties levied on
goods imported from Puerto Rico into the continental United States.[11] In
Downes v Bidwell,[12] the most significant of the *Insular Tariff Cases*, the Court
held that a tariff imposed by Congress on goods imported from Puerto Rico
into the continental United States, which imposed tariffs of 15 percent of the
generally applicable tariff rates,[13] did not violate the constitutional requirement that "all Duties, Imposts and Excises shall be uniform throughout the
United States."[14] This statement of the holding requires some explanation.
The Constitution flatly forbids the imposition of tariffs on goods brought
from one state to another.[15] It also requires, as previously noted, that all tariffs
"shall be uniform throughout the United States." Thus, if Puerto Rico is part
of the United States for purposes of this uniformity provision, then goods
traveling between Puerto Rico and any of the states must be treated exactly
like goods moving from state to state, which means that they cannot be subject
to duty. Hence the alleged uniformity problem in *Downes* was not that the
tariff statute provided for duties at 15 percent rather than 100 percent of the

regular tariff rate, but that it imposed any duties at all on goods imported from Puerto Rico into the rest of the United States.

Although the Justices in the majority in *Downes* could not agree on a rationale for the decision,[16] the case produced a square holding that at least one provision of the Constitution, which is plainly phrased as a limitation on congressional power, does not apply to congressional legislation respecting the territories in the same way that it must apply to the same or similar legislation respecting the states.[17]

The *Insular Tariff Cases* raised only the seemingly dry question of the territories' tariff status, but it is clear from a full reading of the several opinions, the arguments of counsel,[18] and the historical context that these cases were generally understood to be a broad referendum on the freedom of Congress to deal with the island territories in ways at least facially prohibited by the Constitution. More specifically, the larger question lurking in the background was whether all the provisions in the Bill of Rights concerning civil and criminal procedure had to be fully extended to territories populated, in the pointed and revealing words of Justice Henry Brown, "by alien races, differing from us in religion, customs, laws, methods of taxation and modes of thought."[19] In 1903, two years after *Downes*, the Court explicitly addressed that question, refusing to apply certain of the Constitution's criminal procedure provisions to trials in the island territories,[20] though again the Court reached no clear agreement on a rationale.

By 1922, however, after two decades of litigation,[21] the Court could unanimously treat as settled law a theory — first advanced by Justice Edward White in a concurring opinion in *Downes*,[22] and first seemingly adopted by a majority of the Court in 1904[23] — that has come to be known as the "doctrine of territorial incorporation." The doctrine turns upon a none-too-clear distinction between territories that have and territories that have not been "incorporated into the Union."[24] That decidedly murky phrase appeared, without definition, in Article III of the Louisiana Purchase treaty in 1803, and as employed by the Court in *The Insular Cases*, the phrase probably has something to do with a territory's perceived suitability as a candidate for statehood.[25] If a territory is incorporated, then all provisions of the Constitution are said to be "applicable"[26] to that territory of their own force (or *ex proprio vigore*). If a territory is unincorporated, then only those provisions of the Constitution that are "fundamental"[27] are applicable in that territory *ex proprio vigore*; the rest are applicable only if and to the extent that Congress has so directed.

The Court's most lucid description of the incorporation doctrine is found in *Balzac v Porto Rico* in 1922. The Court explained why "the legislative recognition that federal constitutional questions may arise in litigation in Porto Rico" did not establish that Puerto Rico was an incorporated territory:

> The Constitution of the United States is in force in Porto Rico as it is wherever and whenever the sovereign power of that government is exerted. This has not only been admitted but emphasized by this court in all its authoritative expressions upon the issues arising in the *Insular Tariff Cases*, especially in the *Downes v Bidwell* and the *Dorr Cases*. The Constitution, however, contains grants of power and limitations which in the nature of things are not always and everywhere applicable, and the real issue in the *Insular Tariff Cases* was not whether the Constitution extended to the Philippines or Porto Rico when we went there, but which of its provisions were applicable by way of limitation upon the exercise of executive and legislative power in dealing with new conditions and requirements. The guarantees of certain fundamental personal rights declared in the Constitution, as for instance that no person could be deprived of life, liberty or property without due process of law, had from the beginning full application in the Philippines and Porto Rico, and, as this guaranty is one of the most fruitful in causing litigation in our own country, provision was naturally made for similar controversy in Porto Rico.[28]

The decisions do not explain how to distinguish fundamental from nonfundamental constitutional provisions, but the holdings indicate that the category of "fundamental" provisions does not include the guarantees of jury trial in criminal cases or indictment by grand jury. While the incorporation doctrine has seemed on shaky ground in the Court on several recent occasions,[29] it is still at least nominally applied as the governing test to determine which constitutional provisions apply in particular territorial settings.[30]

There is a torrent of academic criticism of *The Insular Cases*,[31] but from an originalist perspective, a few words here will be sufficient. The Constitution clearly contemplates a difference between the powers of the national government over people in the territories and in the states; the federal government has a general legislative power over the territories that is not limited to the subject matters enumerated in Article I. It is possible that the scope of that general legislative power might be somewhat different in various territorial settings.[32] There are also potential differences between the constitutional power of the national government over territories before and after ratification of the Bill of Rights. There is even a case to be made that federal power over territories in which the United States is the only sovereign is different from federal power over national enclaves within states, where the state and federal governments are potentially overlapping sovereigns.[33] But there is nothing in the Constitution that even intimates that express constitutional limitations on national power apply differently to different territories once that territory is properly acquired. Nor is there anything in the Constitution that marks out certain categories of rights or powers as more or less "fundamental" than others — much less that rights to jury trial would fall on the "nonfundamental" side of the ledger.[34] The doctrine of "territorial incorporation" that emerged from *The Insular Cases* is transparently an invention designed to facilitate the felt needs of a particular moment in American history. Felt needs generally make bad law, and *The Insular Cases* are no exception.

Of course, two-score years before the Spanish-American War another set of felt needs made some even worse law. No discussion of the relationship between the Constitution and the territories would be complete without a brief discussion of the most famous, and infamous, of all territorial cases: *Scott v Sandford*.[35]

Slavery was the subject of several compromises written into the Constitution, all of which delicately managed to avoid using the word *slave*. First, as we have already discussed at length, the Slave Trade Clause forbade Congress from prohibiting the importation of "such Persons as any of the States now existing shall think proper to admit"[36] until 1808 (and Article V placed that provision beyond the amendment power). Second, the Constitution specified that, for purposes of establishing each state's representation in the House of Representatives and for the purposes of direct taxation, state populations would be determined "by adding to the whole Number of free Persons, including those bound to Service for a Term of Years . . . , three fifths of all other Persons,"[37] rather than not counting "other Persons" at all, as the antislavery advocates desired, or counting them as full persons, as the Southern states desired. Third, the Fugitive Slave Clause guaranteed that runaway slaves who escaped into free states would remain slaves regardless of the municipal law of the haven free states.[38]

After the Louisiana Purchase, the slave and free states both worried about the balance of governmental powers that would result from the admission of new states from the acquired territory.[39] Of course, a state entering the union as a slave state could subsequently change its policy, and vice versa. However, abolishing (or introducing) slavery into a culture that had grown accustomed to slavery (or freedom) might prove difficult, so it seemed reasonably likely that each state's destiny for the foreseeable future would be determined by the institutions in place at the time of admission. By the same token, the institutions in place at the time of admission were likely to be determined by those that had taken root during the preadmission period of territorial governance.

After considerable political maneuvering, Congress added to the 1820 statute admitting Missouri to the Union a provision that has come to be known as the Missouri Compromise. This provision declared, subject to a proviso drawn from the Fugitive Slave Clause that requires free states to return escaped slaves, that "[i]n all that territory ceded by France to the United States, under the name of Louisiana, which lies north of thirty-six degrees and thirty minutes north latitude, not included within the limits of [Missouri] . . . , slavery and involuntary servitude, otherwise than in the punishment of crimes . . . , is hereby, forever prohibited."[40] Of course, the word "forever" really meant "as long as the territory is federally governed and Congress does not repeal or amend this statute." One congress cannot bind future congresses in such matters, and once the territory was transformed into states, those states would then determine their own positions on slavery as a matter of local law. Congress could, no doubt, refuse to admit a territory into statehood unless its proposed constitution prohibited slavery, but Congress could not prohibit that state, once admitted, from amending its constitution to permit slavery if it so chose.

Missouri elected to enter the Union as a slave state, and it remained a slave state at all times relevant to the *Dred Scott* case. Illinois was carved out of the Northwest Territory, whose ordinance prohibited slavery, and was more or less a free state from the date of its admission on December 3, 1818.[41] The federally governed Wisconsin Territory, which included the present states of Minnesota and Wisconsin, was free by virtue of the Missouri Compromise.

Dred Scott was born a slave in Virginia. He moved, with his master, to Missouri in 1831, and was shortly thereafter sold to Dr. John Emerson. Emerson joined the army in 1833 and was ordered to Rock Island, Illinois. He took Scott with him, and they both stayed in Illinois for several years. Emerson then went, with Scott in tow, to the federally governed Wisconsin Territory, where Scott met and married, with Emerson's permission, another slave, whom Emerson thereafter acquired. Emerson traveled widely over the next few years, leaving Scott hired out in Wisconsin. Emerson and Scott, after a stopover in Louisiana, both eventually returned to Missouri.

Emerson died in 1843, leaving his property, including Scott, Scott's wife, and their two children, to his surviving spouse and daughter. John Sandford, the named defendant, was Mrs. Emerson's brother and the executor of Emerson's estate.

In 1846, Scott sued for his freedom in Missouri state court, claiming that by virtue of his two-year-long stay in the free state of Illinois he had obtained his freedom, which, once acquired, could not be extinguished by a return to Missouri. At the time of the suit, Missouri precedent was on Scott's side, and indeed Scott prevailed in the lower court. The Missouri Supreme Court, however, used Scott's case to reverse its longstanding rule on the status of (former) slaves who reside more than transiently in free states and held that Scott remained a slave.[42]

Scott then switched to federal court, filing a suit for trespass vi et armis (essentially battery) against Sandford. Scott alleged that Sandford was a citizen of New York and Scott was a citizen of Missouri, thus providing federal jurisdiction under the clause authorizing federal courts to hear "Controversies . . . between Citizens of different States."[43] Scott's argument was twofold. First, he repeated his claim that a two-year stay in Illinois was sufficient to establish his freedom as a matter of state law. This claim was a long shot. The Supreme Court had already indicated in a prior case that the status of slaves who moved from a slave state to a free state and back again was governed by the law of the origin state — in this case Missouri, which had just ruled against Scott.[44] One could argue, as did Justice McLean in dissent in *Dred Scott*, that the law of Missouri on this point should be determined by statute or settled practice rather than by a single decision of a state court,[45] but that was a tough argument to sell. The second, and more important, argument was that Scott's further sojourn into the Wisconsin Territory established his free status as a matter of supreme *federal* law, which Missouri could not then undo by operation of state law.

Scott lost in the lower court on the ground that if Congress could not simply abolish slavery in the states — and everyone agreed that it could not — it could not alter the status of slaves simply by virtue of their entry into federally governed territory. The Supreme Court affirmed on the ground that the federal courts had no jurisdiction over Scott's suit. A plurality of the Court held that descendants of slaves could never be "Citizens" within the meaning of the Diversity Clause, even if those descendants were themselves free. That claim was ridiculous on its face,[46] and it is doubtful whether Chief Justice Taney's views on that point commanded a majority of the Court. The more pertinent holding for our project was the Court's decision that Congress had no power to declare Scott free upon his entry into federal territory. That claim was ridiculous on its face, torso, and internal organs.

The Court spent a great deal of time and energy trying to establish that the Territories Clause applied only to territory in the possession of the United States at the time of ratification.[47] As we have already pointed out in Chapter 1, that is an impossible position to maintain. The language of the Territories Clause is general; the Northwest Territory may have been its primary subject, but that does not exclude application to other territory, including, as Justice Curtis pointed out in dissent, anticipated but unexecuted cessions from North Carolina and Georgia that took effect in, respectively, 1790 and 1802.[48]

Moreover, the Territories Clause — or, more precisely, the Territories and Property Clause — does not distinguish between real and personal property. If the clause does not apply to land acquired by the United States after ratification, it also does not apply to personal property acquired after ratification. The only source of authority to regulate personal property would then be the Sweeping Clause, and the nondelegation doctrine would thereby forbid Congress from broadly entrusting property management to the President.

The Court's determination to limit the scope of the Territories Clause is all the more remarkable because, as Justice Curtis pointed out, the conclusion is irrelevant even on the Court's own reasoning. The Court did not deny that Congress had the power to govern federal territories. It simply maintained that the power was incidental to the power of acquisition. So what? The real question was whether the power to govern, from whatever source it was derived, included the power to prohibit slavery in federal territory. It is certainly easy to reach the conclusion that Congress has such power by reading the Territories Clause as a grant of general legislative authority, but one could reach the same conclusion just as easily even if the power to govern was incidental to the power of acquisition.[49]

The Court's argument thus boiled down to the proposition that "an act of Congress which deprives a citizen of the United States of his liberty or property, merely because he came himself or brought his property into a particular Territory of the United States, and who had committed no offence against the laws, could hardly be dignified with the name of due process of law."[50] Of course, this argument gets off the ground only if the Due Process Clause of the Fifth Amendment applies to territorial legislation. As we explained above, the Court in *Dred Scott* was right that it does so apply, along with the other provisions of the Bill of Rights that limit federal power. The general power to govern conferred by the Territories Clause is constrained by generally applicable constitutional provisions, including provisions in the Bill of Rights. On that point, the Court in *Dred Scott* was one large step ahead of the Court in *The Insular Cases* (which, admittedly, would have reached the same conclusion about the scope of the Due Process Clause on the facts of *Dred Scott*, either or both because the Louisiana Territory would have been regarded as "incorporated" or because the Due Process Clause would have been regarded as "fundamental"). The next step, however, is to find a violation of due process in a law that abolishes the status of slavery in federal territory. The Court provided no argument for this point, because none can be given.

Put aside the rather large question whether the Due Process Clause addresses anything beyond executive and judicial procedures for deprivations of property and, perhaps, statutes that regulate those procedures. (Of course, that is rather like putting aside the question whether political discourse is "speech" under the First Amendment or rifles are "arms" under the Second Amendment; but indulge us for the moment.[51]) If Congress bans the possession of certain substances on federal territory, it is not unconstitutional to confiscate such items if they are brought into the territory, even if they are legal under the law of the origin state. Contraband does not cease to be contraband simply because some jurisdictions permit it. It is even clearer that ending the status of slavery did not constitute a deprivation of property without due process of law (or, for that matter, a taking of private property for public use without just compensation). It was universally agreed that slavery was entirely the product of municipal law and had no grounding in natural law or common law. That is why the Fugitive Slave Clause was inserted into the Constitution; otherwise, slaves who managed to escape onto free soil, where there was no municipal law to sustain the slave relationship, would have been free upon reaching the free haven. The Missouri Compromise recognized the principle behind the Fugitive Slave Clause by providing for the return of escaped slaves (though because the Fugitive Slave Clause applied by its terms only to slaves who escape from one *state* into another *state*, it is doubtful whether that concession was constitutionally required), but there is no reason why free federal territory would not otherwise function like free state territory. People who did not want to lose their slaves in federal territory needed to leave them behind.

Hard cases sometimes make bad law. In *Dred Scott*, an easy case made terrible law.

Conclusion: Imperial Reflections

Was Thomas Jefferson right in 1809 about the Constitution's suitability for empire? It depends.

First, it depends on what one means by *empire*. The Constitution readily accommodates an increase in the number of states in the union. As long as territorial acquisitions are designed to serve the purposes of statehood, territory can be acquired through the Treaty Clause, the Sweeping Clause, or some combination of the two. Governing that territory in a fashion that prepares the population for statehood does present some formal problems in light of the structural imperatives of the Appointments Clause and Article III. Because territorial executives and legislatures necessarily carry into effect federal law, they must be "Officers of the United States," appointed in conformity with the Appointments Clause, rather than locally selected officials. The President and Congress, however, can circumvent that difficulty if they so choose by "rubber-stamping" the formally nonbinding actions of local territorial officials. There is no such way of getting around the requirement that the "judicial Power" be exercised in federal territories only by Article III judges, but constitutions have generated worse results.

If, however, an "empire" includes territories that are not intended to become equal parts of the larger American polity, the Constitution is not so hospitable. If we are right that the Treaty Clause and the Sweeping Clause, the two vehicles for territorial acquisition, are both implementational powers that carry into effect other enumerated powers, then any territory that is not acquired with an eye toward admission as a state must serve some other enumerated constitutional power. The larger the territory, the harder it is to make that kind of case. And small territories, such as Guam, Wake, and Midway, whose acquisition can be constitutionally validated by the naval power, are not the stuff of which colonial empires are made. The imperialists of the nineteenth century, and their subsequent intellectual ancestors, may well have envisioned a traditional European-style empire for America. Jefferson had no sympathy for any such visions, and the Constitution has little more.

At least, the Constitution does not sanction the direct construction of such an empire. But just as practical, even if not formal, territorial self-governance can be achieved by following constitutional forms with an eye toward their evasion, could one indirectly construct an empire by following the proper forms for acquisition but never delivering on the promises that they require? Puerto Rico was a plausible candidate for statehood in 1899. It is still a plausible candidate for statehood in 2003. Can Congress hold it as a territory for another 104 years, and 104 more after that? If an initial acquisition is constitutionally legitimate, as the acquisition of Puerto Rico clearly was, does it ever cease to be a legitimate possession from the passage of time? Does it matter if a territory that was acquired with thoughts of statehood ceases to be a plausible candidate at some future time?

In keeping with our fascination for form over function, the constitutionally relevant moment is the moment of acquisition. Once the acquisition has been constitutionally validated, the acquired territory becomes "Territory . . . belonging to the United States," and there is nothing in the Territories Clause that requires Congress either to admit a territory as a state or to dispose of it (perhaps by granting independence) if statehood ever ceases to be an option. If Congress ultimately decides to hold legitimately acquired territory as a permanent colony, the Constitution does not forbid it (though the next Congress, or the next, can always switch sides again). Of course, under the Constitution as properly construed, territorial governance requires full compliance with a wide range of constitutional rights, including some distinctively Anglo-American procedural devices whose mandated use might make territorial governance inconvenient or impossible in some circumstances. The American Constitution, contrary to the case law of the past century, does not permit full-fledged colonialism in which territorial inhabitants are treated as subjects beyond the range of the Constitution. Accordingly, the cost of back-door colonialism might be very high. But if Congress really wants to bear the cost, the Constitution does not stand in the way.

Second, the Constitution's suitability for empire depends on what one means by "the Constitution." For many people, the Constitution is something far more complex than the document that was ratified by nine states as of June 21, 1788. If one views the Constitution as a set of social practices that bear a contingent (and quite possibly marginal) relationship to the document on display at the National Archives, one may have a very different view of the relationship between the Constitution and territorial acquisition and governance. The Constitution that we have in mind, however, is the one that is self-referentially described in Article VI, which declares that "[t]his Constitution" — not a set of social practices, not a set of moral aspirations, not a set of principles that emerges from a process of reflective equilibrium engaged in by elite twenty-first century academics, but "[t]his Constitution" — is "the Supreme Law of the Land." We do not in any way mean to denigrate the value of understanding social practices or moral aspirations.[1] They may well be better guides to political action than a dead document from the late eighteenth century. But as a purely intellectual matter, it is hard to understand why one would call anything other than that dead document "the Constitution," unless it is to capture the rhetorical ground that often accompanies equivocation.

Third, the answers to questions about American empire may depend on what one means by "the meaning of the Constitution." If the Constitution's meaning depends on historically concrete eighteenth-century mental states — original *understandings* rather than original *meanings* — it is possible that some of the answers that we have reached in this book might change. But it is also possible that they wouldn't. Original meanings and original understandings converge in a wide range of cases; we leave it to others to sort out how, if at all, they would differ in the context of territorial acquisitions and governance.

Finally, from the standpoint of original meaning, the constitutional fate of empire depends on a host of factual and legal contingencies. We reach the various conclusions in this book with widely varying degrees of confidence. We are very confident that peacetime military governments and territorial criminal trials conducted by adjudicators other than Article III judges are unconstitutional. We are much less confident that the Treaty Clause only confers power to make implementational law, and accordingly we are much less confident in our conclusions about the constitutional rules for territorial acquisition. Even within the framework for acquisitions that we adopt, there are many unanswered questions. The possibilities for American territorial acquisition depend to some extent on how tight a fit the Treaty Clause (and, for that matter, the Sweeping Clause) requires between means and ends. They depend to some extent on factual questions concerning the prospects for statehood of particular territories at the time of acquisition. And they depend to some extent on some basic epistemological points that we have largely skirted: what is the standard of proof, and who bears the burden of meeting that standard, for various propositions about constitutional meaning?

Regardless of whether Jefferson was right or wrong, he has sent us on a challenging journey. We hope that the journey has proved valuable to the reader, even if he or she has chosen to disembark at different ports along the way.

Notes

Introduction

1. Thomas Jefferson to the President of the United States (James Madison), Apr 27, 1809, *in* 12 *The Writings of Thomas Jefferson* 275, 277 (Albert Ellery Bergh ed., 1905).

2. *Id.*

3. *The Federalist* No. 10, at 82–84 (Clinton Rossiter ed., New American Library, 1961).

4. James Madison, *Notes of Debates in the Federal Convention of 1787*, at 410 (Adrienne Koch ed., 1966).

5. US Const art IV, § 3, cl 1. In full, the clause reads: "New States may be admitted by the Congress into this Union, but no new State shall be formed or erected within the Jurisdiction of any other State; nor any State be formed by the Junction of two or more States, or Parts of States, without the Consent of the Legislatures of the States concerned as well as of the Congress."

6. *Id.* art I, § 8, cl 17; *id.* art IV, § 3, cl 2. The latter clause is subject to the proviso: "and nothing in this Constitution shall be so construed as to Prejudice any Claims of the United States, or of any particular State."

7. The Constitution refers to the President using a generic male pronoun. We follow that practice without endorsing it.

8. US Const art II, § 2, cl 2.

9. Gerald L. Neuman, *The Nationalization of Civil Liberties*, 99 Colum L Rev 1630, 1646–47 (1999).

10. 252 US 416 (1920).

11. For an articulate expression of fundamentally the same methodology, see Vasan Kesavan and Michael Stokes Paulsen, *The Interpretive Force of the Constitution's Secret Drafting History*, - Geo LJ - (2003) (forthcoming). Our presentation here builds on a previous discussion in Gary Lawson and Guy Seidman, *The First "Establishment" Clause: Article VII and the Post-Constitutional Confederation*, 78 Notre Dame L Rev 83, 87–93 (2002).

12. A complete theory of interpretation must do much more: it must provide *principles of admissibility* that determine what materials are relevant for establishing meaning, *principles of significance* that determine the relative weight of admissible evidence, and *standards of proof* that determine how much admissible evidence is necessary in order to justify truth claims about a text. Obviously, it would require a lengthy book to spell out any such theory, originalist or otherwise. One of us intends to write such a book eventually. Until then, see Gary Lawson, *On Reading Recipes . . . and Constitutions*, 85 Geo LJ 1823 (1997); Gary Lawson, *Legal Indeterminacy: Its Cause and Cure*, 19 Harv JL & Pub Pol'y 411 (1996); Gary Lawson, *Proving the Law*, 86 Nw UL Rev 859 (1992).

13. Saikrishna B. Prakash, *Unoriginalism's Law Without Meaning*, 15 Const Comm 529, 541 (1998) (reviewing Jack N. Rakove, *Original Meanings: Politics and Ideas in the Making of the Constitution* (A. A. Knopf, 1996)).

14. Any contemporary reader who thinks it frivolous to speculate whether the standard meaning of *screwdriver* in this context could change in two hundred years either does not have children or has never attempted to assemble a computer table. For an even better example involving the changing meaning of the term *ratchet*, see John Harrison, *Forms of Originalism and the Study of History*, 26 Harv JL & Pub Pol'y 83 (2003).

15. Put another way, reading a document and deciding whether to follow it are two distinct operations. *See* Lawson, *On Reading Recipes . . . and Constitutions*. The nature of the document and the nature of communication tell you how to discern a document's meaning, though not what to do with that meaning once you have it.

More precisely, the nature of the document tells you *part* of what you need to know in order to interpret it. Michael Dorf, in a characteristically thoughtful response to some of Professor Lawson's prior work in this vein, has forcefully denied that interpretation can be divorced from normative concerns because "[w]hether we equate meaning with original public meaning, or with speaker's meaning, or with a dynamic conception of meaning, or with something else, depends on why we care about the meaning of whatever it is we are interpreting." Michael C. Dorf, *Recipe for Trouble: Some Thoughts on Meaning, Translation and Normative Theory*, 85 Geo LJ 1857, 1858 (1997). Professor Lawson has elsewhere agreed that the answers to at least some interpretive questions are "inescapably normative, depending heavily on the end one seeks to serve through interpretation." Gary Lawson, *Proving the Law*, 860. It is crucial, however, to understand the particular respects in which interpretation, of a constitution or anything else, is and is not necessarily a normative enterprise.

Propositions about meaning are propositions. Anything that is true of propositions in general is also true of propositions about meaning. One important truth about propositions is that the *proof* of any proposition requires three elements: *principles of admissibility* that tell you which considerations count for or against a proposition's truth, *principles of significance* that tell you how much (relative) weight to give to different sets of admissible evidence, and *standards of proof* that tell you how much evidence is necessary in order to proclaim the truth value of a proposition.

Normative considerations enter at the last stage, where one determines the *standard of proof* or *level of evidence* that is epistemologically required in order to make a declaration of truth. There is no way to separate that determination from the consequences of a truth declaration; the standard of proof appropriate to an ivory-tower scholar considering the meaning of the Engagements Clause is not necessarily the same as the standard of proof appropriate to the President of the United States in deciding whether a certain state of affairs justifies the launch of thermonuclear missiles. But by the same token, the correct principles of admissibility and significance for documents are objective facts. It is possible to monkey around with the rules of admissibility and significance for a document such as the Constitution, just as it is possible to monkey around with the rules of admissibility and significance for proving ordinary facts about events in the world. The law does it all of the time through rules of evidence. But to do so is deliberately to sacrifice the search for truth in favor of other values. There may, of course, be a good normative case for sacrificing the search for truth about constitutional meaning in favor of other values in many circumstances, but one ought to own up to the trade-off.

16. Steven D. Smith, *Law Without Mind*, 88 Mich L Rev 104 (1989).

17. This presents serious evidentiary problems, especially when people express views in the context of a political debate. To put it as delicately as possible: people, especially political actors, do not always mean what they say or say what they mean.

18. Gary Lawson, *Controlling Precedent: Congressional Control of Judicial Decision-Making*, 18 Const Comm 191, 196 n.20 (2001).

19. Laurence H. Tribe, *Taking Text and Structure Seriously: Reflections on Free-Form Method in Constitutional Interpretation*, 108 Harv L Rev 1221, 1235 (1995). The interchange between Professor Tribe and Professors Bruce Ackerman and David Golove of which this article was a part (*see* Bruce A. Ackerman and David M. Golove, *Is NAFTA Constitutional?*, 108 Harv L Rev 799 (1995); David M. Golove, *Against Free-Form Formalism*, 73 NYU L Rev 1791 (1998)) is one of the most interesting and rewarding exchanges in modern constitutional scholarship.

20. US Const art I, § 8, cl 3.

21. For explorations of some of the issues raised by tribal status, see Sarah H. Cleveland, *Powers Inherent in Sovereignty: Indians, Aliens, Territories, and the Nineteenth Century Origins of Plenary Power over Foreign Affairs*, 81 Tex L Rev 1, 25–82 (2002); Peter Nicolas, *American-Style Justice in No Man's Land*, 36 Ga L Rev 895 (2002); Judith Resnick, *Dependent Sovereigns: Indian Tribes, States, and the Federal Courts*, 56 U Chi L Rev 671 (1989). For analysis of some of the problems posed by Reconstruction, see John Harrison, *The Lawfulness of the Reconstruction Amendments*, 68 U Chi L Rev 375 (2001).

Chapter 1. Fundamentals

1. Our historical narrative is based principally on Henry Adams, 1–2 *History of the United States of America under the First Administration of Thomas Jefferson*

(Antiquarian Press, rep. 1962); Alexander DeConde, *This Affair of Louisiana* (Scribner's, 1976); Dumas Malone, *Jefferson the President: First Term, 1801–1805,* 239–332 (Little, Brown, 1970); and Arthur Preston Whitaker, *The Mississippi Question 1795–1803: A Study in Trade, Politics, and Diplomacy* (P. Smith, 1934). In the interest of editorial economy, we give specific citations to these sources for only a small fraction of the propositions that we have drawn from them.

2. *See* William Earl Weeks, *John Quincy Adams and American Global Empire* 93 (University Press of Kentucky, 1992); Whitaker, *The Mississippi Question,* 13.

3. Letter from James Madison to Charles Pinckney, Nov 27, 1802, *in* 6 *The Writings of James Madison* 462 (Gaillard Hunt ed., 1900).

4. Among the European countries, Spain was the first to discover Louisiana and France was the first to settle it. *See* DeConde, *This Affair of Louisiana,* 4–5. On whether or not discovery without settlement could have supported a Spanish claim in the sixteenth or seventeenth century, see Julius Goebel, *The Struggle for the Falkland Islands: A Study in Legal and Diplomatic History* 116–18 (Yale University Press, 1927) (suggesting "not"); Friedrich August Freiherr von der Heydte, *Discovery, Symbolic Annexation, and Virtual Effectiveness in International Law,* 29 Am J Int'l L 448, 457–61 (1935) (same). Spain never asserted a claim, so France took dominion over the Louisiana Territory by virtue of LaSalle's explorations and the resulting settlements in the late seventeenth century. *See* Binger Herman, *The Louisiana Purchase and Our Title West of the Rocky Mountains, with a Review of Annexation by the United States* 12–14 (1898). In 1762, at the conclusion of the Seven Years' War, France ceded the Louisiana Territory west of the Mississippi River to Spain as a supposed palliative for Spain's loss of Florida to England, though the territory was more of a burden than a benefit to whoever held it. *See* William P. Shepherd, *The Cession of Louisiana to Spain,* 19 Pol Sci Q 439, 451–53 (1904) (describing France's utter disinterest in retaining the Louisiana Territory in 1762). In the 1763 Treaty of Paris, England officially received Florida from Spain and the Louisiana Territory east of the Mississippi River (which became part of the United States in 1783) from France. *See* DeConde, *This Affair of Louisiana,* 28–29.

5. DeConde, *This Affair of Louisiana,* 39.

6. After England acquired Florida from Spain in 1763, England divided the territory at the Apalachicola River (roughly halfway along the Panhandle) into East Florida and West Florida. *See* Isaac Joslin Cox, *The West Florida Controversy, 1798–1813: A Study in American Diplomacy* 11–12 (Johns Hopkins Press, 1918). The northern boundary was, for the most part, set at the 31st parallel, which ranges from a few miles to about fifty miles north of the Gulf of Mexico. *See* Edward Bicknell, *The Territorial Acquisitions of the United States: An Historical Review* 3 (Small, Maynard & Co, 1899); Whitaker, *The Mississippi Question,* 38. This boundary fluctuated under British rule to accommodate settlements north of the line: *see* Cox, *The West Florida Controversy,* 12–13, 29–30; it was definitively settled at the 31st parallel for most of its length by treaty between Spain and the United States in 1795. *See* Treaty of Friendship, Limits and Navigation, Between the United States of America and the King of Spain, art II & IV, 8 Stat 138, 140.

7. *See* Adams, 1 *History of the United States,* 337–38.

8. Treaty of Friendship, Limits and Navigation, Between the United States of America and the King of Spain, art XXII, 8 Stat 138, 152.

9. DeConde, *This Affair of Louisiana*, 96 (quoting the memoirs of Spanish minister Godoy).

10. Napoleon had promised that the royal son-in-law, the Duke of Parma, would be placed on the throne of Etruria (as they renamed the province) with real powers and international recognition. By the summer of 1801, "[t]he young King of Etruria . . . had been sent to Italy, and had there been told that he possessed a kingdom and a crown, — but French armies occupied the territory; French generals administered the government; no foreign Power recognized the new kingdom, and no vestige of royal authority went with the royal title." Adams, 1 *History of the United States*, 374–75. Matters had not improved by the summer of 1802. *See id.*, 399–400.

11. The story of the negotiations and their political context is told in *id.*, 403–46; Adams, 2 *History of the United States*, 1–42; DeConde, *This Affair of Louisiana*, 107–72.

12. Treaty Between the United States of America and the French Republic, Apr. 30, 1803, art I, 8 Stat 200, 202 ("The First Consul of the French Republic . . . doth hereby cede to the United States in the name of the French Republic for ever and in full Sovereignty the said territory, with all its rights and appurtenances as fully and in the Same manner as they have been acquired by the French Republic in virtue of the above mentioned Treaty concluded with his Catholic Majesty.").

13. *Id.* art III.

14. Letter from Thomas Jefferson to John Dickinson, Aug 9, 1803, *in* 8 *The Writings of Thomas Jefferson* 262 (Paul L. Ford ed., 1895).

15. For expressions of Jefferson's belief in the need for a constitutional amendment, see Letter from Thomas Jefferson to John C. Breckinridge, Aug 18, 1803, *in id.*, 244; Letter from Thomas Jefferson to William Dunbar, July 17, 1803, *in id.*, 254; Letter from Thomas Jefferson to Benjamin Austin, July 18, 1803, *quoted in* Everett S. Brown, *The Constitutional History of the Louisiana Purchase* 23 (A. M. Kelley, 1920). For Jefferson's proposed amendments, see 10 *The Writings of Thomas Jefferson* 3–12 (Paul L. Ford ed., 1905). Jefferson's shifting positions on the federal government's power to acquire Louisiana are detailed in Brown, *The Constitutional History of the Louisiana Purchase*, 17–29, as is a sampling of people who shared Jefferson's doubts in one form or another (*id.*, 29–34).

16. *American Insurance Co. v 356 Bales of Cotton*, 26 US (1 Pet.) 511, 542 (1828).

17. 12 *Annals of Cong* 454 (1803) (statement of Rep. Mitchill); *id.*, 457 (statement of Rep. Sandford); *id.* (statement of Rep. Smilie); *id.*, 50 (statement of Sen. Taylor).

18. US Const amend X ("The powers not delegated to the United States by the Constitution, nor prohibited by it to the States, are reserved to the States respectively, or to the people.").

19. 12 *Annals of Cong* 454 (1803). In fairness to Rep. Sandford, he identified himself as "a plain Western farmer," *id.*, and the concept of a limited government of enumerated powers is neither intuitive nor self-evident even to trained legal minds. For a less charitable assessment of Rep. Sandford, see David P. Currie, *The Constitution in Congress: Jefferson and the West, 1801–1809*, 39 Wm & Mary L Rev 1441, 1464 n.127 (1998) ("Even a plain Western farmer, one would think, ought to read the Constitution that defines his authority.").

20. 12 *Annals of Cong* 468. *See also id.*, 467 ("had I been asked anywhere but, in this House, whether a sovereign nation had a right to acquire new territory, I should have thought the question an absurd one. It appears to me too plain and undeniable to admit of demonstration").

21. *Id.*, 436.

22. *Id.*, 473 ("It does appear to me that the right of acquiring territory must be included in the treaty-making power").

23. US Const art I, § 8, cl 1.

24. 12 *Annals of Cong* 472 (1803).

25. Jeffrey T. Renz, *What Spending Clause? (Or the President's Paramour): An Examination of the Views of Hamilton, Madison, and Story on Article I, Section 8, Clause 1 of the United States Constitution*, 33 John Marshall L Rev 81, 87 (1999).

26. *See Helvering v Davis*, 301 US 619, 640 (1937); *United States v Butler*, 296 US 1, 78 (1936).

27. For an excellent modern treatment of the debate, see John C. Eastman, *Restoring the "General" to the General Welfare Clause*, 4 Chapman L Rev 63 (2001).

28. *See* Renz, *What Spending Clause?*, 137–44.

29. US Const art I, § 8, cl 17 (emphasis added).

30. 12 *Annals of Cong* 473 (1803).

31. *See*, e.g., *South Dakota v Dole*, 483 US 203 (1987); *Spending Clause Symposium*, 4 Chapman L Rev 1–230 (2001).

32. David E. Engdahl, *The Spending Power*, 44 Duke LJ 1, 49 (1994).

33. US Const art I, § 8, cl 2.

34. David E. Engdahl, *The Basis of the Spending Power*, 18 Seattle UL Rev 215, 222 (1995).

35. US Const art I, § 9, cl 7.

36. *Id.* art IV, § 3, cl 2.

37. *See* Engdahl, *The Basis of the Spending Power*.

38. *See*, e.g., James Madison, *Notes of Debates in the Federal Convention of 1787*, at 402 (Adrienne Koch ed., 1966) (reporting Oliver Ellsworth's query that "[o]ught not every man who pays a tax, to vote for the representative who is to levy and dispose of his money?"); Jonathan Elliot, 1 *Debates on the Adoption of the Federal Constitution* 74 (1859) [hereinafter "*Elliot's Debates*"] (reporting that Benjamin Franklin during the debate on the Articles of Confederation thought it "extraordinary" that some states "would not confederate with us, unless we would let them dispose of our money"); *id.*, 76 (describing John Adams's rhetorical question during the debate on the Articles of Confederation that, in a partnership of unequal partners, "Is it just that they should equally dispose of the moneys of the partnership?").

39. For the various taxing clauses, see US Const art I, § 8, cl 1; *id.* art I, § 9, cls 4–6. For the various appropriation clauses, see *id.* art I, § 7, cl 1; art I, § 8, cl 12; *id.* art I, § 9, cl 7. For other financial provisions, see *id.* art I, § 8, cl 2; *id.* art I, § 8, cls 5–6.

40. *Cf.* Akhil Reed Amar, *The Bill of Rights: Creation and Reconstruction* 178–79 (Yale University Press, 1998) (arguing that the word *abridge* can have different meanings in different constitutional contexts); Akhil Reed Amar, *Intratextualism*, 112 Harv L Rev

747, 774–75 (1999) (explaining that the word *person* does not always have the same meaning throughout the Constitution).

41. *The Records of the Federal Convention of 1787*, 367 (Max Farrand ed., 1911).

42. *See* Engdahl, *The Basis of the Spending Power*, 256–58.

43. *Id.* art I, § 8, cl 18.

44. The label was originally employed by antifederalists as a criticism of the clause's potentially expansive character, but the term gained near-universal acceptance, including acceptance by *The Federalist*. *See The Federalist* No. 33, at 203 (Alexander Hamilton) (Clinton Rossiter ed., New American Library, 1961).

45. *See* Engdahl, *The Basis of the Spending Power*, 251–56.

46. It would be quite jarring, of course, if the federal government did not have the power to pay off the Revolutionary War debt, which was a subject of considerable concern during the founding. But the Sweeping Clause provides ample authority for that task. The Constitution enumerates the power "[t]o borrow Money on the credit of the United States." US Const art I, § 8, cl 2. A creditor who fails to pay debts will soon have no credit. Accordingly, it is "necessary and proper for carrying into Execution" the borrowing power to pay off preexisting debt. And Article VI, section 1 neatly makes the pre-ratification debt an obligation of the new government. *See id.* art VI, § 1 ("All Debts contracted and Engagements entered into, before the Adoption of this Constitution, shall be as valid against the United States under this Constitution, as under the Confederation.").

47. *Id.* art II, § 2, cl 2.

48. *See* Vasan Kesavan, *The Treaty-Making Power and American Federalism: An Originalist Proof for* Missouri v Holland (unpublished manuscript, Dec 9, 2001).

49. *See id.*, n. 3.

50. *See*, e.g., Martin H. Flaherty, *Are We to Be a Nation? Federal Power vs. "States Rights" in Foreign Affairs*, 70 U Colo L Rev 1277 (1999); Gerald L. Neuman, *The Nationalization of Civil Liberties Revisited*, 99 Colum L Rev 1630, 1650–55 (1999).

51. In 1999, this question was the subject of a 303-page exchange in the pages of the *Columbia Law Review* between John Yoo, who defends the view that at least some treaties are not self-executing, and Martin Flaherty and Carlos Vazquez, who defend a stronger vision of self-execution. *Compare* John C. Yoo, *Globalism and the Constitution: Treaties, Non-Self-Execution, and the Original Understanding*, 99 Colum L Rev 1955 (1999); John C. Yoo, *Treaties and Public Lawmaking: A Textual and Structural Defense of Non-Self-Execution*, 99 Colum L Rev 2218 (1999), *with* Martin S. Flaherty, *History Right?: Historical Scholarship, Original Understanding, and Treaties As "Supreme Law of the Land,"* 99 Colum L Rev 2095 (1999); Carlos Manuel Vazquez, *Laughing at Treaties*, 99 Colum L Rev 2154 (1999). For an alternative view that would give self-executing effect only to treaties that do not conflict with existing statutory law, see Vasan Kesavan, *The Three Tiers of Federal Law* (unpublished manuscript, June 4, 2002).

52. This question has prompted modern debates that approach in length, intensity, and variety the recent debates on self-execution. *Compare* Bruce A. Ackerman and David M. Golove, *Is NAFTA Constitutional?*, 108 Harv L Rev 799 (1995) (treaties and executive agreements are interchangeable because of an unwritten constitutional amendment)

with Laurence H. Tribe, *Taking Text and Structure Seriously: Reflections on Free-Form Method in Constitutional Interpretation*, 108 Harv L Rev 1221 (1995) (treaties and executive agreements are not interchangeable because the Constitution does not contain amendments written in invisible ink) *with* John C. Yoo, *Laws As Treaties?: The Constitutionality of Congressional-Executive Agreements*, 99 Mich L Rev 757 (2001) (treaties and executive agreements are sometimes interchangeable because of contemporary practice).

53. *See Reid v Covert*, 354 US 1, 5–6, 15–18 (1957) (plurality opinion); *id.*, 56 (Frankfurter, J., concurring in the result).

54. *See* Robert Anderson IV, *"Ascertained in a Different Way": The Treaty Power at the Crossroads of Contract, Compact, and Constitution*, 69 Geo Wash L Rev 189 (2001) (arguing that the treaty power is limited to provisions resulting from the good-faith negotiations of the parties); Curtis Bradley, *The Treaty Power and American Federalism*, 97 Mich L Rev 390 (1998) (arguing, based largely on modern developments, for federalism-based limitations on the treaty power); Curtis Bradley, *The Treaty Power and American Federalism, Part II*, 99 Mich L Rev 98 (2000) (same); David M. Golove, *Treaty-Making and the Nation: The Historical Foundations of the Nationalist Conception of the Treaty Power*, 98 Mich L Rev 1075, 1083–84 (2000) (claiming some limits to the treaty power based on the separation of powers).

55. *See*, e.g., Anderson, *"Ascertained in a Different Way"*, 206 ("For the Framers, domestic legislation effected by treaty simply would not have been a 'treaty' in their minds.").

56. *See*, e.g., Caleb Nelson, *The Treaty Power and Self-Execution: A Comment on Professor Woolhandler's Article*, 42 Va J Int'l L 801, 812–14 (2002).

57. *See* Golove, *Treaty-Making and the Nation*, 1104–27.

58. *See id.*, 1210–37.

59. 252 US 469 (1920). Today, under modern understandings of Congress's power to "regulate Commerce . . . among the several States," US Const art I, § 8, cl 3, it is virtually certain that Congress would be allowed to pass a statute to protect migratory birds without recourse to a treaty.

60. For a thorough (albeit decidedly unsympathetic) detailing of the progress, and near passage, of the Bricker Amendment, see Duane Tananbaum, *The Bricker Amendment Controversy: A Test of Eisenhower's Political Leadership* (Cornell University Press, 1988).

61. *See* Kesavan, *The Treaty-Making Power and American Federalism*.

62. *See* Christopher Rebel J. Pace, *The Art of War under the Constitution*, 95 Dickinson L Rev 557, 562–65 (1991); John C. Yoo, *The Continuation of Politics by Other Means: The Original Understanding of War Powers*, 84 Cal L Rev 167, 265 (1996). Congress could enact a statute declaring peace, and perhaps that statute would have domestic consequences if other statutes are contingently triggered by such a legislative declaration, but the declaration does not end the war in any meaningful legal sense.

63. Gerald L. Neuman, *The Nationalization of Civil Liberties*, 99 Colum L Rev 1630, 1646–47 (1999).

64. *Compare* Bradley, *The Treaty Power and American Federalism*, 415–16 (claiming that Jefferson's views were widely held); George A. Finch, *The Need to Restrain the*

Treaty-Making Power of the United States within Constitutional Limits, 48 Am J Int'l L 57, 61 (1954) (same) *with* Golove, *Treaty-Making and the Nation*, 1188 (arguing that Jefferson's views were idiosyncratic). One need not be a historian to sense that Professor Golove has much the better of this argument. A casual reading of founding-era materials shows that Jefferson's view was very far from commanding a consensus.

65. Thomas Jefferson, *A Manual of Parliamentary Practice for the Use of the Senate of the United States*, in *Jefferson's Parliamentary Writings* 353, 420–21 (Wilbur Samuel Howell ed., 1988).

66. It also identifies the President as a branch of the legislature, which does not speak well of Jefferson's skill as a constitutional interpreter. Fortunately, we do not invoke Jefferson as an authority but instead independently examine whether his views of the treaty power are correct.

67. *See* Flaherty, *Are We to Be a Nation?*, 1306 ("Few would dispute that requirement, early on articulated by Thomas Jefferson, that treaties not be pretextual"); Golove, *Treaty-Making and the Nation*, 1090 n.41; Louis Henkin, *The Constitution, Treaties, and International Human Rights*, 116 U Pa L Rev 1012, 1024–25 (1968).

68. On the importance of constitutional form, even at the expense of substance, see Vasan Kesavan and Michael Stokes Paulsen, *Is West Virginia Unconstitutional?*, 90 Cal L Rev 291 (2002).

69. Letter from Thomas Jefferson to Wilson Cary Nicholas, Sept 7, 1803, *in* 8 *The Writings of Thomas Jefferson* 247 n.1 (Paul L. Ford ed., 1897).

70. US Const art I, § 3, cl 4 & 6.

71. S Rep No 79, 28th Cong, 2d Sess (1845), *reprinted in* 6 *Compilation of Reports of Committee on Foreign Relations, US Senate, 1789–1901*, at 78, 81–82 (1901). As we shall later see, this committee's constitutional acumen was not always much better than its clarity of expression, but it does show that Jefferson was not wholly idiosyncratic.

72. *See* 32 *Cong Rec* 497 (1899) (statement of Sen. Hoar).

73. For a detailed treatment of the near passage of the various forms of the "Bricker Amendment," see Tananbaum, *The Bricker Amendment Controversy*.

74. Whether that is enough to establish our proposed meaning as "correct" raises questions that go far beyond our project. If, for example, a proposition about constitutional meaning is true only if it can be established beyond a reasonable doubt, then any clause that generates enough uncertainty to prevent any single interpretation from meeting that threshold will be literally meaningless. Needless to say, that is a problem that we cannot address here.

75. *See* US Const art II, § 2, cl 2.

76. *Id.* art I, § 10, cl 1.

77. *Id.* art I, § 10, cl 3.

78. *Id.* art VI, cl 2.

79. On standard doctrine, see Caleb Nelson, *Preemption*, 88 Va L Rev 225 (2002). On original meaning, see Kesavan, *The Three Tiers of Federal Law*.

80. US Const amend 1.

81. *Cf.* Nelson, *The Treaty Power and Self-Execution*, 811–12 (noting that the First Amendment, by its terms, seems not to apply to treaties).

82. *See* Daniel A. Farber, *The First Amendment* 1 (Foundation Press, 1998).

83. "No state shall make or enforce any law which shall abridge the privileges or immunities of citizens of the United States." US Const amend XIV, § 1. For the proposition that the Privileges or Immunities Clause protects some First Amendment rights against discriminatory state action, see John Harrison, *Reconstructing the Privileges or Immunities Clause*, 101 Yale LJ 1385 (1992). For the proposition that the Privileges or Immunities Clause may also protect some First Amendment rights against even non-discriminatory state action, see Akhil Reed Amar, *The Bill of Rights and the Fourteenth Amendment*, 101 Yale LJ 1193 (1992).

84. As one Federalist pamphleteer put it in 1788: "examine the plan [of the Constitution], and you will find that the liberty of the press and the laws of Mahomet are equally affected by it." Hugh Williamson, *Remarks on the New Plan of Government* (1788), *reprinted in* Bernard Schwartz, 1 *The Bill of Rights: A Documentary History* 550, 551 (Chelsea House, 1971). For other expressions of this view by prominent founding-era figures, see Gary Lawson and Patricia B. Granger, *The "Proper" Scope of Federal Power: A Jurisdictional Interpretation of the Sweeping Clause*, 43 Duke LJ 267, 318–19 (1993).

85. The other provisions of the Bill of Rights present a more complicated story. Amendments 2–8 do not make specific reference to Congress. Indeed, they do not even make specific reference to the federal government, though Chief Justice John Marshall was surely correct to conclude in *Barron v Baltimore*, 32 US (7 Pet.) 242, 250 (1833), that the context of the Bill of Rights demonstrates that it does not limit state governments. It makes sense that those other amendments are not limited to Congress, because they deal with subjects that implicate potential abuses of the executive or judicial power. The Second Amendment, which protects the right to keep and bear arms, limits Congress but also prevents the President from disarming the militia through his power as military commander-in-chief. Similarly, the Third Amendment, which limits the quartering of soldiers, also obviously addresses the President's power over the military. The Fourth Amendment's requirement of reasonable searches and seizures constricts the President's power to execute the laws, and the requirement of probable cause for warrants limits the judicial power to immunize executive agents from civil suits. The Fifth Amendment's criminal process provisions clearly constrain the executive's prosecutorial power and the judicial power to compel testimony through contempt orders. The Due Process Clause is paradigmatically a restriction on arbitrary executive or judicial action. The Sixth, Seventh, and Eighth Amendments all target potential abuses of the judicial process. The only exceptional provision may be the Takings Clause of the Fifth Amendment, which is perhaps the most difficult provision in the Bill of Rights to explicate. For our expedition into the swamp, see Gary Lawson and Guy Seidman, *Taking Notes: Subpoenas and Just Compensation*, 66 U Chi L Rev 1081 (1999).

86. US Const art I, § 9, cl 1 (emphasis added).

87. *See id.* art V.

88. *Id.* art I, § 9, cl 8 (emphasis added).

89. As for the other Article I, section 9 prohibitions that do not make specific reference to congressional actions, one could plausibly say either that the absence of such reference makes them generally applicable to all federal action or that the specific reference to "the United States" in the Nobility Clause demands the opposite inference. The placement of

these provisions in Article I does not create a presumption that they apply only to Congress because some of them, such as the prohibition on withdrawal of funds without an appropriation (*id*. art I, § 9, cl 7) are clearly aimed at executive and judicial actors.

90. *Id*. art I, § 1, cl 1.

91. *Id*. art I, § 3, cl 1. It also means, inter alia, that two-thirds of the Senate cannot expel the Vice President. *See id*. art I, § 5, cl 2 ("[e]ach House may . . . , with the Concurrence of two thirds, expel a Member").

92. Theoretical conceptions, of course, are important because they help define otherwise ambiguous terms and provide the background conventions against which the Constitution's compromise was constructed.

93. *See* John Harrison, *The Constitutional Origins and Implications of Judicial Review*, 84 Va L Rev 333 (1998).

94. US Const art I, § 1.

95. The classic comparative study of the Vesting Clauses is Steven G. Calabresi and Kevin H. Rhodes, *The Structural Constitution: Unitary Executive, Plural Judiciary*, 105 Harv L Rev 1153 (1992).

96. US Const art II, § 1, cl 1.

97. *Id*. art III, § 1.

98. *See* Steven G. Calabresi, *The Vesting Clauses As Power Grants*, 88 Nw UL Rev 1377 (1994); Steven G. Calabresi and Saikrishna B. Prakash, *The President's Power to Execute the Laws*, 104 Yale LJ 541, 570–79.

99. Gary Lawson and Christopher D. Moore, *The Executive Power of Constitutional Interpretation*, 81 Iowa L Rev 1267, 1281–82 (1996). Of course, the view that the Article II Vesting Clause is a grant of power rather than a mere designation of office has its share of critics; *see* Gary Lawson, *The Rise and Rise of the Administrative State*, 107 Harv L Rev 1231, 1242–43 (1994) (listing scholars who maintain that the clause merely designates the presidential office), and the view is at least implicitly rejected by much modern Supreme Court doctrine. But what these critics do not lack in numbers they lack in substance. By far the best argument against the "power grant" reading of the Article II Vesting Clause is Lawrence Lessig and Cass R. Sunstein, *The President and the Administration*, 94 Colum L Rev 1, 46–52 (1994)—and it isn't very good. In addition to the counterpunch thrown by Professors Calabresi and Prakash in *The President's Power to Execute the Laws*, see also the recent rebuttal by Professor Prakash. Saikrishna B. Prakash, *The Essential Meaning of Executive Power*, Ill L Rev —— (2004) (forthcoming).

100. Several of the Article I enumerations grant powers to entities other than Congress. Some of the provisions in sections 2–5 of Article I grant powers to the individual legislative branches concerning such matters as appointment of legislative officers, the qualifications of members of the legislature, and impeachment. *See* US Const art I, §2, cl 5; *id*. art I, § 3, cl 5–6; *id*. art. I, § 5, cl 1–3. Other provisions in those sections grant power to nonlegislative actors, such as giving the Vice President power to preside over the Senate and cast tie-breaking votes (*id*. art I, § 3, cl 4) and the Chief Justice power to preside over presidential impeachment trials (*id*. art I, § 3, cl 6).

101. *Id*. art III, § 2, cl 1.

102. *Id.* art II, § 2, cl 1 ("The President shall be Commander in Chief of the Army and Navy of the United States, and of the Militia of the several States, when called into the actual Service of the United States").

103. *Id.* art II, § 2, cl 1 ("he may require the Opinion, in writing, of the principal Officer in each of the executive Departments, upon any Subject relating to the Duties of their respective Offices").

104. *Id.* art II, § 2, cl 2 (appointments); *id.* art II, § 3 (adjournment).

105. *Id.*

106. The classic study of the drafting of the Treaty Clause, which emphasizes that the participants in the Constitutional Convention probably did not intend for the clause's placement in Article II to settle this issue, is Jack N. Rakove, *Solving a Constitutional Puzzle: The Treatymaking Clause As a Case Study*, 1 Persp in Am Hist 233 (1984). Such evidence of drafting intentions is relevant to an inquiry into original *understanding*, but is considerably less decisive to an inquiry into original *meaning* that focuses on the perceptions (whether actual or hypothetical) of the public to whom the Constitution was addressed.

107. Saikrishna B. Prakash and Michael D. Ramsey, *The Executive Power over Foreign Affairs*, 111 Yale LJ 231, 292 (2000). Indeed, virtually every important thinker who influenced the founding generation thought of treaty making as an executive function. *See* Prakash and Ramsey, 265–72; Yoo, *Globalism and the Constitution*, 1990–97.

108. *See,* e.g., James Madison, Letters of Helvidius, Aug 24, 1793, *in* 6 *The Writings of James Madison* 138–88 (Gaillard Hunt ed., 1906): "If we consult, for a moment, the nature and operation of the two powers to declare war and to make treaties, it will be impossible not to see, that they can never fall within a proper definition of executive powers. The natural province of the executive magistrate is to execute laws, as that of the legislature is to make laws. All his acts, therefore, properly executive, must presuppose the existence of the laws to be executed. A treaty is not an execution of laws; it does not presuppose the existence of laws. It is, on the contrary, to have itself the force of a *law*, and to be carried into *execution*, like all *other laws*, by the *executive magistrate.*"

Other members of the founding generation expressed similar views at various times. *See* Golove, *Against Free-Form Formalism*, 1873–75 (noting that James Madison, George Mason, and James Wilson at the Constitutional Convention viewed the treaty power as legislative in character and that Alexander Hamilton took conflicting positions at different times).

109. *See id,* 1873–74.

110. John Norton Moore, *Treaty Interpretation, the Constitution, and the Rule of Law,* 42 Va J Int'l L 163, 192 (2001).

111. The Senate does gain power from the Treaty Clause via the requirement of its "Advice and Consent" and two-thirds approval for the making of treaties. Whether this power is purely a negative power of disapproval or a stronger power to participate in the shaping of treaties is an interesting question that we do not address. For an illuminating exploration, see Rakove, *Solving a Constitutional Puzzle.* For whatever this may be worth to the debate: it seems very difficult to read a provision calling for "Advice and Consent" as requiring only consent without advice.

112. Pacificus No. 1, June 29, 1793, *in The Papers of Alexander Hamilton* 42 (Harold C. Syrett ed., 1969).

113. *See The Federalist* No. 75, at 418 (Hamilton) ("Though several writers on the subject of government place that [treaty-making] power in the class of executive authorities, yet this is evidently an arbitrary disposition. For if we attend carefully to its operation, it will be found to partake more of the legislative than of the executive character, though it does not seem strictly to fall within the definition of either of them.").

114. Prakash, *The Essential Meaning of Executive Power*.

115. This proposition, and its implications for the nondelegation doctrine, is explored in Gary Lawson, *Delegation and Original Meaning*, 88 Va L Rev 327, 337–40 (2002).

116. US Const art I, § 8, cl 18.

117. For an excellent overview of the historical debate and a defense of a minimalist conception of the executive power, see Henry P. Monaghan, *The Protective Power of the Presidency*, 93 Colum L Rev 1 (1993).

118. *See* Prakash and Ramsey, *The Executive Power over Foreign Affairs*. Of course, to say that it is hard to dispute is not to say that no one has ever disputed it. James Madison disputed it with considerable fervor in his exchange with Alexander Hamilton concerning the President's power to issue the Neutrality Proclamation of 1793. But the weight of the evidence, as Professors Prakash and Ramsey have convincingly demonstrated, strongly supports the idea that the standard eighteenth-century understanding of "executive Power" included a foreign affairs component.

119. *See id.*, 263–64. In this respect, cases such as *Dames and Moore v Regan*, 453 US 654 (1981), which permitted the President to halt pending judicial proceedings by executive order, are clearly wrong.

120. *See* Lawson and Granger, *The "Proper" Scope of Federal Power*.

121. *See* David E. Engdahl, *Constitutional Federalism in a Nutshell* 20 (2d ed., West, 1987).

122. For the argument of the Bank's opponents, see 17 US (4 Wheat.), 367 (argument of Mr. Jones). For the argument of the Bank's proponents, see *id.*, 324–25 (argument of Mr. Webster); *id.*, 356–57 (argument of attorney general); *id.*, 386–88 (argument of Mr. Pinckney).

123. *See id.*, 413 (*necessary* means "convenient, or useful").

124. *See* Lawson and Granger, *The "Proper" Scope of Federal Power*, 288.

125. Grants of authority can, of course, be ministerial rather than discretionary. In that circumstance, there is no need for a principle of reasonableness, for the agent has no discretion that can be unreasonably exercised.

126. 5 Co Rep 99b (1598).

127. 23 H 8 c V, § 3, cl 2–3, 4 Stat at Large 223, 224 (1531). Technically, the statute of 1531 expired by its own terms after twenty years, but it was continued indefinitely in 1549. *See* 3 & 4 Ed 6 c 8, 5 Stat at Large 341 (1549).

128. 5 Co Rep 99b–100a.

129. 6 H 6 c V 3 Stat at Large 108, 110 (1427). The vitality of this statute was specifically confirmed in the 1531 enactment. *See* 23 H 8, c V, § 6, 4 Stat at Large 227.

130. 5 Co Rep 99b–100a.

131. *See* Stanley de Smith, Harry Woolf, and Jeffrey Jowell, *Judicial Review of Administrative Action* 297–98 (5th ed., Sweet & Maxwell, 1995); H. W. R. Wade and C. F. Forsyth, *Administrative Law* 353 (8th ed., Oxford University Press, 2000).

132. 2 W Bl 924 (1828) (reporting cases from Westminster Hall from 1746 through 1779).

133. *Id.*, 924–25.

134. *Id.*, 925.

135. Wade and Forsyth, *Administrative Law*, 353.

136. William Blackstone, 3 *Commentaries on the Laws of England* 74 (1765).

137. *See* de Smith, Woolf, and Jowell, *Judicial Review of Administrative Action*, 596. For general discussions of the Continental principle of proportionality, see Jurgen Schwarze, *European Administrative Law* 677–88 (Sweet & Maxwell, 1992); Robert Thomas, *Legitimate Expectations and Proportionality in Administrative Law* 77–85 (Hart, 2000).

138. Its adoption has, however, often been urged in modern times (*see* Thomas, *Legitimate Expectations and Proportionality*, 86–110), and the principle "may well infiltrate British law" through decisions of the European Court of Human Rights, which engages in proportionality review. Wade and Forsyth, *Administrative Law*, 368.

139. *See* de Smith, Woolf, and Jowell, *Judicial Review of Administrative Action*, 593.

140. Wade and Forsyth, *Administrative Law*, 368.

141. *See* de Smith, Woolf, and Jowell, *Judicial Review of Administrative Action*, 603–05.

142. The difference between "ill-advised" and "unconstitutional" is relevant if the President's actions give rise to a private-law cause of action that is not barred by immunity. If the act is unconstitutional, then the actors could not claim actual legal authorization for their conduct.

143. Again, the answer could be legally relevant if there is not an absolute judicial immunity from civil lawsuits. The Supreme Court has said that there is absolute immunity even for actions taken in bad faith without jurisdiction. *See Bradley v Fisher*, 80 US (13 Wall.) 335, 347 (1871). We plan to explore the correctness of this determination, as well as larger questions of executive and sovereign immunity, in a subsequent work.

144. *See* A. V. Dicey, *Introduction to the Study of the Law of the Constitution* 3–11 (8th ed., Liberty Classics, 1982).

145. Thomas, *Legitimate Expectations and Proportionality*, 79 (quoting R. *Ministry of Agriculture, Fisheries and Food, ex parte Fedesa*, ECR (1990)).

146. US Const art II, § 1, cl 5.

147. For a similar example, see William E. Mikell, *The Extent of the Treaty-Making Power of the President and Senate of the United States, Pt. II*, 7 U Pa L Rev 528, 530–31 (1909).

148. The Article V amending authorities, of course, are expressly granted the power to alter the Constitution's structural arrangements. And accordingly, their authority is expressly limited by the proviso that no state may be deprived of its equal suffrage in the Senate without its consent.

149. At that convention, Henry Abbott observed that "[i]t is feared by some people, that, by the power of making treaties, they might make a treaty engaging with foreign

powers to adopt the Roman Catholic religion in the United States." 4 *Elliot's Debates*, 191–92 (statement of Henry Abbott). James Iredell's tepid response was simply that "[t]he power to make treaties can never be supposed to include a right to establish a foreign religion among ourselves, though it might authorize a toleration of others." *Id.*, 194 (statement of James Iredell).

150. *See* William E. Mikell, *The Extent of the Treaty-Making Power of the President and Senate of the United States*, 7 U. Pa L Rev 435, 443 (1909).

151. Patrick Henry was particularly vocal on this score. *See* 3 *Elliot's Debates*, 315 (statement of Patrick Henry) ("The important right of making treaties is upon the most dangerous foundation. The President, and a few senators, possess it in the most unlimited manner"). Other prominent antifederalists shared his concerns. *See id.*, 509 (statement of George Mason) ("The President and Senate can make any treaty whatsoever"); Letter IV from the Federal Farmer, Oct 12, 1787, *reprinted in* 14 *The Documentary History of the Ratification of the Constitution* 43–44 (John P. Kaminski and Gaspare J. Saladino eds., State Historical Society of Wisconsin, 1986) ("It is not said that these treaties shall be made in pursuance of the constitution, nor are there any constitutional bounds set to those who shall make them. . . . This power in the president and senate is absolute"); Brutus II, Nov 1, 1787, *reprinted in* 13 *The Documentary History of the Ratification of the Constitution* 529 (John P. Kaminski and Gaspare J. Saladino eds., State Historical Society of Wisconsin, 1986) ("I do not find any limitation, or restriction, to the exercise of this [treaty] power"). James Madison's response to these concerns at the Virginia ratifying convention was vague and general: "I conceive that, as far as the bills of rights in the states do not express any thing foreign to the nature of such things, and express fundamental principles essential to liberty, and those privileges which are declared necessary to all free people, these rights are not encroached on by this government." 3 *Elliot's Debates*, 516 (statement of James Madison).

152. *See* Flaherty, *Are We to Be a Nation?*, 1308–09.

153. *See* John O. McGinnis and Michael B. Rappaport, *Our Supermajoritarian Constitution*, 80 Tex L Rev 703 (2002).

154. Even in a post–Seventeenth Amendment world, there can be a real difference between the majorities required to elect a senator and a representative in any state that conducts House elections by district and has more than one district.

155. What happens under this theory if Congress has already acted depends on the hierarchical status of treaties and laws. *See* Kesavan, *The Three Tiers of Federal Law*.

156. Letter from William Cary Nicholas to Thomas Jefferson, Sept 3, 1803, *quoted in* Brown, *The Constitutional History of the Louisiana Purchase*, 27.

157. 3 *Elliot's Debates*, 507 (statement of George Nicholas).

158. For a detailed demonstration of this basic point, see Pace, *The Art of War under the Constitution*, 562–67.

159. US Const art IV, § 4.

160. *See* St. George Tucker, 1 *Blackstone's Commentaries App.* 366 (William Young Birch & Abraham Small, 1803) ("The possibility of undue partiality in the federal government in affording its protection to one part of the union in preference to another, which may be invaded at the same time, seems to be provided against, by that part of this clause which guarantees such protection to each of them.").

161. *See* Convention Between His Most Christian Majesty and the United States of America, for the Purpose of defining and establishing the Functions and Privileges of their respective Consuls and Vice-Consuls, 8 Stat 106 (1859) (providing the text of the convention); *Journal of the Executive Proceedings of the Senate of the United States* 8–9 (1828) (providing the text of the Senate's approval).

162. Golove, *Treaty-Making and the Nation,* 1150.

163. US Const art II, § 3.

164. William Blackstone, 1 *Commentaries on the Laws of England* 246.

165. *See* Joseph Story, 3 *Commentaries on the Constitution* § 1562 (Hilliard, Gray & Co, 1833) ("as public functionaries, they [ambassadors] are entitled to all of the immunities and rights, which the law of nations has provided at once for their dignity, their independence, and their inviolability.").

166. *See id.* § 1559 (suggesting that a presidential power to receive consuls can be inferred, even though consuls "are not diplomatic functionaries, or political representatives of a foreign nation; but are treated in the character of mere commercial agents").

167. Treaty of Amity, Commerce and Navigation, Nov 19, 1794, United States–Great Britain, art 9, 8 Stat 116, 122.

168. Golove, *Treaty-Making and the Nation,* 1099.

169. *See* Lawson and Seidman, *Taking Notes,* 1106–07. For a more detailed defense of this position, see Gary Lawson, *Legal Indeterminacy: Its Cause and Cure,* 19 Harv JL & Pub Pol'y 411 (1996).

170. Thomas Jefferson, 1 *The Writings of Thomas Jefferson* 329 (Paul L. Ford ed., 1904).

171. US Const art IV, § 3, cl 1.

172. Northwest Ordinance of 1787, Art V, 1 Stat 51, 53.

173. Letter from Levi Lincoln to Thomas Jefferson, Jan 10, 1803, *reprinted in* Brown, *The Constitutional History of the Louisiana Purchase,* 19.

174. Letter from Gouverneur Morris to Henry W. Livingston, Dec 4, 1803, *reprinted in* 4 *The Founders' Constitution* 548 (Philip B. Kurland and Ralph Lerner eds., University of Chicago Press, 1987).

175. *See,* e.g., 8 *Annals of Cong* 55 (1803) (statement of Sen. Tracy) ("The article of the Constitution, if any person will take the trouble to examine it, refers to domestic States only, and not at all to foreign States. . . . The words of the Constitution are completely satisfied, by a construction which shall include only the admission of domestic States, who were all parties to the Revolutionary war, and to the compact."); *id.,* 433 (statement of Rep. Griswold) ("Congress may admit new States, — but according to my construction of this article, are confined to the territory belonging to the United States at the formation of the Constitution — to the territory then within the United States.").

176. Story, 3 *Commentaries on the Constitution* § 1310.

177. Articles of Confederation art XI ("Canada, acceding to this confederation, and joining in the measures of the united states, shall be admitted into, and entitled to all the advantages of this union; but no other colony shall be admitted into the same, unless such admission be agreed to by nine states.").

178. 10 US (6 Cranch) 332, 336–37 (1810).

179. *See United States v Gratiot*, 39 US (14 Pet.) 526, 537–38 (1840).

180. 60 US (19 How.) 393, 432–43, 448–49 (1857). For a painstaking breakdown of the various Justices' positions on this question, see David P. Currie, *The Constitution in the Supreme Court: The First Hundred Years 1789–1888*, at 268–69 (University of Chicago Press, 1985).

181. *National Bank v County of Yankton*, 101 US 129, 132 (1880).

182. Letter from Albert Gallatin to Thomas Jefferson, Jan 1803, *reprinted in* Brown, *The Constitutional History of the Louisiana Purchase*, 21.

183. 8 *Annals of Cong* 56 (1803) (statement of Sen. Tracy).

184. *Id.*, 454 (statement of Rep. Thatcher).

185. *Id.*, 462 (statement of Rep. Griswold).

186. *Id.*, 56 (statement of Sen. Tracy).

187. *Id.*, 58 (statement of Sen. Tracy).

188. *Id.*, 45 (statement of Sen. Pickering).

189. *See* US Const art V ("no Amendment which may be made prior to the Year One thousand eight hundred and eight shall in any Manner affect the first and fourth Clauses in the Ninth Section of the first Article; and . . . no State, without its Consent, shall be deprived of its equal Suffrage in the Senate").

190. Robert Knowles, *The Balance of Forces and the Empire of Liberty: States' Rights and the Louisiana Purchase*, 88 Iowa L. Rev 343 (2003)("Under the structure of the Constitution, it is insufficient to guarantee each state that it will exist on an equal footing with the others. In order to respect the sovereignty of the states as well as the national government, the states' approval must be sought through the constitutional amendment process — in which the states themselves share equal power in re-interpreting the Constitution — whenever profound changes in the nature of the union may diminish the ability of existing states to have their interests represented in the national government.").

191. Treaty Between the United States of America and the French Republic, Apr. 30, 1803, art III, 8 Stat 200, 202.

192. For a summary of this debate, see Brown, *The Constitutional History of the Louisiana Purchase*, 51–59.

193. *See* 8 *Annals of Cong*, 45 (statement of Sen. Pickering); *id.*, 56–57 (statement of Sen. Tracy).

194. Northwest Ordinance of 1787, art V, 1 Stat 51, 53.

195. Act of Aug 7, 1789, c 8, 1 Stat 50 (1789). The changes conformed the ordinance to the separation-of-powers structure of the new Constitution, such as by restructuring the appointment of territorial officials to comply with the Appointments Clause. *See* Gary Lawson, *Territorial Governments and the Limits of Formalism*, 78 Cal L Rev 853, 868 (1990).

196. US Const art VI, cl 1.

197. *See* Max Farrand, *The Legislation of Congress for the Government of the Organized Territories of the United States, 1789–1895*, at 16–17 (W. S. Hein, 1896).

198. US Const art I, § 8, cl 7.

199. *Id.* art I, § 8, cl 13.

200. *Id.* art I, § 8, cl 2.

201. Lawson and Granger, *The "Proper" Scope of Federal Power*, 331.

Chapter 2. Forms

1. Our principal sources for this section are Henry Adams, 2 *History of the United States of America During the First Administration of Thomas Jefferson* (Anitquarian Press, rep. 1962); Isaac Joslin Cox, *The West Florida Controversy, 1798–1813: A Study in American Diplomacy* (Johns Hopkins University Press, 1918); and Alexander De-Conde, *This Affair of Louisiana* (Scribner's, 1976).

2. Treaty Between the United States of America and the French Republic, Apr 30, 1803, art III, 8 Stat 200, 202.

3. Actually, France maintained possession of the territory until 1764, though the cession became final on November 13, 1762. *See* Binger Herman, *The Louisiana Purchase and Our Title West of the Rocky Mountains, with a Review of Annexation by the United States* 17 (1898).

4. Adams, 2 *History of the United States of America*, 43.

5. The conversation is quoted in DeConde, *This Affair of Louisiana*, 174.

6. Adams, 2 *History of the United States of America*, 27.

7. The arguments against the American claim to West Florida under the Louisiana Purchase were elegantly collected and summarized by the counsel for plaintiffs in *Foster v Neilson*, 27 US (2 Pet.) 253, 256–72, 293–99 (1829).

8. Act of Feb 24, 1804, ch 13, § 4, 2 Stat 251, 252.

9. *Id.* § 11, 2 Stat 254.

10. This intriguing story is told in detail in Cox, *The West Florida Controversy*. For a compacted version, see Frank Lawrence Owsley Jr. and Gene A. Smith, *Filibusters and Expansionists: Jeffersonian Manifest Destiny, 1800–1821*, at 7–9 (University of Alabama Press, 1997).

11. It is unclear why the views of an interested party about the strength of its own title should be given weight, but that is a matter for another time.

12. Treaty of Amity, Settlement and Limits Between the United States of America and His Catholic Majesty, the King of Spain, Feb 22, 1819, United States–Spain, art II, 8 Stat 252 [hereinafter "Adams-Onis Treaty"]. Although the treaty was initially ratified by the Senate on February 24, 1819, Spain did not ratify the treaty until October 5, 1820, at which point the Senate reratified it. The treaty formally took effect on February 22, 1821. These machinations are recounted in William Earl Weeks, *John Quincy Adams and American Global Empire* 168–73 (University Press of Kentucky, 1992).

13. Adams-Onis Treaty art VI.

14. *See* Owsley and Smith, *Filibusters and Expansionists*.

15. Our narrative in this discussion is drawn largely from Justin H. Smith, *The Annexation of Texas* (Macmillan, 1919).

16. The vote in favor of annexation was 3,277 to 91. *See* John Cornyn, *The Roots of the Texas Constitution: Settlement to Statehood*, 26 Tex Tech L Rev 1089, 1123 (1995).

17. *See* Edward Bicknell, *The Territorial Acquisitions of the United States: An Historical Review* 64–65 (1899) (the people of the Republic of Texas "were mostly Americans who had come in there. All their political ideas were American. They were of what we may call, for the sake of a name, the Anglo-Saxon race; while the Mexicans were of another stock.").

18. *See* Smith, *The Annexation of Texas*, 277 (Northern opposition); 240–42, 273–75 (relations with Mexico); 297 (Polk's campaign); 243–44, 240–41, 258–59 (personality politics).

19. Particularly in an era when Senators were directly selected by states, it is not impossible to imagine circumstances in which a majority in both houses might be harder to come by than a two-thirds majority in the Senate.

20. *See* Act of Mar 1, 1845, Res No 7, 5 Stat 797 (1845).

21. The vote was 4,245 to 267. *See* http://www.tsl.state.tx.us/ref/abouttx/annex ation/timeline.html.

22. *See* S Rep No 79, 28th Cong, 2d Sess (1845), *reprinted in 6 Compilation of Reports of Committee on Foreign Relations, US Senate, 1789–1901*, at 78, 89–90, 94–95 (1901).

23. *See*, e.g., *Cong Globe*, 28th Cong, 2d Sess 95 (1845) (statement of Rep. Winthrop); *id.*, 108 (statement of Rep. Smith); *id.*, 119 (statement of Rep. Hamlin); *id.*, 121 (statement of Rep. Sample); *id.*, 137 (statement of Rep. Davis); *id.*, 321 (statement of Sen. Simmons).

24. *See* Act of Apr 2, 1790, ch 6, 1 Stat 106 (accepting cession of land from North Carolina); Act of May 10, 1800, ch 50, § 10, 2 Stat 69, 70 (authorizing federal commissioners to accept a land cession from Georgia).

25. In both the North Carolina and Georgia cessions, the land was committed to eventual statehood by virtue of the extension of the Northwest Ordinance to the ceded lands. It is a nontrivial question whether the United States could accept a cession of land for the sole purpose of raising money, with no expectation of statehood or use. Under the Property Clause, Congress has power to "dispose of" land belonging to the United States. Does that mean that Congress can use the Sweeping Clause to acquire land in order to carry into execution the power to dispose of it? This seems a bit too much like bootstrapping to make sense. Once Congress has legitimately acquired land, it can choose to dispose of it pursuant to the Property Clause, but that does not mean that the original acquisition can be justified as a means of implementing the disposal power. Nor is it obvious that the United States can purchase land for resale in order to make money — no more than it is obvious that the United States can buy a private steel business in order to improve its finances.

26. Bruce Ackerman and David Golove, *Is NAFTA Constitutional?*, 108 Harv L Rev 799, 834–35 (1995). Representative Owens also got it right during the 1845 debates. *See Cong Globe*, 28th Cong, 2d Sess 109 (1845).

27. Our principal source for this section is Frederick Merk, *The Oregon Question: Essays in Anglo-American Diplomacy and Politics* (Harvard University Press, 1967).

28. Adams-Onis Treaty art III.

29. *See* Convention Between the United States of America and Russia, Apr 5/17, 1824, 8 Stat 302. The agreement has two dates because Russia at that time used a different calendar.

30. Treaty of Boundaries, Jun 15, 1846, United States–Great Britain, 9 Stat 869.

31. Congress did not actually enact legislation for the Oregon Territory until 1848 (*see* Act of Aug 14, 1848, ch 177, 9 Stat 323), but it could have done so two years earlier.

32. *See Oregon History: The "Oregon Question" and Provisional Government*, http://bluebook.state.or.us/cultural/history10.htm.

33. Additionally, a number of attempts were made prior to 1846 to extend federal laws to Oregon. Proposed legislation for Oregon was introduced as early as 1824 (*see Gale and Seaton's Register*, 18th Cong, 2d Sess 44 [1824]), and other efforts followed. *See*, e.g., A Bill To extend portions of the laws of the United States over the Territory of Oregon, S 331, 26th Cong, 1st Sess, Apr 28, 1840 (proposing the extension of federal criminal laws to Oregon). It is useful to know whether these bills would have been constitutional had they actually passed.

34. *See* Herman, *The Louisiana Purchase and Our Title West of the Rocky Mountains*, 55–56, 59, 70–71.

35. *See id.*, 56–58.

36. *See* Richard A. Epstein, *Possession As the Root of Title*, 13 Ga L Rev 1221 (1979).

37. On the important role of Christianity in the doctrine of discovery, see Henry Wheaton, *Elements of International Law* 305–06 (2d ed., Little, Brown & Co, 1863); Steven T. Newcomb, *The Evidence of Christian Nationalism in Federal Indian Law: The Doctrine of Discovery*; Johnson v McIntosh, *and Plenary Power*, 20 NYU Rev L & Social Change 303 (1993).

38. *See* Julius Goebel, *The Struggle for the Falkland Islands: A Study in Legal and Diplomatic History* 89–118 (Yale University Press, 1927); James Simsarian, *The Acquisition of Legal Title to Terra Nullius*, 53 Pol Sci Q 111, 111, 123–24 (1936); Friedrich August Freiherr von der Heydte, *Discovery, Symbolic Annexation and Virtual Effectiveness in International Law*, 29 Am J Int'l L 448, 452–54 (1935).

39. *But see* Charles H. Ambler, *The Oregon Country, 1810–1830: A Chapter in Territorial Expansion*, 30 Miss Valley Hist Rev 3, 3 n.1 (1943) (suggesting that Spain might have had some rights by virtue of discovery).

40. The British took over Astoria as a result of the War of 1812. Whether they did so by purchase just before the war or by conquest during the war was a matter of some doubt. The answer was important, because the Treaty of Ghent in 1814 restored the status quo ante by stipulating that "[a]ll territory, places, and possessions whatsoever taken by either party from the other during the war . . . shall be restored without delay." Treaty of Peace and Amity, Dec 24, 1814, United States–Great Britain, 8 Stat 218. If Astoria had not been "taken . . . during the war," but instead had been bought before the war, it would not fall within the terms of the treaty. The resolution of that question, although intriguing, does not affect the question of the timing of America's initial claim to Oregon.

41. *See* Curtis A. Bradley and Jack L. Goldsmith, *The Current Illegitimacy of International Human Rights Litigation*, 66 Fordham L Rev 319, 361; Sarah H. Cleveland, *Powers Inherent in Sovereignty: Indians, Aliens, Territories, and the Nineteenth Century Origins of Plenary Power over Foreign Affairs*, 81 Tex L Rev 1, 23 (2002); Zephyr Rain Teachout, Note, *Defining and Punishing Abroad: Constitutional Limits on the Extraterritorial Reach of the Offenses Clause*, 48 Duke LJ 1305, 1317–18 (1999).

42. Act of Aug 18, 1856, c 164, 11 Stat 119 (codified at 48 USC §§ 1411–19 (2000)).

43. *Id.* §§ 1411, 1417–18.

44. US Const art I, § 8, cl 10.

45. *Id.* art IV, § 3, cl 2.

46. 137 US 202 (1890).

47. *Id.*, 211.

48. *Id.*, 212.

Chapter 3. Limits

1. Treaty of Peace, Friendship, Limits, and Settlement with the Republic of Mexico, Feb 2, 1848, United States–Mexico, art V, 9 Stat 922 [hereinafter "Treaty of Guadalupe Hidalgo"].

2. Gadsden Treaty, Dec 30, 1853, United States–Mexico, art I, 10 Stat 1031.

3. Treaty of Guadalupe Hidalgo art IX.

4. Gadsden Treaty art V ("All the provisions of the . . . ninth . . . article[] of the treaty of Guadalupe Hidalgo, shall apply to the territory ceded by the Mexican Republic in the first article of the present treaty").

5. *See* Frederick Merk, *Manifest Destiny and Mission in American History: A Reinterpretation* 107–08 (Knopf, 1963).

6. Treaty of Guadalupe Hidalgo art X.

7. The agreement guaranteed joint navigational and fishing rights in the Pacific Ocean. The United States pledged not to make any settlements north of the 54-40 latitude and Russia pledged not to establish settlements south of that line. *See* Convention Between the United States of America and Russia, Apr 5/17, 1824, 8 Stat 302.

8. The boundary between Alaska and British Columbia was not definitively settled until decades later. *See* Convention of Boundaries: Alaska and Canada, Jan 24, 1903, United States–Great Britain, 32 Stat 1961.

9. For surveys of the transaction, see Paul S. Holbo, *Tarnished Expansion: The Alaska Scandal, the Press, and Congress, 1867–1871*, at 1–35 (University of Tennessee Press, 1983); Ronald J. Jensen, *The Alaska Purchase and Russian–American Relations* (University of Washington Press, 1975); Frank A. Golder, *The Purchase of Alaska*, 25 Am Hist Rev 411 (1920).

10. For an engaging account of the occupation and early (non)governance of Alaska, see Ted C. Hinckley, *The Americanization of Alaska, 1867–1897* (Pacific Books, 1972).

11. *See*, e.g., *Cong Globe*, 40th Cong, 2d Sess 473–74 (1868) (statement of Rep. Cullum); *id.*, 466–67 (statement of Rep. Miller); *id.*, 380–82 (statement of Rep. Price); *id.*, 392, 395–96, 399 (statement of Rep. Washburn).

12. *See generally* Holbo, *Tarnished Expansion*; Jensen, *The Alaska Purchase*, 123–31.

13. Treaty concerning the Cession of the Russian Possessions in North America by his Majesty the Emperor of all the Russias to the United States of American, Art III, 15 Stat 542 (1867).

14. Max Farrand, *Territory and District*, 5 Am Hist Rev 676, 678 (1900).

15. *Id.*, 679–80.

16. Edward Bicknell, *The Territorial Acquisitions of the United States: An Historical Review*, 75–77 (1899). *See also* Hinckley, *The Americanization of Alaska*, 35–36 (noting ground for doubts in 1867 about Alaska's eventual statehood).

17. Gary Lawson, *Delegation and Original Meaning*, 88 Va L Rev 327, 377 (2002).

18. Although the Senate approved the Alaska treaty with only two dissenting votes, the

debate in the House concerning whether to appropriate the money for the purchase was more vigorous. Many representatives thought it was a bad bargain, but none expressly declared that Alaska could never become a state. Perhaps the closest approximation of this view was Representative Butler's objection to acquiring territory populated with nonhomogeneous races. *See Cong Globe*, 40th Cong, 2d Sess 402 (1868) (statement of Rep. Butler).

19. *See* Richard E. Welch Jr., *American Public Opinion and the Purchase of Russian America*, 17 Am Slavic & E European Rev 481 (1958) (surveying the editorial attitudes of forty-eight American newspapers about the acquisition of Alaska and not mentioning any expressions of doubt about future statehood). Indeed, at least one newspaper correspondent projected Sitka as a future San Francisco with a population of fifty thousand within ten years of acquisition. *See id.*, 485. The reality, of course, was somewhat different. In 1877, a government customs official described Sitka as a " 'Deserted Village,' " *see* Hinckley, *The Americanization of Alaska*, 104, and by the end of the nineteenth century Sitka's population probably did not exceed one thousand. *See id.*, 242.

20. *See* Jensen, *The Alaska Purchase*, 63–64.

21. *See id.*, 91–92.

22. Our principal source for this discussion is Julius W. Pratt, *Expansionists of 1898: The Acquisition of Hawaii and the Spanish Islands* (Johns Hopkins University Press, 1936).

23. Act of July 7, 1898, 30 Stat 750.

24. *See* Sen Rep No 681, 55th Cong, 2d Sess (1897).

25. Pratt, *Expansionists of 1898*, 154 (quoting Carl Schurz, *Manifest Destiny*, 87 Harpers New Monthly Magazine 737–46).

26. *See* Goran Rystad, *Ambiguous Imperialism: American Foreign Policy and Domestic Politics at the Turn of the Century* 25, 29 (Esselte Studium, 1975).

27. 31 *Cong Rec* 6665 (1898) (statement of Sen. Hoar).

28. *See id.*, 6141 (statement of Sen. Morrill).

29. Albert J. Beveridge, "The March of the Flag," Sept 16, 1898, *available at* http://www.fordham.edu/halsall/mod/1898beveridge.html (last visited on Sept 27, 2002).

30. Act of Nov 23, 1993, 107 Stat 1510.

31. Vasan Kesavan and Michael Stokes Paulsen, *Is West Virginia Constitutional?*, 90 Cal L Rev 291 (2002). They argue that the more difficult question (to which they also answer "yes") is whether a state can ever be formed wholly out of territory from a single other state. Similar reasoning may explain (though that is a subject for another day) how the Reconstruction Amendments could possibly be constitutional. *See* John Harrison, *The Lawfulness of the Reconstruction Amendments*, 68 U Chi L Rev 375 (2001).

32. For an encyclopedic and engaging treatment of the war, see Ivan Musicant, *Empire by Default: The Spanish-American War and the Dawn of the American Century* (H. Holt, 1998).

33. At the time, the island was known as "Porto Rico." Congress changed the territory's name to its current spelling in 1932. *See* Act of May 17, 1932, ch 190, 47 Stat 158. We use the modern spelling unless the original form appears in quoted material.

34. Treaty of Paris, Dec 10, 1898, United States–Spain, art I–III, 30 Stat 1754.

35. Letter from Thomas Jefferson to James Madison, Oct 24, 1823, *in* 15 *The Writings of Thomas Jefferson* 477, 479 (Albert Ellery Bergh ed., 1905).

36. *See* Musicant, *Empire by Default*, 47, 79.

37. *See* Louis A. Perez Jr., *Incurring a Debt of Gratitude: 1898 and the Moral Sources of United States Hegemony in Cuba*, 104 Am Hist Rev 356, 356–59 (1999).

38. Guam covers 209 square miles.

39. *See* 32 *Cong Rec* 327 (1898) (statement of Sen. Teller) ("Nobody wants to make Cuba or Porto Rico or the Philippines States of the Union. . . . And yet, in the course of time, if they shall become fitted, they may become States and admitted to the Union.").

40. Speech of Adlai Stevenson, "The Democratic Party," Jan 7, 1899, *reprinted in* 32 *Cong Rec* 1538 (1899).

41. *Id.*

42. *Id.*, 964. Clay's comments made clear that his concerns were not constitutionally based.

43. *Id.*, 640.

44. *See* David Starr Jordan, "False Steps By a Nation Are Hard to Retrace," *reprinted in Republic or Empire? The Philippine Question* 273, 278 (The Independence Co, 1899) (address by president of Stanford University stating that "[w]e make slave nations out of the Philippines, but never make free States in the sense in which the name State applies to Maine or Iowa or California").

45. Richard Hofstadter, *Manifest Destiny and the Philippines, in American Imperialism in 1898*, at 54, 54 (Theodore P. Green ed., Heath, 1955).

46. Luzon covers 40,420 square miles, or roughly two hundred times the area of Guam.

47. 32 *Cong Rec* 96 (1898).

48. C. S. Olcott, 2 *The Life of William McKinley* 110–11 (Houghton Mifflin, 1916).

49. Musicant, *Empire by Default*, 601.

50. For a detailed examination of these territories and their current status, see Stanley K. Laughlin Jr., *The Law of United States Territories and Affiliated Jurisdictions* (Lawyers Cooperative, 1995). For a shorter summary, see Jon M. Van Dyke, *The Evolving Legal Relationships between the United States and Its Affiliated US-Flag Islands*, 14 U Haw L Rev 445 (1992).

51. *See* Convention between the United States of America, Germany, and Great Britain to Adjust Amicably the Question Between the Three Governments in Respect to the Samoan Group of Islands, Dec 2, 1899, United States–Germany–Great Britain, 31 Stat 1878.

52. *See* Articles of Cession of Tutuila and Aunu'u, Apr 17, 1900, *reprinted in* Am Samoa Code Ann § 2; Cession of Manua Islands, July 16, 1904, *reprinted in* Am Samoa Code Ann §§ 9–11.

53. Act of Feb 20, 1929, ch 281, 45 Stat 1253 (codified at 48 USC § 1661(a)(2000)).

54. Convention for the Construction of a Ship Canal, Nov 18, 1903, United States–Panama, 33 Stat 2234 [hereinafter "Panama Canal Treaty"].

55. The same considerations obviously justified the acquisition of the American naval

base at Guantánamo in Cuba. *See* Sedgwick W. Green, *The Applicability of American Laws to Overseas Areas Controlled by the United States*, 68 Harv L Rev 781, 792–93 (1955).

56. For a short summary of the events leading up to the treaty, see Gregory M. Huckabee, *Suffering the Slings and Arrows of the Panama Canal Treaty*, 40 Naval L Rev 65, 65–68 (1992).

57. Panama Canal Treaty art III, 33 Stat 2235.

58. Convention Respecting the Virgin Islands, United States–Denmark, Jan 25, 1917, 39 Stat 1706 (1917). For a thorough history of the half century of negotiations leading up to the final purchase, see Charles Callan Tansill, *The Purchase of the Danish West Indies* (Johns Hopkins University Press, 1932).

59. For a discussion of the different forms of affiliation with the United States, *see* Laughlin, *The Law of United States Territories and Affiliated Jurisdictions*, 91–104.

60. Act of July 18, 1847, 61 Stat 3301.

61. *See United States v Tiede*, 86 FRD 227 (US Ct for Berlin 1979).

62. Gerald L. Neuman, *Anomalous Zones*, 48 Stan L Rev 1197 (1996). Professor Neuman was primarily discussing Guantánamo Bay, and his chief interest concerned the applicability of the Constitution to governance in that zone rather than the permissibility of its acquisition.

63. *Cong Globe*, 40th Cong, 2d Sess 454 (statement of Rep. Delano).

Chapter 4. Constitutional Architecture I

1. Stanley K. Laughlin Jr., *The Application of the Constitution in United States Territories: American Samoa, A Case Study*, 2 U Haw L. Rev 337, 343 (1980–81).

2. US Const art I, § 8, cl 17.

3. *Id*. art IV, § 3, cl 2.

4. *Late Corp. of the Church of Jesus Christ of Latter-Day Saints v United States*, 136 US 1, 42 (1890) ("general and plenary" power); *National Bank v County of Yankton*, 101 US 129, 133 (1880) ("full and complete authority").

5. *See*, e.g., *Fleming v Page*, 50 US (9 How.) 603 (1850); *American Ins. Co. v 356 Bales of Cotton*, 26 US (1 Pet.) 511 (1828); *United States v Rice*, 17 US (4 Wheat.) 246 (1819). For an excellent summary of these principles, see Charles E. Magoon, *Reports on the Law of Civil Government in Territory Subject to Military Occupation By the Military Forces of the United States* 11–15 (Hein, 1903).

The Constitution states that "[t]he President shall be Commander in Chief of the Army and Navy of the United States." US Const art II, § 2, cl 1. As we have previously explained, however, the President's war-making powers actually stem from the first sentence of Article II, which declares that "[t]he executive Power shall be vested in a President of the United States of America." *Id*. art II, § 1, cl 1. The Commander-in-Chief Clause simply clarifies the President's role in order to forestall any attempt by Congress to infer a power of troop direction from its explicit Article I war-making powers.

6. *Commonwealth of N. Mariana Islands v Atalig*, 723 F2d 682, 687 (9th Cir 1984).

7. *United States v Wheeler*, 435 US 313, 321 (1978).

8. An Ordinance for the Government of the Territory of the United States north-west of the river Ohio (1787), *reprinted at* 1 Stat 50, 51 n. (a) (1789).

9. *See* Act of Mar 26, 1804, ch 38, § 4, 2 Stat 283, 284 (Louisiana); Act of Mar 3, 1823, ch 28, § 5, 3 Stat 750, 751 (Florida); Act of May 17, 1884, ch 53, § 9, 23 Stat 24, 26–27 (Alaska).

10. *See Snow v United States ex rel Hempstead*, 85 US (18 Wall.) 317, 320 (1873) ("It is, indeed, the practice of the government to invest these dependencies with a limited power of self-government as soon as they have sufficient population for the purpose."); *Clinton v Englebrecht*, 80 US (13 Wall.) 434, 441 (1872) ("The theory upon which the various governments for portions of the territory of the United States have been organized, has ever been that of leaving to the inhabitants all the powers of self-government consistent with the supremacy and supervision of National authority").

11. *See The Federalist* No. 43, at 272–73 (J. Madison) (Clinton Rossiter ed., New American Library, 1961) ("[A] municipal legislature for local purposes, derived from their own suffrages, will of course be allowed [the citizens of the district]").

12. *See* St. George Tucker,1 *Blackstone's Commentaries App.* 278 (William Young Birch & Abraham Small, 1803): "It has been said, that it was in contemplation to establish a subordinate legislature, with a governor to preside over the district. But it seems highly questionable whether such a substitution of legislative authority is compatible with the constitution; unless it be supposed that a power to exercise exclusive legislation in all cases whatsoever, comprehends an authority to delegate that power to another subordinate body. If the maxim be sound, that a delegated authority cannot be transferred to another to exercise, the project here spoken of will probably never take effect."

13. *See* Joseph Story, 3 *Commentaries on the Constitution* § 1218 (Hilliard, Gray & Co, 1833) ("the corporations of the three cities within [the District of Columbia's] limits possess and exercise a delegated power of legislation under their charters, granted by congress, to the full extent of their municipal wants, without any constitutional scruple, or surmise of doubt").

14. Act of Oct 31, 1803, ch 1, § 2, 2 Stat 245, 245.

15. *See* 8 *Annals of Cong* 499 (1803) (statement of Rep. Randolph).

16. *Id.*, 499 (statement of Rep. Elliott). *See also id.*, 508 (repeating Rep. Elliott's concerns about delegation).

17. *See id.*, 498 (statement of Rep. Griswold).

18. *Id.*, 500 (statement of Rep. Randolph).

19. *Id.* (statement of Rep. Griswold).

20. *Id.*, 510 (statement of Rep. Jackson).

21. *See id.*, 506 (statement of Rep. Eustis).

22. Representative Nicholson tried to argue that there was no delegation to the President because power under the bill was not to be exercised by the President but by presidential appointees. *See id.*, 501 (statement of Rep. Nicholson). Apart from the fact that the bill, and the final law, specified that all powers were to be "exercised in such manner, as the President of the United States shall direct," it was not explained why delegations to presidential appointees are constitutionally better than delegations to the President. Representative Mitchill suggested that the rules for delegations might be

different under the Territories Clause than under other constitutional provisions (*see id.*, 503–04), but he did not explain why.

23. 195 US 138 (1904). There were prior challenges to territorial delegations that were nonserious and nonconstitutional. In the course of arguing that admiralty jurisdiction in the territories could be vested only in courts created by Congress, counsel in *American Insurance Co. v 356 Bales of Cotton*, 26 US (1 Pet.) 511 (1828), maintained: "It is said that Congress has given to the territorial legislature all the rights of legislation they have. Legislative powers cannot be delegated. *Delegatus non potest delegare.*" *Id.*, 540. There were no prior or subsequent mentions of this argument, and it seems to have been regarded by all concerned as a make-weight, at best. Statutory challenges to particular exercises of territorial legislative authority were common prior to 1904. *See District of Columbia v John R. Thompson Co.*, 346 US 100, 106 and n.5 (1953) (collecting cases).

24. *See* Act of July 1, 1902, ch 1369, § 1, 32 Stat 691, 691–92.

25. *Dorr v United States*, 195 U.S. 138, 153 (1904).

26. 301 US 308 (1937).

27. Revenue Act of 1934, ch 277, § 602 1/2, 48 Stat 680, 763–64. By this time, Congress had granted the Philippines a very substantial degree of local autonomy. *See* Philippine Independence Act, ch 84, 48 Stat 456 (1934).

28. *See* Brief of Petitioner Cincinnati Soap Co, 58–59, *Cincinnati Soap Co.* (No. 659); Brief for Petitioner Haskins Bros. & Co, 47–49, 52 *Cincinnati Soap Co.* (No. 687); Reply Brief for Petitioner Haskins Bros. & Co, 15–16, *Cincinnati Soap Co.* (No. 687).

29. *Cincinnati Soap Co*, 323.

30. 346 US 100 (1953).

31. *See* Brief for Respondent 22, *District of Columbia v John R. Thompson Co.* (No. 617) ("It is settled that while the Congress may delegate to the Government of the District of Columbia the power to make municipal and police regulations, Congress, under the Constitution having exclusive legislative power over the District of Columbia, cannot delegate to the District the power to enact legislation.").

32. 346 US, 106–09.

33. *See* Gary Lawson, *Territorial Governments and the Limits of Formalism*, 78 Cal L Rev 853, 900–901 (1990).

34. *See* Gary Lawson, *Delegation and Original Meaning*, 88 Va L Rev 327 (2002). *See also* Michael B. Rappaport, *The Selective Nondelegation Doctrine and the Line Item Veto: A New Approach to the Nondelegation Doctrine and Its Implications for* Clinton v City of New York, 76 Tul L Rev 265 (2001).

35. 764 F2d 1285 (9th Cir 1985), *cert denied*, 475 US 1081 (1986).

36. 48 USC § 1423a (2000). At the time of the *Sakamoto* case, the statute gave the legislature of Guam power over "all subject of legislation of local application." 48 USC § 1423a (1994). The language was changed in 1998. *See* Pub L 105–291, § 4, 112 Stat 2786 (1998).

37. Petition for a Writ of Certiorari to the United States Court of Appeals for the Ninth Circuit 3, *Sakamoto* (No. 85–552).

38. Initially, the procedure was as follows: Sakamoto sold the merchandise, accepted payment, and then checked it in for the customer at the airport. The airlines discontinued

this practice in 1976 when DFS pointed out that the practice violated Federal Aviation Administration regulations. Sakamoto then had his employees simply deliver the merchandise to customers at the airport check-in counters, in open defiance of the exclusive franchise. The GAA put a halt to this operation in 1977. Next, Sakamoto tried delivering the goods to the departing customers' hotels, loading the goods onto tour buses, and then having his employees carry the goods from the buses to the check-in counters. In 1979 the GAA again instructed Sakamoto to stop making terminal deliveries. Sakamoto's last-ditch effort was to pay the tour agents and bus drivers to carry the merchandise into the terminal for the customers. The GAA was not amused and in 1980 issued what became the final warning letter. *See Sakamoto v Duty Free Shoppers, Ltd*, 613 FSupp 381, 385–86 (D Guam 1983).

39. Try as we might, we cannot find a Dormant Commerce Clause in the Constitution. Cf. US Const art I, § 8, cl 3 (granting Congress power "[t]o regulate Commerce with foreign Nations, and among the several States, and with the Indian Tribes"). The Supreme Court is either more perceptive or less fastidious than we. *See Tyler Pipe Indus., Inc. v Washington State Dep't of Revenue*, 483 US 232, 259–65 (1987) (Scalia, J., concurring in part and dissenting in part) (criticizing the Court's "negative commerce clause" jurisprudence); Martin H. Redish and Shane V. Nugent, *The Dormant Commerce Clause and the Constitutional Balance of Federalism*, 1987 Duke LJ 569 (arguing that the idea of a Dormant Commerce Clause has no textual basis in the Constitution and is unsupported by nontextual theory).

Even on the assumption that something called a "Dormant Commerce Clause" exists, the court was correct to reject the claim in *Sakamoto. See* 764 F2d at 1286–88. The Dormant Commerce Clause doctrine was invented by courts because of the perceived tension between congressional power to regulate interstate commerce and the independent regulatory authority of state governments. Guam, unlike the states, has only the regulatory authority specifically conferred on it by Congress. It makes no more sense to apply the Dormant Commerce Clause to Guam than it does to apply it to the Federal Reserve Board or the Securities and Exchange Commission. Nor has Congress declared by statute that the Dormant Commerce Clause doctrine is applicable to Guam. *See* 48 USC § 1421b(u) (2000) (listing constitutional provisions applicable to Guam, but not mentioning the Commerce Clause).

40. See *United States v Cooper Corp*, 312 US 600, 606 (1941) (dictum); *Jet Courier Servs., Inc. v Federal Reserve Bank*, 713 F2d 1221, 1228 (6th Cir. 1983).

41. *See* 48 USC § 1423i (2000); *National Bank v County of Yankton*, 101 US 129, 133 (1880).

42. *United States v Wheeler*, 435 US 313, 321 (1978) (quoting *Domenech v National City Bank of New York*, 294 US 199, 204–205 (1935)).

43. *See* 613 F Supp at 386–88; 764 F2d at 1288–89; Brief for the United States as Amicus Curiae 10–12, *Sakamoto* (No. 85–552).

44. US Const art II, § 2, cl 2.

45. 424 US 1, 126 (1976). In other words, a federal appointee is an officer subject to the Appointments Clause if he or she is important enough to be subject to the Appointments Clause. Circular, perhaps, but essentially accurate.

46. 48 USC § 1422 (2000) (emphasis added).

47. Organic Act of Guam, ch 512, 64 Stat 384 (1950) (codified as amended at 48 USC §§ 1421–24 (2000)).

48. *Id.* § 6(a), 64 Stat at 386.

49. Pub L No 90–497, 82 Stat 842 (1968) (codified as amended at 10 USC § 335 (2000), 48 USC §§ 1421a–1421d, 1421f, 1422–1422d, 1423b, 1423h–1423i (2000)).

50. Conceivably, one could resolve the issues in *Sakamoto* without addressing constitutional issues by reasoning that even if Guam is not technically a federal agency, it is sufficiently agencylike to escape the coverage of the federal antitrust laws as a matter of statutory construction. But that would be cheating.

51. *See* Saikrishna Bangalore Prakash, *Field Office Federalism*, 79 Va L Rev 1957 (1993).

52. An Ordinance for the Government of the Territory of the United States north-west of the river Ohio (1787), *reprinted at* 1 Stat 50, 51 n. (a) (1789).

53. Act of Aug 7, 1789, ch 8, 1 Stat 50, 51.

54. *Id.* § 1, 1 Stat 53. Other amendments specified that the territorial secretary was to act in the governor's absence (*id.* § 2, 1 Stat 53); all required reports were to be filed with the President (*id.* § 1, 1 Stat 52–53); and the President rather than Congress was to exercise the removal power (*id.* § 1, 1 Stat 53).

55. *See* Act of May 26, 1790, ch 14, 1 Stat 123 (Tennessee, then known only as the Territory of the United States, south of the river Ohio); Act of Apr 7, 1798, ch 28, § 3, 1 Stat 549, 550 (Mississippi); Act of May 7, 1800, ch 41, § 3, 2 Stat 58, 59 (Indiana); Act of Mar 26, 1804, ch 38, §§ 2, 12, 2 Stat 283, 283, 287 (Orleans and Louisiana); Act of Jan 11, 1805, ch 5, § 3, 2 Stat 309, 309 (Michigan); Act of Feb 3, 1809, ch 13, § 3, 2 Stat 514, 515 (Illinois); Act of June 4, 1812, ch 95, §§ 2, 12, 2 Stat 743, 744, 746 (Missouri); Act of Mar 3, 1817, ch 59, § 2, 3 Stat 371, 372 (Alabama); Act of Mar 2, 1819, ch 49, §§ 3, 9, 3 Stat 493, 494, 495 (Arkansas); Act of Mar 30, 1822, ch 13, §§ 2, 8, 3 Stat 654, 655, 657 (Florida); Act of Mar 3, 1823, ch 28, §§ 2, 10, 3 Stat 750, 750–51, 753 (Florida); Act of Apr 20, 1836, ch 54, §§ 2, 11, 5 Stat 10, 11, 14 (Wisconsin); Act of June 12, 1838, ch 96, §§ 2, 11, 5 Stat 235, 236, 238 (Iowa); Act of Aug 14, 1848, ch 177, §§ 2, 11, 9 Stat 323, 324, 327 (Oregon); Act of Mar 3, 1849, ch 121, §§ 2, 11, 9 Stat 403, 404, 407 (Minnesota); Act of Sept 9, 1850, ch 49, §§ 3, 12, 9 Stat 446, 447, 450 (New Mexico); Act of Sept 9, 1850, ch 51, §§ 2, 11, 9 Stat 453, 453, 456 (Utah); Act of Mar 2, 1853, ch 90, §§ 2, 11, 10 Stat 172, 173, 176 (Washington); Act of May 30, 1854, ch 59, §§ 2, 12, 20, 30, 10 Stat 277, 278, 281, 284, 288 (Nebraska and Kansas); Act of Feb 28, 1861, ch 59, §§ 2, 11, 12 Stat 172, 172, 175 (Colorado); Act of Mar 2, 1861, ch 83, §§ 2, 11, 12 Stat 209, 210, 213 (Nevada); Act of Mar 2, 1861, ch 86, §§ 2, 11, 12 Stat 239, 239–40, 242 (Dakota); Act of Feb 24, 1863, ch 56, § 2, 12 Stat 664, 665 (Arizona); Act of Mar 3, 1863, ch 117, §§ 2, 11, 12 Stat 808, 809, 812 (Idaho); Act of May 26, 1864, ch 95, §§ 2, 11, 13 Stat 85, 86, 90 (Montana); Act of July 25, 1868, ch 235, §§ 2, 11, 15 Stat 178, 178, 181–82 (Wyoming); Act of May 17, 1884, ch 53, §§ 2, 9, 23 Stat 24, 24, 26 (Alaska); Act of May 2, 1890, ch 182, §§ 2, 14, 26 Stat 81, 82, 88 (Oklahoma); Act of Apr 12, 1900, ch 191, § 17, 31 Stat 77, 81 (temporary civil government for Puerto Rico); Act of Apr 30, 1900, ch 339, §§ 66, 67, 31 Stat 141, 153 (Hawaii); Act of June 6, 1900, ch 786, §§ 2, 10, 31 Stat 321, 321–22, 325 (Alaska); Act of Mar 2, 1901, ch 803, 31 Stat

895, 910 (military government for the Philippines); Act of July 1, 1902, ch 1369, § 1, 32 Stat 691, 691–92 (temporary civil government for the Philippines); Panama Canal Act, ch 390, §§ 4, 7, 37 Stat 560, 561, 564 (1912) (Panama Canal Zone); Act of Aug 29, 1916, ch 416, § 21, 39 Stat 545, 552 (permanent government for the Philippines); Act of Mar 2, 1917, ch 145, § 12, 39 Stat 951, 955 (permanent government for Puerto Rico); Act of Feb 20, 1929, ch 281, § (c), 45 Stat 1253, 1253 (Eastern Samoa); Organic Act of the Virgin Islands of the United States, ch 699, § 20, 49 Stat 1807, 1812 (1936) (Virgin Islands); *see also* Act of June 30, 1954, ch 423, § 1, 68 Stat 330, 330 (Trust Territory of the Pacific Islands).

The one possible exception during this period was the District of Columbia government from 1812 through 1871. When Congress initially incorporated the city of Washington, Congress provided for a presidentially appointed mayor. *See* Act of May 3, 1802, ch 53, § 5, 2 Stat 195, 196. The city's charter was amended in 1812 to provide for the election of the mayor by the popularly elected members of local boards (*see* Act of May 4, 1812, ch 75, §§ 1, 3, 2 Stat 721, 721–23), and amended again in 1820 to provide for direct popular election of the mayor (*see* Act of May 15, 1820, ch 104, § 3, 3 Stat 583, 584). This regime lasted until 1871, when the city was reconstituted as a territory with a presidentially appointed governor. *See* Act of Feb 21, 1871, ch 62, § 2, 16 Stat 419, 419. Note, however, that the 1812 statute authorized the elected mayor only to "see that the laws of the *corporation* be duly executed." Act of May 4, 1812, ch 75, § 3, 2 Stat 721, 723 (emphasis added). This wording stands in marked contrast to the typical nineteenth-century charge to territorial governors to "take care that *the laws* be faithfully executed." *See*, e.g., Act of Mar 26, 1804, ch 38, § 2, 2 Stat 283, 283 (Orleans and Louisiana) (emphasis added), presumably meaning all locally applicable federal laws, and the more explicit typical twentieth-century charge to "be responsible for the faithful execution of the laws of Porto Rico *and of the United States applicable in Porto Rico.*" Act of Mar 2, 1917, ch 145, § 12, 39 Stat 951, 955 (emphasis added). (The 1820 charter amendment contained no general declaration of the mayor's executive power.) Thus Congress may not have thought (correctly or incorrectly) that it was giving the elected mayor of the District of Columbia the authority to execute the laws of the United States.

56. *See* Act of Aug 5, 1947, ch 490, § 1, 61 Stat 770, 770–71. This provision was repealed when Puerto Rico's constitution took effect. *See* Act of July 3, 1950, ch 446, § 5, 64 Stat 319, 320. *See also* P.R. Const art IV, § 1 (providing for an elected governor).

57. *See* Guam Elective Governor Act, Pub L No 90–497, § 1, 82 Stat 842, 842 (1968) (codified as amended at 48 USC § 1422 (2000)); Virgin Islands Elective Governor Act, Pub L No 90–496, § 4, 82 Stat 837, 837 (1968) (codified as amended at 48 USC § 1591 (2000)); Am Samoa Rev Const art IV, § 2. Samoa is governed administratively by the Secretary of the Interior. *See* 48 USC § 1661(c) (2000); Exec. Order No 10,264, 16 Fed. Reg. 6419 (1951), *reprinted in* 48 USC § 1662 note (2000), who approved and promulgated a Samoan constitution effective as of July 1, 1967. The constitutional provision mandating an elected governor, who has authority to execute United States laws (*see* Am Samoa Code Ann § 4.0111(a) (1981)) was promulgated by the Secretary in 1977. *See* Order No 3009, 42 Fed Reg 48,398 (1977).

58. The legislative histories of the statutes pertaining to Puerto Rico, Guam, and the Virgin Islands do not mention the issue. *See* S Rep No 422, 80th Cong, 1st Sess (1947)

(Puerto Rico); HR Rep No 455, 80th Cong, 1st Sess (1947) (Puerto Rico); 93 Cong Rec 7076–79, 10,402–03 (1947) (Puerto Rico); HR Rep No 1521, 90th Cong, 2d Sess (1968) (Guam); S Rep No 1704, 89th Cong, 2d Sess (1966) (Guam); HR Rep No 1520, 89th Cong, 2d Sess (1966) (Guam); 114 Cong Rec 17,438–45, 23,044–47 (1968) (Guam); 112 Cong Rec 10,545–51, 25,977–79 (1966) (Guam); HR Rep No 1522, 90th Cong, 2d Sess (1968) (Virgin Islands); S Rep No 1705, 89th Cong, 2d Sess (1966) (Virgin Islands); HR Rep No 1519, 89th Cong, 2d Sess (1966) (Virgin Islands); 114 Cong Rec 17,445–50, 23,047–50, 23,692 (1968) (Virgin Islands); 112 Cong Rec 10,551–53, 25,979–81 (1966) (Virgin Islands).

59. Story, 3 *Commentaries on the Constitution of the United States* § 667.

60. *Benner v Porter*, 50 US (9 How.) 235, 242 (1850).

61. *Scott v Sandford*, 60 US (9 How.) 393, 448–49 (opinion of the Court); *see also id.*, 623 (Curtis, J., dissenting) (agreeing with the majority on this point).

62. *Downes v Bidwell*, 182 US 244, 289–90 (White, J., concurring).

63. 22 US (9 Wheat.) 738 (1824); 22 US (9 Wheat.) 904 (1824).

64. Act of Apr 10, 1816, ch 44, § 7, 3 Stat 266, 269.

65. *See* 22 US (9 Wheat.) at 817–18. That conclusion was not inevitable, though its correctness is of no concern here. *See* David P. Currie, *The Constitution in the Supreme Court: The First Hundred Years, 1789–1888*, at 102 n.80 (University of Chicago Press, 1985) (noting the Court's earlier contrary conclusion in *Bank of the United States v Devaux*, 9 US (5 Cranch) 61, 85–86 (1809)).

66. US Const art III, § 2, cl 1.

67. 22 US (9 Wheat.) at 823.

68. Courts have in fact read the "arising under" language in the general federal question statute, 28 USC § 1331 (2000), more narrowly than Marshall read the Constitution in *Osborn*. *See* Peter Nicolas, *American-Style Justice in No Man's Land*, 36 Ga L Rev 895, 1017 (2002). This narrow reading can be correct as a matter of statutory interpretation without calling into question Marshall's constitutional analysis.

69. 85 US (18 Wall.) 317 (1873).

70. *See* Act of Sept 9, 1850, ch 51, §§ 10–11, 9 Stat 453, 456.

71. *Id.* §§ 4, 6, 9 Stat at 454.

72. *Snow*, 318. The territorial statute also provided for the election of district attorneys with similar authority over crimes in their districts. *See id.*

73. *Id.*, 322.

74. *See* Transcript of Record 6–7, *Snow* (No. 424).

75. We have been unable to locate the Utah Supreme Court's opinion. The statement of the case in the United States Reports says only that "[t]he Supreme Court of the Territory, assuming that the Supreme Court and the District Courts of Utah were courts of the United States, were of the opinion that the attorney of the United States was the proper person; and adjudged accordingly." *Snow*, 319. The sparse record before the United States Supreme Court provides no elaboration. Whatever the Utah Supreme Court might have meant, its assumption that Utah's territorial courts were courts of the United States had been rejected in *Clinton v Englebrecht*, 80 US (13 Wall.) 434, 447 (1872). Snow's counsel, in a one-paragraph brief, sought what amounted to summary reversal on the strength of *Clinton*. *See* Brief for Plaintiff in Error, *Snow* (No. 424). The United States

filed a three-page brief which made no reference to the status of the Utah territorial courts. *See* Brief for the United States, *Snow* (No. 424).

76. *See Snow*, 322 ("The power given to the [Territorial] legislature . . . extends to all rightful subjects of legislation consistent with the Constitution and the organic act itself. And there seems to be nothing in either of these instruments which directly conflicts with the Territorial law.").

77. *See id.*, 321 ("The question is . . . whether the act of the Territorial legislature was authorized by the organic act."); Brief for the United States 2, *Snow* (No. 424) (characterizing the case strictly in statutory terms).

78. Brief for the United States 3, *Snow* (No. 424).

79. *See Snow*, 322.

80. *Id.*, 321.

81. *Id.*

82. This calls to mind the comments of Justice Catron in *Dred Scott*, defending the power of Congress to govern territories under Article IV: "It is due to myself to say, that it is asking much of a judge, who has for nearly twenty years been exercising jurisdiction, from the western Missouri line to the Rocky Mountains, and, on this understanding of the Constitution [that Congress has power under Article IV to govern territories], inflicting the extreme penalty of death for crimes committed where the direct legislation of Congress was the only rule, to agree that he had been all the while acting in mistake, and as an usurper." *Scott v Sandford*, 522–23 (Catron, J., concurring).

83. A possible exception might be the provisions for self-governance applicable to the original Northwest Territory by virtue of the Northwest Ordinance. The Engagements Clause of Article VI constitutionalized those arrangements and may therefore have provided affirmative authorization for elected legislators and other officials.

Chapter 5. Constitutional Architecture II

1. US Const art III, § 1.

2. 48 USC § 1424(b) (2000); *see also id.* § 1612(a) (same provision for a district court of the Virgin Islands).

3. *Id.* § 1424b(a); *see also id.* § 1614(a) (same provision for a district judges of the Virgin Islands).

4. *See id.* § 1424b(a) (tying judicial pay to Article III salaries; *see also id.* § 1614(a) (same for judges in the Virgin Islands). On the absence of constitutional protection for territorial judges, see *McAllister v United States*, 141 US 174, 180 (1891) (Alaska district court judge could be removed by President); *United States v Fisher*, 109 US 143, 145 (1883) (Congress could prescribe a lower salary for a territorial justice than was fixed in a prior statute).

The Samoan courts, which have general civil and criminal jurisdiction (*see* Am Samoa Code Ann § 3.0103 (1981)), are even further removed from the Article III model. The chief justice and an associate justice are appointed for indefinite terms by the Secretary of the Interior (Am Samoa Rev Const art III, § 3 (1967)), who may remove them for cause (Am Samoa Code Ann § 3.1001(a) (1981)). As in Guam, the justices' salaries are not constitutionally guaranteed. For more detailed descriptions of the various territorial court schemes, see Peter Nicolas, *American-Style Justice in No Man's Land*, 36 Ga L Rev 895, 986–93 (2002).

5. Act of Feb 27, 1801, ch 15, § 11, 2 Stat 103, 107. This appears to have been the first time that territorial judges were given a term of years rather than tenure during good behavior. *Cf.* Act of May 7, 1800, ch 41, § 3, 2 Stat 58, 59 (Indiana) (providing for tenure during good behavior); Act of May 26, 1790, ch 14, § 1, 1 Stat 123, 123 (Tennessee) (same); Act of Apr 7, 1798, ch 28, § 3, 1 Stat 549, 550 (Mississippi) (same); An Ordinance for the Government of the Territory of the United States north-west of the river Ohio (1787), reprinted at 1 Stat 51 n.(a) (same). Terms of years, however, quickly became commonplace. *See* Act of Mar 2, 1819, ch 49, § 7, 3 Stat 493, 495 (Arkansas) (term of four years, and providing for removal by the President); Act of June 4, 1812, ch 95, § 10, 2 Stat 743, 746 (Missouri) (term of four years, and providing for removal); Act of Mar 26, 1804, ch 38, § 5, 2 Stat 283, 284 (Orleans and Louisiana) (territorial judges "shall hold their offices for the term of four years").

6. *See* 5 US (1 Cranch), 155, 157, 162, 167, 172 (1803). If Marbury had in fact held his office at the President's pleasure, then President Jefferson's instructions to Madison to refuse to deliver Marbury's commission could be seen as a tacit exercise of the removal power, leaving Marbury with no claim on the office, commission, or salary, and leaving Marshall with no opportunity to side with Marbury on the merits before reaching the decisive jurisdictional issue.

7. 7 US (3 Cranch) 159, 160 n* (1805) (reporting the circuit court opinion of 1803).

8. *See* Act of Feb 27, 1801, ch 15, § 11, 2 Stat 103, 107.

9. Act of May 3, 1802, ch 52, § 8, 2 Stat 193, 195.

10. *See More*, 160 n*.

11. *Id.*

12. *Id.* The government suggested that the fees-for-services provision was not a provision for compensation "at stated Times," and could thus be reduced without violating the terms of Article III. *See id.*, 161 n*. Judge Cranch, however, held that the phrase "at stated times" could include something like "when the service is rendered." *Id.* "And," he added, "we are rather to incline to this construction, than to suppose the command of the Constitution to have been disobeyed." *Id.* The "command" he had in mind was presumably the requirement that judges receive some "Compensation," which would have been violated if More's fees were unlawful.

13. *Id.*, 164 n*–165 n* (Kilty, J., dissenting).

14. *Id.* (argument of Jones). In response to the objection that More's office was not governed by Article III under the 1801 statute because the office had a limited term of five years (instead of having a term for "good behavior"), Jones responded that "[i]t is not the tenure, but the essence and nature of the office which is to decide this question," and that "[i]f the limitation to five years makes a difference, it would be an evasion of the constitution." *Id.*, 167.

15. *Id.*, 168 (argument of Mason, counsel for the United States) (emphasis in original).

16. *Id.*, 168–69 (argument of Jones).

17. That problem is of considerable interest in its own right. The same act of Congress that created More's office, Act of Feb 27, 1801, ch 15, § 11, 2 Stat 103, 106, also created the District of Columbia circuit court that decided his case. *See id.* § 3, 2 Stat at 105. The

act provided for Supreme Court review of "any final judgment, order or decree in said circuit court, wherein the matter in dispute, exclusive of costs, shall exceed the value of one hundred dollars." *Id.* § 8, 2 Stat 106. Marshall construed this language, and in particular the words "matter in dispute," to refer exclusively to civil cases. *See* 7 US, 173–74. Marshall reasoned that an affirmative statutory description of the Supreme Court's appellate jurisdiction must be read to prohibit the exercise of powers other than those described and that Congress had therefore implicitly used its power to define exceptions to the Supreme Court's appellate jurisdiction in order to preclude the Court from reviewing criminal cases decided by the circuit court of the District.

18. 7 US (3 Cranch) 331 (1806).

19. Act of Mar 3, 1803, ch 20, § 6, 2 Stat 215, 216.

20. Act of May 8, 1792, ch 33, § 2, 1 Stat 271, 272.

21. 7 US (3 Cranch), 336. This assumes, quite reasonably, that Congress was using the words *executive* and *judicial* in something resembling their constitutional senses.

22. 10 US (6 Cranch) 332 (1810).

23. *Id.*, 337.

24. 22 US (9 Wheat.) 738 (1824).

25. When *American Insurance Co.* was decided in 1828, the Court had already held—correctly—in *Corporation of New Orleans v Winter*, 14 US (1 Wheat.) 91 (1816), that citizens of territories were not citizens of any state for purposes of diversity jurisdiction in the Article III circuit courts. *Cf. National Mut. Ins. Co. v Tidewater Transfer Co.*, 337 US 582 (1949) (revisiting the issue with respect to District of Columbia citizens). As was just explained, that result could lead to the conclusion that Congress does not have the power under Article III to authorize territorial tribunals to hear claims by or against territorial citizens that are substantively founded on the law of a state. If true, the result is interesting, and perhaps unfortunate, but hardly grounds for reading Article III out of the Constitution. If the use of a territorial choice-of-law rule to determine the applicability of state substantive law is enough to support "arising under" jurisdiction, then there is no jurisdictional gap. Alternatively, cases brought in territorial courts simply must be grounded in federal or territorial law. C'est la vie.

26. *See* Act of Jan 9, 1815, ch 21, § 1, 3 Stat 164, 164–65; Act of Feb 27, 1815, ch 60, § 1, 3 Stat 216, 216.

27. 18 US (5 Wheat.) 317 (1820).

28. US Const art I, § 8, cl 1. By locating the power to tax in this clause, rather than in Congress's legislative power over the District, Marshall avoided the potentially thorny question whether the power over the District authorizes taxes for general revenues or only for local purposes. *See Loughborough*, 318.

29. *Id.*, 318–19.

30. *Id.*

31. 26 US (1 Pet.) 511 (1828). From the date of its issuance, the decision has generally been cited as *American Insurance Co. v Canter. See*, e.g., *Freytag v Commissioner of Internal Revenue*, 501 US 868, 889 (1991); *id.*, 909 (Scalia, J., concurring in part and concurring in the judgment); *Northern Pipeline Constr. Co. v Marathon Pipe Line Co.*, 458 US 50, 64 (1982) (plurality opinion); *Clinton v Englebrecht*, 80 US (13 Wall.) 434, 447 (1872); *Benner v Porter*, 50 US (9 How.) 235, 240 (1850). *But see Ngiraingas v*

Sanchez, 495 US 182, 204 (1990) (Brennan, J., dissenting) (citing the case as *American Ins. Co. v 356 Bales of Cotton*); *United States v Dalcour*, 203 US 408, 427 (1906) (same). Compare *United States v Coe*, 155 US 76, 80 (1894) (argument of counsel citing the case as *American Insurance Co. v 356 Bales of Cotton*); *with id.*, 85 (opinion of the Court citing the case as *American Insurance Co. v Canter*). A WESTLAW search on September 25, 2002, revealed that of the twenty-five then most recent law review citations to the case, twenty-three cited it as *American Insurance Co. v Canter*. That citation is wrong. Although process was issued against Canter in personam (*see* 26 US (1 Pet.) at 513), the case was primarily an action in rem for possession of specific bales of cotton (or their proceeds upon sale). *See id.; Canter v American Insurance Co.*, 28 US (3 Pet.) 307, 315 (1830). The captions in the record reflect this view: *see* Record at 1, *American Insurance. Co.*, 26 US (1 Pet.) 511 (No. 1415) (available on microfilm, US Nat'l Archives Microfilm Publications, Microcopy No. 214, Roll 74, frame no. 667) [hereinafter Record], as do the captions in the *United States Reports* (26 US (1 Pet.) at 511).

32. Act of May 26, 1824, ch 163, § 1, 4 Stat 45, 45. This statute amended the territory's organic act, which originally provided for only two superior courts. *See* Act of Mar 3, 1823, ch 28, § 7, 3 Stat 750, 752. The organic act also created the territorial legislative council referred to in the text, which consisted of the governor plus thirteen presidentially appointed "fit and discreet persons of the territory" (*id.* § 5, 3 Stat at 751), who had power "over all rightful subjects of legislation." *Id.*

33. *See* Act of May 26, 1824, ch 163, § 1, 4 Stat 45, 45 (describing jurisdiction over territorial matters); *id.* § 2, 4 Stat at 45 (vesting "the same jurisdiction" as was possessed by the Kentucky district court).

34. Judiciary Act of 1789, ch 20, § 9, 1 Stat 73, 77. The Kentucky and Maine district courts had, in addition to the jurisdiction conferred generally on federal district courts, all the original jurisdiction of a circuit court. *See id.* § 10, 1 Stat at 77–78. That additional jurisdiction was not relevant to any issue in *American Insurance Co.*

35. Record, 7 (quoting Florida Territorial Legislative Council Act of July 4, 1823, § 1, repealed by Florida Territorial Legislative Council Act of Nov 23, 1828, *reprinted in Public Acts of the Legislative Council of the Territory of Florida* 259 (J. Duval ed., 1839)). The record in this case is handwritten, so our reproduction of its punctuation and capitalization may not be entirely accurate.

36. A number of differences existed between the duties of justices of the peace and notaries public in Florida in the 1820s. *Cf.* Florida Territorial Legislative Council Act of Feb 15, 1834 (establishing schedule of fees for justices of the peace, notaries public, and others), *reprinted in Public Acts of the Legislative Council of Florida*, 212–13. But as far as the salvage statute was concerned, their duties were identical. *Cf.* Record, 13, 17–18 (indicating that notaries were generally regarded as judges of some sort).

37. Act of Mar 3, 1823, ch 28, § 10, 3 Stat 750, 753. The full text of the statute makes clear that this limitation applied to local judges created by territorial legislatures as well as by Congress.

38. The record states only that between 300 and 356 bales of cotton showed up in Charleston under the control of Canter. *See* Record, 2.

39. *See* 26 US (1 Pet.) at 514, 515 n* (circuit court opinion of Johnson, J.).

40. They advanced two insignificant arguments as well. First, they made an ill-defined

challenge to the power of the Florida legislature to establish salvage courts. See *id.*, 515. Second, they argued that jurisdiction was appropriate only in the superior courts because of the provision of the organic act giving those courts original jurisdiction in all civil actions arising under territorial laws and involving more than $100. *See id.*; Act of May 26, 1824, ch 162, § 1, 4 Stat 45, 45. As Justice Johnson pointed out in his opinion on circuit (*see American Insurance Co.*, 522 n*), nothing in this provision (apart from the arguments discussed in the text) foreclosed concurrent original jurisdiction over such actions in inferior territorial courts.

41. The Court pointed out that the jurisdiction of the Florida superior courts tracked that of the Kentucky district court only in cases "arising under the laws and Constitution of the United States" (*American Insurance Co.*, 545), which Article III makes clear are jurisdictionally distinct from admiralty. *See id.*, 545–46. Hence the provision giving the two courts "the same jurisdiction" in cases arising under federal law did not establish that in admiralty cases Congress had vested exclusive territorial jurisdiction in the superior courts. Counsel for the insurance companies, anticipating this obvious problem, argued that all cases involving territorial tribunals necessarily arise under federal law within the meaning of Article III, citing *Osborn v Bank of the United States. See American Insurance Co.*, 536 (argument of Mr. Whipple, counsel for claimants). The Court did not even mention, much less respond to, this argument, which the insurance companies plainly viewed as the backbone of their statutory claim. Perhaps the Court felt (correctly) that Justice Johnson's opinion on circuit had dealt adequately with this argument. In any event, the issue was resolved by Congress in 1826 in favor of exclusive superior court admiralty jurisdiction — one year too late to do the insurance companies any good. *See* Act of May 15, 1826, ch 46, § 1, 4 Stat 164, 164 (the Florida superior courts "shall have original and exclusive cognisance of all civil causes of admiralty and maritime jurisdiction").

42. *American Insurance Co.*, 528 (argument of Mr. Ogden) (emphasis in original).

43. *Id.*, 546.

44. Perhaps it is rash to claim that the insurance companies "at no time" made such an argument, as the record of the case does not contain the parties' briefs. Nonetheless, if any such argument had been made even in passing, one would expect some mention of it in the record (which included both lower court opinions), the summary of the arguments of counsel in the *United States Reports*, or the Court's opinion. There is none, other than the district court's somewhat cryptic holding that neither state nor territorial courts can exercise admiralty jurisdiction. *See* Record, 32.

45. We stand alone on many questions. This is not one of them. Such luminaries as David Currie, Martin Redish, and Charles Alan Wright have all criticized the decision. *See* Gary Lawson, *Territorial Governments and the Limits of Formalism*, 78 Cal L Rev 837, 892 n.238 (1990). For a compendium of other criticisms (lodged within a relatively rare defense of the decision), see Christopher D. Man, *Extradition and Article III: A Historical Examination of the "Judicial Power of the United States"*, 10 Tulane J Int'l & Comp L 37, 90–91 (2002).

46. That possibility calls to mind one of the many intriguing aspects of *American Insurance Co.* The insurance companies' statutory arguments against the jurisdiction of the salvage court turned in large measure on whether the cause was one "arising under" the laws of the United States within the meaning of the statute establishing the jurisdiction of

the Florida superior courts. If the cause did "arise under" federal law, then the provision of the organic act giving the superior courts the same jurisdiction as federal district courts in such cases would apply. Additionally, since the district courts had exclusive jurisdiction over admiralty cases, it could then at least be argued that the territorial admiralty jurisdiction was vested exclusively in the superior courts. The insurance companies cited *Osborn* and argued to Justice Johnson in the circuit court that all activities of the Florida courts indeed presented cases arising under federal law, just as did all activities of the Bank of the United States. *See American Insurance Co.*, 520 n*. Justice Johnson, who had been the lone dissenter in *Osborn* (*see* 22 US (9 Wheat.), 871 (Johnson, J., dissenting)), gave the following memorable response: "I have taken a week to reflect upon this question alone, and I cannot withhold from the gentleman, who argued the cause for the libelants, an acknowledgment, that I have not been able to draw any line of discrimination, between this and the decided cause, which satisfies my mind. Yet, I am thoroughly persuaded that the learned men who decided that cause, never contemplated that such an application would have been given of their decision. I am happy in the prospect that this cause will finally be disposed of elsewhere, not doubting, that the mental acumen of those who decided the other, will be found fully adequate to distinguish or reconcile the two cases, on grounds which have escaped my reflections. At present, I must content myself with observing, that it is too much to require of a Court, upon mere analogy, to sustain an argument, that not only proves too much, if it proves any thing, but which leads, in fact, to positive absurdity." *American Insurance Co.*, 521–22 n* (circuit court opinion of Johnson, J.).

In fact, Justice Johnson did have, and indeed relied upon, a perfectly good basis for distinguishing *American Insurance Co.* from *Osborn*; he simply could not pass up an opportunity to tweak the *Osborn* majority. (The majority did not respond to this challenge, or to the insurance companies' argument, when the case reached the Supreme Court.) *Osborn* involved the interpretation of Article III, while *American Insurance Co.* involved the interpretation of a statute. If the statute vesting jurisdiction in the superior courts of Florida had used the words "arising under" in their full constitutional sense (as construed by *Osborn*), then it would have been meaningless for that statute also either to grant or to limit the jurisdiction of the Florida territorial courts by reference to the jurisdiction of the Kentucky court. Each and every case arising in the Florida territory would have arisen under federal law, which is a most implausible interpretation of the terms of the organic act. *See id.* at 520 n*. The same reasoning supports the result in *Puerto Rico v Russell & Co.*, 288 US 476, 483–85 (1933) (despite the holding in *Osborn* with regard to federal corporations, a suit does not arise under United States law merely because it involves a territorial government whose existence derives from an act of Congress).

47. *See Clinton v Englebrecht*, 80 US (13 Wall.) 434, 447 (1872) (the status of territorial courts as other than constitutional courts of the United States "was decided long since in *The American Insurance Company v Canter*, and in the later case of *Benner v Porter*.") (footnotes omitted). *Benner v Porter* dealt with the status of territorial tribunals after their home territory became a state, holding that statehood automatically abolishes all territorial institutions. *See* 50 US (9 How.) 235, 244–45 (1850).

48. 411 US 389, 410 (1973).

Chapter 6. War and Peace

1. For a thorough description of the rules of military governance, see Charles E. Magoon, *Reports on the Law of Civil Government in Territory Subject to Military Occupation By the Military Forces of the United States* (Hein, 1903).

2. 57 US (16 How.) 164 (1854).

3. *See* Ronald D. Rotunda and John E. Nowak, *Treatise on Constitutional Law: Substance and Procedure* (3d ed., West, 1999); Laurence H. Tribe, *American Constitutional Law* (3d ed., Foundation Press, 2000).

4. *See* Jerome A. Barron, C. Thomas Dienes, Wayne McCormack, and Martin H. Redish, *Constitutional Law: Principles and Policy* (4th ed., West, 1992); Paul Brest and Sanford Levinson, *Processes of Constitutional Decisionmaking* (3d ed., Little, Brown, 1992); Daniel A. Farber, William N. Eskridge Jr., and Philip P. Frickey, *Constitutional Law: Themes for the Constitution's Third Century* (2d ed., West, 1998); Gerald Gunther and Kathleen M. Sullivan, *Constitutional Law* (13th ed., Foundation Press, 1997); Douglas W. Kmiec and Stephen B. Presser, *The American Constitutional Order* (Anderson, 1998); William B. Lockhart, Yale Kamisar, Jesse H. Choper, Steven H. Shiffrin, and Richard H. Fallon Jr., *The American Constitution* (8th ed., Foundation, 1996); Geoffrey R. Stone, Louis M. Seidman, Cass R. Sunstein, and Mark L. Tushnet, *Constitutional Law* (3d ed., Little, Brown, 1996).

5. We have found twenty-five articles in the WESTLAW and LEXIS databases that cite *Cross v Harrison*. One of those articles was written by one of the present authors. *See* Gary Lawson, *Territorial Governments and the Limits of Formalism*, 78 Cal L Rev 853, 906 n.322 (1990). Twenty-two of the articles cite *Cross*, without any discussion, for very general propositions of law. *See* Russel Lawrence Barsh and James Youngblood Henderson, *Contrary Jurisprudence: Tribal Interests in Navigable Waterways Before and After Montana v United States*, 56 Wash L Rev 627 (1981); David J. Bederman, *Extraterritorial Domicile and the Constitution*, 28 Va J Int'l L 451 (1988); Stephen L. Carter, *The Constitutionality of the War Powers Resolution*, 70 Va L Rev 101 (1984); Carol Chomsky, *The United States–Dakota War Trials: A Study in Military Injustice*, 43 Stan L Rev 13 (1990); Robert N. Clinton, *Original Understanding, Legal Realism, and the Interpretation of "This Constitution,"* 72 Iowa L Rev 1177 (1987); David P. Currie, *The Constitution in the Supreme Court: Full Faith and the Bill of Rights, 1889–1910*, 52 U Chi L Rev 867 (1985); David P. Currie, *The Constitution in the Supreme Court: Article IV and Federal Powers, 1836–1864*, 1983 Duke LJ 695; Jonathan C. Drimmer, *The Nephews of Uncle Sam: The History, Evolution, and Application of Birthright Citizenship in the United States*, 9 Geo Immigration LJ 667 (1995); L. Benjamin Ederington, *Property as a Natural Institution: The Separation of Property from Sovereignty in International Law*, 13 Am U Int'l L Rev 263 (1997); David M. Golove, *Against Free-Form Formalism*, 73 NYU L Rev 1791 (1998); Sedgwick W. Green, *Applicability of American Laws to Overseas Areas Controlled by the United States*, 68 Harv L Rev 781 (1955); Cap't Timothy Guiden, *Defending America's Cambodian Incursion*, 11 Ariz J Int'l & Comp Law 215 (1994); Deborah D. Herrera, *Unincorporated and Exploited: Differential Treatment for Trust Territory Claimants — Why Doesn't the Constitution Follow the Flag?*, 2 Seton Hall Const LJ 593 (1992); Karl Manheim and Edward P. Howard, *A

Structural Theory of the Initiative Power in California, 31 Loy LA L Rev 1165 (1998); Maj. Scott R. Morris, *The Laws of War: Rules by Warriors for Warriors*, 1997 Army Lawyer 4; Gerald L. Neuman, *Whose Constitution?*, 100 Yale LJ 909 (1991); Maj. Michael A. Newton, *Continuum Crimes: Military Jurisdiction over Foreign Nationals Who Commit International Crimes*, 153 Military L Rev 1 (1996); Efren Rivera Ramos, *The Legal Construction of American Colonialism: The Insular Cases (1901–1922)*, 65 Rev Jur UPR 225 (1996); Cap't Annamary Sullivan, *The President's Power to Promulgate Death Penalty Standards*, 125 Military L Rev 143 (1989); Roger M. Sullivan, *The Power of Congress under the Property Clause: A Potential Check on the Effect of the* Chadha *Decision on Public Land Legislation*, 6 Pub Land L Rev 65 (1985); David L. Roland, *Casenote*, 17 St Mary's LJ 1085 (1986); Paul S. Rosenzweig, *Comment: Functional Equivalents of the Border, Sovereignty, and the Fourth Amendment*, 52 U Chi L Rev 1119 (1985). One article contains a brief description of the case as a small part of a sweeping survey of caselaw concerning aspects of sovereignty. Sarah H. Cleveland, *Powers Inherent in Sovereignty: Indians, Aliens, Territories, and the Nineteenth Century Origins of Plenary Power over Foreign Affairs*, 81 Tex L Rev 1, 192 (2002). The remaining author on this list is very much aware of the events in California during that time but does not focus on their constitutional dimension. *See* Myra K. Saunders, *California Legal History: The Legal System under the United States Military Government, 1846–1849*, 88 Law Libr J 488 (1996).

At least one article that pays significant attention to *Cross* does not appear in the LEXIS or WESTLAW databases. *See* David J. Bederman, *Article II Courts*, 44 Mercer L Rev 825, 851 (1993). Professor Bederman is among the few scholars to appreciate the significance of the issues raised in *Cross*.

6. For an eminently readable discussion of the events leading up to and during the Mexican–American War, see Paul H. Bergeron, *The Presidency of James K. Polk* 65–113 (University Press of Kansas, 1987).

7. *See* Letter from W. L. Marcy, Secretary of War, to Brig. Gen. S. W. Kearny or officer of the US Army highest in rank in California, Mexico, Jan 11, 1847, *reprinted in* S Doc No 18, 31st Cong, 1st Sess, 242–46 [hereinafter "S Doc No 18"].

8. *See* US Const art I, § 8, cl 1 ("The Congress shall have Power To lay and collect Taxes, Duties, Imposts and Excises, to pay the Debts and provide for the common Defense and general Welfare of the United States; but all Duties, Imposts and Excises shall be uniform throughout the United States."); *id*. art I, § 9, cl 5 (no federal duties may be laid on exports from states); *id*. art I, § 9, cl 5 (no vessels bound to or from a state shall be made to pay duties in another state); *id*. art I, § 10, cls. 2–3 (no state shall, without congressional consent, impose any duties except as "absolutely necessary" for executing inspection laws or in case of actual or imminent invasion).

9. Prior to *Cross*, the Supreme Court had expressly recognized this power, both when the United States occupies foreign territory (*see Fleming v Page*, 50 US (9 How.) 603 (1850)) and when foreign nations occupy American soil (*see United States v Rice*, 17 US (4 Wheat.) 246 (1819)).

10. The letter instructing the military authorities to impose the duties stated that the money collected was "to be applied to the purposes of the war, and among these purposes is the support of the temporary civil government." Letter from W. L. Marcy, Sen Doc No

18, at 245. Congress could, of course, have funded the government without recourse to such import fees, but according to Secretary Marcy, there was no reason to expect any money from Congress "much within a year from this time." *Id.* Thus the military government was left to rely for its operation on import fees and any other internal sources of revenue that it could find.

11. Treaty of Peace, Friendship, Limits, and Settlement, Feb 2, 1848, United States–Mexico, 9 Stat 922 [hereinafter "Treaty of Guadalupe Hidalgo"].

12. Proclamation of R. B. Mason to the People of California (Aug 7, 1848), *reprinted in* S Doc No 18, at 566–67.

13. Letter from H. W. Halleck, Lieutenant, to Captain J. L. Folsom, Collector, San Francisco, CA (Aug 9, 1848), *reprinted in id.*, 568.

14. Act of Mar 3, 1849, ch 112, 9 Stat 400.

15. 9 Stat 452 (1850). For detailed accounts of the California constitutional convention, see Joseph Ellison, *The Struggle for Civil Government in California, 1846–50 (Pt. 2)*, 10 Q Cal Hist Soc 129, 150–54 (1931); Myra K. Saunders, *California Legal History: The California Constitution of 1849*, 90 Law Libr J 447 (1998).

16. Mason took "office" as governor on May 31, 1847. *See* Proclamation of R. B. Mason, May 31, 1847, *reprinted in* S Doc No 18, at 313–14.

17. Messages had to be physically carried from the eastern United States to California, and that was no small feat. Consider Collier's account of his journey to his new post: "I am at last at my post. The delay attendant upon my arrival has been to me a great source of anxiety, and given me much trouble.... I have suffered much of hardship, of privation, and toil, and encountered no little of peril. We were compelled, for several days in succession, to fight our way through hostile bands of Indians, but escaped without the loss of life on our part, and with but one man wounded, he having both bones of his arm broken. It is with great regret that I have to state, also, that in crossing the Colorado, four persons were drowned, and that one of the number was Captain Thorn, of New York, who was in command of the dragoons. At some future period I hope to give you some account of my pilgrimmage, and of the miserable country we have passed over." Letter from J. Collier to W. M. Meredith, Secretary of the Treasury, Nov 13, 1849, *reprinted in id.*, 24.

18. As a colonel in the military, of course, Mason had been properly appointed as an officer of the United States. But that office did not include, as part of its normal duties, serving as the peacetime governor of a federal territory. A new appointment was clearly needed for a post of that magnitude — just as the Secretary of Defense could not be given authority to administer federal antipollution laws without a separate appointment. *See Weiss v United States*, 510 US 163, 173–76 (1994) (discussing when an officer's new duties require a separate appointment); *id.*, 196 (Scalia, J., concurring) (same).

19. The post of customs collector is undoubtedly an inferior office, so that if Mason was properly appointed as governor, Congress could likely have permitted him, as one of the "Heads of Departments," to appoint customs collectors. *But see Freytag v Commissioner of Internal Revenue*, 501 US 868, 886 (1991) (stating, in a 5 to 4 decision, that the chief judge of the Tax Court cannot be one of the constitutional "Heads of Departments" because "Departments" means only "executive divisions like the Cabinet-level departments"). Interestingly, however, when Congress finally authorized the appointment of a

246 Notes to Pages 155–62

customs collector on March 3, 1849, it chose to employ presidential appointment along with Senate confirmation. *See* 9 Stat 400, § 2.

20. There were similar problems with the governance of New Mexico. *See* Bederman, *Article II Courts*, 838–39.

21. Letter from R. B. Mason, Colonel, to R. Jones, Adjutant General (Aug 19, 1848), *reprinted in* S Doc No 18, 573–74 (emphasis added).

22. Letter from James Buchanan, Secretary of the United States of America, to William V. Vorhies, Oct 7, 1848, *reprinted in id.*, 7–8.

23. The Tucker Act, which waives sovereign immunity for claims for damages against the United States founded on statutes, regulations, or the Constitution, was not enacted in anything resembling its present form until 1887. Act of Mar 3, 1887, ch 359, 24 Stat 505.

24. Although it was a garden-variety common-law suit, the case was initially heard in a federal trial court in the Southern District of New York. The defendant no doubt invoked a statutory removal provision pertaining to suits under, or under color of, the customs laws. *See* Act of Mar 3, 1817, ch 109, § 2, 3 Stat 396.

25. *See Harlow v Fitzgerald*, 457 US 800, 813–19 (1982) (setting out the framework for the modern law of official immunity). For a useful summary of the ways in which qualified immunity poses a serious bar to official liability, see Cornelia T. L. Pillard, *Taking Fiction Seriously: The Strange Results of Public Officials' Individual Liability Under Bivens*, 88 Geo LJ 65, 80–90 (1999).

26. The full scope of this principle is illustrated by *Little v Barreme*, 6 US (2 Cranch) 170 (1804), in which a United States naval officer was held personally liable for damages resulting from obedience to an unlawful presidential order to naval commanders.

27. *Waite v Santa Cruz*, 184 US 302, 323 (1902).

28. *See* Kathryn A. Clokey, Note, *The De Facto Officer Doctrine: The Case for Continued Application*, 85 Colum L Rev 1121, 1122 (1985).

29. 159 US 596 (1895).

30. *See Cocke v Halsey*, 41 US (16 Pet.) 71, 84–88 (1842).

31. *See Norton v Shelby County*, 118 US 425, 440–42 (1886); *see also McLaughry v Deming*, 186 US 49, 63 (1902) (holding that the de facto officer doctrine cannot apply to an improperly constituted court-martial).

32. *See* George S. Harris, *The Validity of Acts of Officers Occupying Offices Created Under Laws Declared Unconstitutional*, 3 U Newark L Rev 123, 125–31 (1938); Clifford L. Pannam, *Unconstitutional Statutes and De Facto Officers*, 2 Fed L Rev 37, 50–57 (1966); Note, *The De Facto Officer Doctrine*, 63 Colum L Rev 909, 914–15 (1963).

33. 48 US (7 How.) 1 (1849).

34. 74 US (7 Wall.) 700 (1869).

35. 48 US (7 How.) at 38–39.

36. *Id.*, 40–41.

37. *Id.*, 41–45.

38. As an aside: The Court probably should have found more troubling than it did the question whether even governmental authorization could help the defendants in *Luther*. The Court assumed without much analysis that the state of martial law was enough

justification for the defendants' actions to close off tort liability. *See id.*, 45–46. That issue, however, was not as easily in the defendants' favor as the Court made it appear. *See id.*, 58–88 (Woodbury, J., dissenting).

39. *See Texas v White*, 720–31.

40. *Id.*, 733

41. *Id.*

42. *Cf.* Steven G. Calabresi and Gary Lawson, *Equity and Hierarchy: Reflections on the Harris Execution*, 102 Yale LJ 255 (suggesting that federalism is an appropriate part of remedial balancing for federal courts).

43. It surely includes criminal law. Does de facto authority therefore mean a free ride for all criminals? The answer may depend on how clearly one can identify a category of malum in se offenses. On the other hand, the right answer may be simply that a criminal prosecuted by the federal government has a constitutional right to be prosecuted only in accordance with strictly enforced constitutional norms.

44. 57 US (16 How.) at 189–91.

45. Mason announced the ratifications by proclamation on August 7, 1848. He claimed to have received official notification on August 6, 1848 (*see* Letter from R. B. Mason to Brig. Gen. R. Jones, Aug 23, 1848, *reprinted in* S Doc No 18, at 577), and there is no reason to doubt his veracity.

46. The answer to this question in modern law is actually something like, "Military occupation is permissible until the President says otherwise." *See* Bederman, *Article II Courts*, 861–62. This doctrine has no remotely plausible constitutional foundation.

47. *Cross v Harrison*, 190.

48. Treaty of Guadalupe Hidalgo arts III–IV.

49. *See* Ingrid Detter De Lupis, *The Law of War* 297–98 (Cambridge University Press, 1988).

50. Treaty of Guadalupe Hidalgo art III.

51. *Id.*

52. *Id.*

53. *Id.* art IV. The provision also called for the return to Mexico of all captured weapons and other property.

54. *Id.*

55. 50 US (9 How.) 127 (1850).

56. *Id.*, 148.

57. Treaty of Guadalupe Hidalgo art VIII, XI.

58. Letter from James Buchanan to William V. Vorhies, Oct 7, 1848, *reprinted in* S Doc No 18, at 9. We are not as certain as was Buchanan that Madison, Wilson, Hamilton, et al. would have regarded a peacetime military government as "the best form of civil government ever established amongst men."

59. *See Cross v Harrison*, 191 ("But after the ratification of the treaty, California became a part of the United States, or a ceded, conquered territory.").

60. *Id.*, 191–92 (emphasis added).

61. Proclamation of R. B. Mason to the People of California (Aug 7, 1848), *reprinted in* S Doc No 18, at 566 (emphasis added).

62. *See* Joseph Ellison, *The Struggle for Civil Government in California, 1846–1850 (Pt. 1),* 10 Q Cal Hist Soc 3, 11–13 (1931).

63. Proclamation of R. B. Mason to the People of California (Aug 7, 1848), *reprinted in* S Doc No 18, at 566.

64. *See* Ellison, *The Struggle for Civil Government in California (Pt. 2),* 132–36. On the role of slavery generally in debates over territorial governance, see Richard White, *"It's Your Misfortune and None of My Own": A History of the American West* 155–60 (University of Oklahoma Press, 1991).

65. *See* US Comm'n on Civil Rights, *Language, Rights, and New Mexico Statehood* (2000), *available at* http://ourworld.compuserve.com/homepages/JWCRAWFORD/nmocon.htm (last visited Oct 20, 2000).

66. Letter from H. W. Halleck to Capt. J. L. Folsum (Aug 9, 1848), *reprinted in* S Doc No 18, at 632. Halleck, incidentally, went on to become President Lincoln's chief of staff during part of the Civil War, and he published a major treatise on international law.

67. It would take a separate article to establish this proposition. Fortunately, we have written it. *See* Gary Lawson and Guy Seidman, *When Did the Constitution Become Law?,* 76 Notre Dame L Rev 1 (2002).

68. Letter from H. W. Halleck to Capt. J. L. Folsum, Aug 9, 1848, *reprinted in* S Doc No 18, at 632.

69. *See Cross v Harrison,* 192.

70. *See* Act of Mar 2, 1799, ch 22, §§ 27–28, 1 Stat 627, 648.

71. Letter from H. W. Halleck, Brevet Captain, to E. H. Harrison, US Customs Collector (Feb 24, 1849), *reprinted in* S Doc No 18, at 670–71.

72. *Id.,* 671.

73. Letter from Persifor F. Smith, Brevet Major General, to R. Jones, Brigadier General (Apr 5, 1849), *reprinted in id.,* 694.

74. The need for imports into California was so great that the authorities permitted (upon the payment of "duties") entry of goods from foreign-owned ships, which was forbidden by the general customs laws. As the commander-in-chief of the Pacific naval forces explained to Collier upon his arrival in San Francisco, "Mr. Harrison, your predecessor, will doubtless make you fully acquainted with all that has been done by the naval and military commanders on this station for the collection of duties, and for the relief of the suffering community, whose wants and necessities were of that urgent nature as to compel the ruling authorities to adopt their measures to meet the urgent wants of the in-pouring emigrants, rather than strict obedience to legislative enactment." Letter from Thos. AP C. Jones to Col. Collier, Nov 12, 1849, *reprinted in id.,* 34. Collier ended the practice upon taking office. *See* Letter from J. Collier to Thos. AP C. Jones, Nov 15, 1849, *reprinted in id.,* 35: "I am aware also of the necessity which seemed to justify the exercise of that discretion. It must be admitted, however, that it was in violation of the revenue laws. . . . I should exceedingly regret that the strict enforcement of those laws should inflict injury upon any portion of my countrymen; but I am not vested with *discretionary* powers upon such subjects. . . . [W]hile I may lament that any portion of our countrymen who are engaged in the mining district should feel the effects in the increased price of provisions, we have, on the other hand, the satisfaction of knowing that another class, that of the American ship-builders and ship-owners, will enjoy that protection which the

law intended to give them, that the great interest of our *own* commerce will be promoted, and that the law of the land is respected and maintained."

75. Of course, the plaintiff's ships and goods that were involved in the illegal landing of goods would have been subject to forfeiture as well. The lack of authorization cuts in both directions. If Harrison did not have the power to collect customs duties, he also did not have the power to make legal an otherwise illegal entry of goods into San Francisco. But that would be a separate case that had no proper bearing on the disposition of the plaintiff's simple assumpsit action.

76. *Cross v Harrison*, 193–94.

77. *Id.*, 195.

78. 54 US (13 How.) 115 (1852).

79. Technically, the *Insular Tariff Cases* was the name given by the Supreme Court to a series of decisions in 1901 that dealt with the tariff status of the new territories acquired by the United States as a result of that war. *See De Lima v Bidwell*, 182 US 1, 2 (1901). For convenience, however, we use the term *"The Insular Cases"* to refer to the range of decisions, effectively ending in 1922 with *Balzac v Porto Rico*, 258 US 298 (1922), that discussed the applicability of various constitutional restrictions to the extracontinental "insular" territories. For an excellent and readable discussion of the cases, see Owen M. Fiss, *Troubled Beginnings of the Modern State, 1888–1910*, 225–26 (1993).

80. 182 US 222 (1901).

81. The Court's entire discussion of this point was: "We have no doubt, however, that, from the necessities of the case, the right to administer the government of Porto Rico continued in the military commander after the ratification of the treaty, and until further action by Congress. *Cross v Harrison*, above cited." *Id.*, 234.

82. *Id.*

83. *Id.*, 236.

84. *Id.*, 234.

85. *Id.*, 235–36.

86. 214 US 260 (1909).

87. *Id.*, 264.

88. *Id.*, 265–66.

89. *Id.*

90. Letter of R. B. Mason, Colonel, to R. Jones, Adjutant General (Aug 19, 1848), *reprinted in* S Doc No 18, at 574.

91. Letter from James Buchanan, Secretary of State, to William V Voorhies (Oct 7, 1848), *reprinted in id.*, 7.

92. *Id.*

93. *Id.*, 8.

94. *Cong Globe*, 30th Cong, 2d Sess 5 (1848). It is interesting to contrast the statement made on January 23, 1850, by President Zachary Taylor in response to a Senate resolution asking, inter alia, whether he had appointed anyone as civil or military governor of California since March 4, 1849: "On coming into office, I found the military commandant of the department of California exercising the functions of civil governor in that Territory; and left, as I was, to act under the treaty of Guadalupe Hidalgo, without the aid of any legislative provision establishing a government in that Territory, I thought it best

not to disturb that arrangement, made under my predecessor, until Congress should take some action on that subject. I therefore did not interfere with the powers of the military commandant, who continued to exercise the functions of civil governor as before; but I made no such appointment, conferred no such authority, and have allowed no increased compensation to the commandant for his services." S Doc No 18, at 1.

95. Mason appears from this saga to have been an honest person with no pretensions of grandeur. Indeed, it is hard to study these events without feeling a great sadness, and some measure of admiration, for Colonel Mason. His comments after the conclusion of the treaty of peace demonstrate a keen awareness of the precariousness of his legal situation, and his comments during his wartime administration show a detailed and precise knowledge of the nature of military governance. *See* Letter of R. B. Mason to L. W. Boggs, June 2, 1847, *reprinted in id.*, 305–06 (correctly describing the legal origins and limits of military rule). He took the extraordinary step of asking to be relieved from his post. And when that day finally came, he died shortly after returning home. *See* Saunders, *California Legal History*, 510 n.135.

96. Myra K. Saunders, *California Legal History: A Review of Spanish and Mexican Legal Institutions*, 87 Law Libr J 487, 506 (1996). For a detailed description of the Mexican institutions that were in place in 1846, see *id.*, 495–504.

97. This was acknowledged by State Department official John Clayton in a letter of April 3, 1849, giving instructions to a presidential agent being sent to California: "The laws of California and New Mexico, as they existed at the conclusion of the treaty of Guadalupe Hidalgo, regulating the relations of the inhabitants with each other, will necessarily remain in force in those Territories. Their relations with their former government have been dissolved, and new relations created between them and the government of the United States; but the existing laws regulating the relations of the people with each other will continue until others, lawfully enacted, shall supersede them." Letter from John M. Clayton to Hon. Thomas Butler King, Apr 3, 1849, *reprinted in* S Doc No 18, at 10.

98. *See* Ellison, *The Struggle for Civil Government in California (Pt. 1)*, 17; Saunders, *California Legal History: A Review of Spanish and Mexican Legal Institutions*, 506. But that is a far cry from chaos.

99. *See* Ellison, *The Struggle for Civil Government in California (Pt. 1)*, 9–11.

100. *See* Ellison, *The Struggle for Civil Government in California (Pt. 2)*, 138–40.

101. *See* Ellison, *The Struggle for Civil Government in California (Pt. 1)*, 23–25. Implied consent is more a game than a theory. As one of us has written elsewhere, "[t]he problem with tacit consent is that it is almost always about one hundred parts tacit to one part consent." Gary S. Lawson, *An Interpretivist Agenda*, 15 Harv JL & Pub Pol'y 157, 160 n.9 (1992).

102. *See* Saunders, *California Legal History: A Review of Spanish and Mexican Legal Institutions*, 488.

103. *See* Kenneth C. Martis and Gregory A. Elmes, *The Historical Atlas of State Power in Congress, 1790–1990*, at 58 (1993).

104. Letter from J. L. Folsom, Captain, to W. T. Sherman, Lieutenant (Aug 14, 1848), *reprinted in* S Doc No 18, at 589.

105. Letter from R. B. Mason, Colonel, to R. Jones, Brigadier General (Mar 6, 1849), *reprinted in id.*, 625.

106. Letter from Persifor F. Smith, Brevet Major General, to R. B. Mason, Colonel (Mar 6, 1849), *reprinted in id.*, 691.

107. Saunders, *California Legal History: A Review of Spanish and Mexican Legal Institutions*, 489. For more details on the governance structure of mining colonies, see Rodman Wilson Paul, *Mining Frontiers of the Far West, 1848–1880*, 22–25 (Holt, Rinehart & Winston, 1963); Andrea G. McDowell, *From Commons to Claims: Property Rights in the California Gold Rush*, 14 Yale JL & Humanities 1 (2002).

Chapter 7. Bulwark or Façade?

1. The classic exposition of the continuity between the Bill of Rights and the original Constitution is Akhil Reed Amar, *The Bill of Rights as a Constitution*, 100 Yale LJ 1131 (1991).

2. US Const art I, § 9, cls 1, 3–6.

3. *Id.* art I, § 9, cl 7.

4. *Id.* art I, § 9, cls 2, 8. In addition, federal officials are forbidden from accepting benefits from foreign sovereigns. *See id.* art I, § 9, cl 8.

5. *See* Gary Lawson and Patricia B. Granger, *The "Proper" Scope of Federal Power: A Jurisdictional Interpretation of the Sweeping Clause*, 43 Duke LJ 267 (1993).

6. *See* Gary Lawson, *The Bill of Rights As an Exclamation Point*, 33 U Rich L Rev 511 (1999).

7. 32 US (7 Pet.) 242 (1833).

8. US Const amend VII.

9. On this point, at least, Chief Justice Taney was right in *Dred Scott. See Scott v Sandford*, 60 US (19 How.) 393, 451 (1857).

10. For longer versions of the story, see Owen M. Fiss, *Troubled Beginnings of the Modern State, 1888–1910*, 225–26 (1993); Frederick Coudert, *The Evolution of the Doctrine of Territorial Incorporation*, 26 Colum L Rev 823 (1926).

11. The first, and least important, of these cases was *De Lima v Bidwell*, 182 US 1 (1901). In *De Lima*, the Supreme Court held that, as a matter of statutory construction, Puerto Rico ceased to be a "foreign country" within the meaning of the generally applicable tariff law (Dingley Act, ch 11, 30 Stat 151, 151 (1897)) upon its cession to the United States by Spain (182 US at 200). The Court applied the same reasoning in the other *Insular Tariff Cases. See Goetze v United States*, 182 US 221 (1901) (Hawaiian Islands); *Fourteen Diamond Rings v United States*, 183 US 176 (1901) (Philippines).

12. 182 US 244 (1901).

13. *See* Foraker Act, ch 191, § 3, 31 Stat 77, 77 (1900).

14. US Const art I, § 8, cl 1.

15. *Id.* art I, § 9, cl 6 ("nor shall Vessels bound to, or from, one State, be obliged to enter, clear, or pay Duties in another").

16. *Compare* 182 US 179, 182 (dictum) (opinion of Brown, J.) ("[T]he Constitution is applicable to territories . . . only when and so far as Congress shall so direct," at least with

respect to "what may be termed artificial or remedial rights, which are peculiar to our own system of jurisprudence.") *with id.*, 342 (White, Shiras, and McKenna, JJ., concurring) (the Uniformity Clause did not bind Congress in legislating for Puerto Rico "because the island had not been incorporated into the United States, but was merely appurtenant thereto as a possession") *with id.*, 345 (Gray, J., concurring) (agreeing "in substance" with the concurring opinion of Justice White).

17. *See also Dooley v United States*, 183 US 151 (1901) (upholding a duty on goods brought into Puerto Rico from the continental United States, notwithstanding the Constitution's prohibition on taxes or duties "on Articles exported from any State").

18. *See generally The Insular Cases, Comprising the Records, Briefs, and Arguments of Counsel in the Insular Cases of the October Term, 1900, in the Supreme Court of the United States, Including the Appendixes Thereto*, HR Doc No 509, 56th Cong, 2d Sess (A. Howe ed., 1901) (reprinting the lower court record, briefs, and arguments of counsel).

19. *Downes*, 287. The sentiments voiced by Justice Brown found expression in other Supreme Court opinions over the next twenty years: "The jury system needs citizens trained to the exercise of the responsibilities of jurors. . . . Congress has thought that a people like the Filipinos or the Porto Ricans, trained to a complete judicial system which knows no juries, living in compact and ancient communities, with definitely formed customs and political conceptions, should be permitted themselves to determine how far they wish to adopt this institution of Anglo-Saxon origin, and when" (*Balzac v Porto Rico*, 258 US 298, 310 (1922)); "If the right to trial by jury were a fundamental right which goes wherever the jurisdiction of the United States extends . . . it would follow that, no matter what the needs or capacities of the people, trial by jury, and in no other way, must be forthwith established, although the result may be to work injustice and provoke disturbance rather than to aid the orderly administration of justice. If the United States, impelled by its duty or advantage, shall acquire territory peopled by savages, and of which it may dispose or not hold for ultimate admission to Statehood, if this doctrine is sound, it must establish there the trial by jury. To state such a proposition demonstrates the impossibility of carrying it into practice" (*Dorr v United States*, 195 US 138, 148 (1904)).

20. *See Hawaii v Mankichi*, 190 US 197 (1903) (5–4 decision, with two Justices concurring specially) (no constitutional or statutory right to indictment by grand jury or conviction by a unanimous petit jury in the Hawaiian Islands).

21. *See Ocampo v United States*, 234 US 91 (1914) (9–0 decision) (no constitutional or statutory right to indictment by grand jury in the Philippines); *Dowdell v United States*, 221 US 325 (1911) (8–1 decision) (no statutory right — and by implication no constitutional right — to indictment by grand jury in the Philippines); *Dorr v United States*, 195 US 138 (1904) (8–1 decision, with three concurring Justices specifically repudiating much of the majority's reasoning) (no constitutional or statutory right to jury trial in the Philippines); *cf. Grafton v United States*, 206 US 333 (1907) (while the same offense may be tried in federal and state courts without raising double jeopardy problems, that is not true when the same offense is sought to be tried in federal and territorial courts, since the latter derive their powers from the United States rather than from an independent source

of sovereignty); *Gonzalez v Williams*, 192 US 1 (1904) (citizens of Puerto Rico are not aliens within the meaning of the immigration laws); *Kepner v United States*, 195 US 100 (1904) (prohibition on double jeopardy applies to the Philippines by statute); *Mendezona v United States*, 195 US 158 (1904) (following holding in *Kepner*). *Compare Rasmussen v United States*, 197 US 516 (1905) (constitutional right to jury trial applies in Alaska because the territory was incorporated into the United States by treaty manifesting the intention to grant citizenship to the inhabitants) *with id.*, 528 (Harlan, J., concurring) (constitutional right to jury trial applies in Alaska because it applies in all territories) *and id.*, 531 (Brown, J., concurring) (constitutional right to jury trial applies in Alaska because Congress so said).

22. *See Downes*, 287 (White, J., concurring).

23. *See Dorr*, 148–49.

24. *Balzac*, 305.

25. *See United States v Verdugo-Urquidez*, 494 US 259, 268 (1990) (describing unincorporated territories as possessions "not clearly destined for statehood"); *Granville-Smith v Granville-Smith*, 349 US 1, 5 (1955) (referring to unincorporated territories as "possessions of the United States not thought of as future States"); *see also* Coudert, *The Evolution of the Doctrine of Territorial Incorporation*, 834 ("I surmise, although it is not wholly clear, that Mr. Justice White thought incorporation as a Territory implied a promise of ultimate statehood."). As a description of the original intendment of the incorporation doctrine, this at least has the virtue of explaining why, at the turn of the century, Alaska was regarded as incorporated (*see Rasmussen v United States*, 197 US 516, 525 (1905)) while the distant islands teeming with "alien races" (*Downes*, 287) were not. *Cf. Downes*, 391 (Harlan, J., dissenting) ("I am constrained to say that this idea of 'incorporation' has some occult meaning which my mind does not apprehend. It is enveloped in some mystery which I am unable to unravel.").

26. *Id.*, 292 (White, J., concurring).

27. *Balzac*, 312.

28. *Id.*, 312–13.

29. *See Reid v Covert*, 354 US 1, 14 (1957) (plurality opinion) ("[I]t is our judgment that neither the [*Insular Tariff*] cases nor their reasoning should be given any further expansion."); *Torres v Puerto Rico*, 442 US 465, 475–76 (1979) (Brennan, Stewart, Marshall, and Blackmun, JJ., concurring) (agreeing with, and citing, the plurality sentiment expressed in *Reid v Covert*).

30. *See Verdugo-Urdiquez*, 268–70; *Torres*, 468–71.

31. *See*, e.g., Gerald L. Neuman, *Whose Constitution?*, 100 Yale LJ 909 (1991); Efren Rivera Ramos, *The Legal Construction of American Colonialism: The Insular Cases (1901–1922)*, 65 Rev Jur UPR 225 (1996); Gabriel A. Terrasa, *The United States, Puerto Rico, and the Territorial Incorporation Doctrine: Reaching a Century of Constitutional Authoritarianism*, 31 John Marshall L Rev 55 (1997).

32. The District Clause gives Congress the power of "exclusive Legislation" over the District of Columbia and federal enclaves, while the Territories Clause gives Congress the power to enact "needful Rules and Regulations" concerning territories. If the word "needful" limits the scope of Congress's general legislative jurisdiction, then Congress

might have broader power over the District and federal enclaves than it has over territories, and what counts as a "needful" regulation could vary from one territory to another depending on local circumstances.

33. *See* David E. Engdahl, *State and Federal Power over Federal Property*, 18 Ariz L Rev 283 (1976).

34. For an analysis of the fundamental (by any understanding of that term) role of juries in the American constitutional order, see Akhil Reed Amar, *The Bill of Rights: Creation and Reconstruction* 81–118 (Yale University Press, 1998).

35. 60 US (19 How.) 393 (1857).

36. US Const art I, § 9, cl 1.

37. *Id.* art I, § 2, cl 3.

38. *Id.* art IV, § 2, cl 2: "No Person held to Service or Labour in one State, under the Laws thereof, escaping into another, shall, in Consequence of any Law or Regulation therein, be discharged from such Service or Labour, but shall be delivered up on Claim of the Party to whom such Service or Labour may be due."

39. For a discussion of this debate and its background, see Robert Knowles, *The Balance of Forces and the Empire of Liberty: States' Rights and the Louisiana Purchase*, 88 Iowa L. Rev 343 (2003).

40. Act of Mar 6, 1820, ch 22, § 8, 3 Stat 545, 548.

41. The Illinois constitution of 1818 purported to prohibit slavery, but it authorized a form of indentured servitude that came close to the mark. *See* Don E. Fehrenbacher, *The Dred Scott Case: Its Significance in American Law and Politics* 86–86 (Oxford University Press, 1978).

42. *Scott v Emerson*, 15 Mo 576 (1851).

43. US Const art III, § 2.

44. *See Strader v Graham*, 51 US (10 How.) 82 (1851).

45. *See Scott*, 555–57 (McLean, J., dissenting).

46. For a brief but devastating compendium of errors, see David P. Currie, *The Constitution in the Supreme Court: The First Hundred Years, 1789–1888*, at 264–66 (University of Chicago Press, 1985). Although the Diversity Clause speaks only of *state* citizenship as the basis for federal court jurisdiction, all of the Justices, including the dissenters, focused instead on the concept of *national* citizenship. Because the original Constitution contained no definition of national citizenship, the ideas of state and national citizenship were necessarily linked. Chief Justice Taney conceded that "every person of every class and description of persons who were at the time of the adoption of the Constitution recognized as citizens in the several States, became also citizens of this new political body." *Scott*, 406. Justice Curtis pointed out that free blacks were indeed citizens in a number of states at the time of ratification — *Scott*, 572–76 (Curtis, J., dissenting) — to which Taney had no response. It would have been more plausible for Taney to argue simply that Scott was not a citizen of Missouri under Missouri law. That was not, however, the way that the case was pleaded, nor would such a holding have prevented other states from conferring constitutionally recognized state citizenship on free blacks. The first sentence of the Fourteenth Amendment deals with the problem by declaring that "[a]ll persons born or naturalized in the United States and subject to the jurisdiction

thereof, are citizens of the United States and of the State wherein they reside." US Const amend. XIV, § 1.

47. *Scott*, 432–42.

48. *Id.*, 605–08, 611–12 (Curtis, J., dissenting).

49. *Id.*, 623–24.

50. *Id.*, 450.

51. For a thorough discussion, see John Harrison, *Substantive Due Process and the Constitutional Text*, 83 Va L Rev 493 (1997).

Conclusion

1. Professor Lawson is untroubled by the prospect of denigrating the third alternative listed above. Professor Seidman keeps his own counsel.

Index

Ackerman, Bruce, 93
Acquisition of property. *See* Spending Clause
Acquisition of territory: by annexation, 92–94; by cession from states, 92–93; by conquest, 21–22, 104; by discovery, 22, 96, 97–98; role of Sweeping Clause in, 30–31, 72, 78; sovereignty as granting right of, 22–23; by treaty, 32, 72, 83. *See also* Annexation; Discovery; Sweeping Clause; Treaty Clause
Adams, Henry, 18
Adams-Onis Treaty: American claims to West Florida confirmed by, 90; East Florida ceded to United States by, 90, 91; inhabitants of East and West Florida incorporated into United States by, 90; signing and ratification of, 90, 224 n.12; Spain's claims to Oregon Territory relinquished by, 94, 96; Spain's claims to Texas confirmed by, 91
Admissions Clause: acquired territory as

within scope of, 3, 4, 73–79, 93; applicability to Northwest Territory of, 73; applicability to state territory of, 110; breadth of, 85; discretion of Congress under, 79–81, 83; exclusivity of power granted by, 78–79, 94; principle of reasonableness as limiting, 82–83; relation to Territories Clause of, 74; text of, 3, 73, 79
Alabama, 89, 90
Alaska Territory: acquisition of, 105; admission to Union of, 105, 107; discovery of, 105; inhabitants of, Joint Convention limiting Russian claims to, 94, 105; legislature for, forbidden by Congress, 124; noncontiguity with mainland of, 106; not incorporated into United States by treaty of acquisition, 106; suitability for statehood of, 106–8
Aliens, 70
Ambassadors: recall of, 51; reception of,